Property Rights in Land

T0331290

Property Rights in Land widens our understanding of property rights by looking through the lenses of social history and sociology, discussing mainstream theory of new institutional economics and the derived grand narrative of national and global economic development.

Written by a collection of expert authors, the chapters delve into social processes through which property relations became institutionalized and were used in social action for the appropriation of resources and rents. This was in order to gain a better understanding of the social processes intervening between the institutionalized 'rules of the game' and their economic and social outcomes.

This collection of chapters is of great interest to those who study economic history, historical sociology and economic sociology, as well as agrarian and rural history.

Rosa Congost is Full Professor in economic history and researcher of the Centre for Research in Rural History at the University of Girona, Spain and ICREA Academy Researcher.

Jorge Gelman is Senior Researcher and current Chair of the Instituto Ravignani, Universidad de Buenos Aires/CONICET, and Full Professor in history at the Universidad de Buenos Aires, Argentina.

Rui Santos is Associate Professor in sociology and researcher at CICS.Nova and IHC at the Nova University of Lisbon, FCSH/Nova, Portugal.

Perspectives in Economic and Social History
Series Editors: Andrew August and Jari Eloranta

Property Rights in Land

Issues in social, economic and
global history

**Edited by Rosa Congost,
Jorge Gelman and Rui Santos**

 Routledge
Taylor & Francis Group

LONDON AND NEW YORK

First published 2017 by Routledge

2 Park Square, Milton Park, Abingdon, Oxfordshire OX14 4RN
52 Vanderbilt Avenue, New York, NY 10017

Routledge is an imprint of the Taylor & Francis Group, an informa business

First issued in paperback 2019

British Library Cataloguing in Publication Data
A catalogue record for this book is available from the British Library

Library of Congress Cataloging in Publication Data
A catalog record for this book has been requested

ISBN: 978-1-8489-3580-8 (hbk)
ISBN: 978-0-367-87606-7 (pbk)

Typeset in Times New Roman
by Keystroke, Neville Lodge, Tettenhall, Wolverhampton

Contents

Illustrations

Figures

Tables

Contributors

Joyce E. Bromley is an independent researcher in modern history, based in the USA. She does research on cultural memories. Her research on post-socialist eastern Germany concerning families returning to their ancestral properties was supported by the Leibniz Institute of Agricultural Development in Transition Economies (IAMO), Halle (Saale) in Germany.

Benedita Câmara teaches at the University of Madeira. She does research in economic and business history in modern Madeira, mainly concerning agriculture and trade, tenancy contracts, and trademarks.

Rosa Congost teaches at the University of Girona in Spain, where she is also a researcher in the Research Group on the History of Rural Societies. She is also an ICREA Academy researcher (Catalan Institution for Research and Advanced Studies) and the President of the European Rural History Organisation. She does research in early modern and modern economic and social history in Spain in comparative perspective, mainly on land property, social inequality and social change in rural societies.

Julio Djenderedjian teaches at the University of Buenos Aires and is a researcher of CONICET at the Instituto de Historia Americana y Argentina 'Dr. Emilio Ravignani' in Buenos Aires, Argentina. He does research in rural history in early modern and modern Argentina, mainly concerning property structures and the development of capitalist agriculture.

Iñaki Iriarte-Goñi teaches at the University of Zaragoza in Spain. He does research in rural and environmental history in modern Spain, mainly concerning common land, property rights, and forestry.

Samuel Garrido teaches at the Universitat Jaume I, in Castellón, Spain. He does research in the economic and rural history of modern Spain in comparative perspective, mainly concerning tenancy contracts and communal institutions.

Jorge Gelman teaches at the University of Buenos Aires and is a researcher of CONICET at the Instituto de Historia Americana y Argentina 'Dr. Emilio Ravignani', which he currently chairs, in Buenos Aires, Argentina. He does research in the economic and social rural history of Argentina and Latin America, mainly on land property and wealth distribution.

José-Miguel Lana teaches at the Public University of Navarra in Spain. He does research in economic and rural history in early modern and modern Spain, mainly concerning common land, land ownership, markets, and agricultural productivity.

Andrea M. Locatelli teaches at the Catholic University in Milan, in Italy. He does research in economic history in modern Lombardy and Italy, mainly concerning institutions and public policy, business, and economic development.

Mats Morell teaches at Stockholm University, in Sweden. He does research in rural history in early modern and modern Scandinavia in comparative perspective, including policy, property rights and agricultural growth.

Eugénia Rodrigues is a researcher at Centro de História da Universidade de Lisboa, in Portugal. She does research in social and political history in early modern and modern Mozambique and the Indian Ocean, including territorial appropriation, intercultural representations, slavery, and gender.

Daniel Santilli teaches at the University of Buenos Aires and is a researcher of CONICET at the Instituto de Historia Americana y Argentina 'Dr. Emilio Ravignani' in Buenos Aires, Argentina. He does research in political and economic history in modern Argentina, including land property, wealth inequality, and welfare.

Rui Santos teaches at Nova University of Lisbon, FCSH/Nova, Portugal, where he is also a researcher at CICS.Nova and IHC. He does research in historical economic sociology in early modern and modern Portugal, mainly on property rights and agrarian contracts in latifundium rural societies.

José Vicente Serrão teaches at the University Institute of Lisbon, in Portugal, where he is also a researcher at CIES-IUL. He does research in rural history in early modern Portugal, as well as imperial and global history, mainly concerning property rights and territorial appropriation.

Paolo Tedeschi teaches at the University of Milan–Bicocca, in Italy and at the University of Luxembourg. He does research in social and economic history in modern Lombardy and the history of European integration, mainly concerning agriculture, business and labour associations, and public policy.

Axel Wolz is a researcher at the Leibniz Institute of Agricultural Development in Transition Economies (IAMO), Halle (Saale) in Germany. He does research on economic and rural development in post-socialist societies, mainly concerning agricultural organizations and cooperatives.

Acknowledgements

To our family and friends, for all the time this has taken us away from them.

Most of the following chapters started out as papers discussed in a conference session that the editors convened on 'Property rights in land: Institutional innovations, social appropriations and path dependence' within the *XVIth World Economic History Conference* held in Stellenbosch, South Africa in July 2012. It is only fitting that we should begin by thanking all participants, authors and audience alike, for the stimulating discussion that took place there. We owe special thanks to Álvaro Ferreira da Silva and Daniel Bromley for having asked the really tough questions.

The editors also wish to thank: Our English proofreader, David Hardisty, for his thorough and patient reading of all the successive drafts we kept sending him; The journal *Historia Agraria*, the Sociedad Española de Historia Agraria and the Universidad de Murcia for having graciously ceded their publication rights in the Spanish original for chapter six in this book; The Spanish Ministry of Economy and Competitiveness (MEC), and the Portuguese Foundation for Science and Tecnology (FCT), without whose support through the research projects (MEC) HAR 2011-25077 and HAR 2014-54891-P at the University of Girona, and the (FCT) strategic project PEst-OE/SADG/UI4067/2014 of the Centre for Sociological Studies at the Nova University of Lisbon (CESNova), respectively, the conference session and the writing of this book would not have been possible.

Introduction

Rosa Congost, Jorge Gelman and Rui Santos

This book reflects our common interest in looking at property rights through the lenses of social history and sociology, in order to discuss the mainstream theory of new institutional economics and the derived grand narrative of economic development. The first steps leading to the book were prompted by the *leitmotiv* of the *XVIth World Economic History Conference* held in Stellenbosch, South Africa in July 2012, entitled 'The roots of economic development'. Most, though not all, of the following chapters started out as papers discussed in a conference session that we convened there on 'Property rights in land: Institutional innovations, social appropriations and path dependence'. We invited Samuel Garrido and Iñaki Iriarte and Jose-Miguel Lana to contribute their chapters at a later stage, in order to broaden the outlook on the management, appropriation and privatization of commons.

We initially chose to approach the subject under the heading of path dependence because this is one cornerstone of the grand narrative of modern economic development within new institutional economic history.[1] Put simply, path dependence is used in that context to explain why modern capitalist development took off in some societies rather than others and why, once it did, it spread so unevenly across the globe. The blame, it is argued, rests on persistent institutional divergence between a few European societies where 'good', economically efficient institutions eventually grew to form the 'roots of economic development', and far more numerous and less fortunate societies, in which such processes did not occur and whose paths were therefore trapped by 'bad' inefficient institutions which did not favour market incentives for productive investment and competitive trade. Even when 'good' institutions were somehow imported, their implementation tended to become either blocked or 'hijacked' by the organizations of the incumbent elites, so that institutional innovations were unable to steer those societies' historical course into a consistent path of development.

This neo-institutional argument transcends national and regional focuses in two ways, both of which raise relevant issues at the global scale as well. On the one hand, it puts forth a general theory to explain the persistence of worldwide patterns of uneven development, in spite of the would-be levelling effects of global competitive markets. On the other, path dependence provides a long-term narrative about the transfer of institutions from the Old to the New Worlds during the age of European empires: as the limited number of Old World societies that created favourable institutions took off on their developmental path, so did those of their colonies which they endowed with such institutions, whereas those which they did not and the colonies of other European countries inherited 'bad' institutions. Not unlike a hereditary disease, inefficient institutions including badly distributed, ill-defined, and insecure property rights, were transferred there, causing post-colonial countries to persistently lag behind. The (admittedly difficult) answer to the problem of promoting global development would lie in creating the social and political conditions for 'good' institutions to take root in the global economy, on the one hand, and in developing societies, on the other, by somehow breaking away from the lock-in of vested interests that have so far precluded effective institutional innovation.

We find the grand narrative of development in new institutional economic history provocative and stimulating but also lacking and biased, both socially and theoretically. Socially, the dichotomy of 'good' versus 'bad' institutions raises the inevitable question of for whom the outcomes of institutions were good or bad. The way in which new 'perfect', 'exclusive' and 'secure' rights of ownership were appropriated by some entailed expropriation from others – a question about distributional consequences and societal integration which cannot be evaded, if the issue is framed in terms of economic development. Theoretically, once questions are raised of appropriation, expropriation and distribution, one has to ask where the agency lies in the process. In this respect, the neo-institutional narrative seems to us to put far too much explanatory weight on rules, norms and beliefs, as well as on the agency of state and elite organizations, mostly to the detriment of the historical analysis of concrete social relations and agency.

The conference session was meant to turn our attention back to social structures and actual social practices, carried out by multiple types of agents to adopt or resist specific sets of rules in concrete situations, striving to keep, to change, to evade or to bend them to their practical interests. Our core argument is that institutions are but one rather rarefied, albeit important, layer in the analysis of property as a social and economic phenomenon. It becomes even more rarefied if they are assumed to be coherent, and the discourse becomes about property as *an* institution, abstracted out of a historical plurality of social norms, rules and enforcements being used to legitimize competing claims for appropriation at given points in space and time.

Ours is not the new institutional economists' emphasis on the efficiency of institutions. Some of us – the editors, the authors and our prospective readers – may feel that the whole debate on the economic efficiency of institutions is pointless and reject it outright. Those will have a social history of property as their ultimate goal and will look at the social processes through which property relations became institutionalized and were used in social action for the appropriation of resources and rents. Others may believe that the efficiency argument does make sense and is worth pursuing. Those will share an interest in a more detailed understanding of the social processes intervening between the 'rules of the game' and their economic outcomes. Even the economists' focus cannot evade the issue – which its more sophisticated versions do not fail to raise, even if they do not fully address it – that institutions as enforceable systems of norms and rules can only produce results through their bearing on concrete actions; hence their outcomes, efficient or otherwise, depend on by whom, how and to what extent rules and norms are appropriated as resources, suffered or resisted against as constraints, and how that balance changes over time.

We believe it is the task of historians and social scientists to embrace and understand the plurality of property institutions and the dynamics of the social relations woven around them. How were property norms and rules disputed and turned into power relations? By which social and political processes did a given set of institutions and social relations come to dominate in specific societies and times? To what degree of hegemony, resistance and hybridity? With which consequences, not just in wealth creation but also in wealth distribution, social stratification and the power structure?[2] Since land is a decisive production factor in preindustrial economies, and it has been our common subject of research for a number of years, we opted to narrow the subject down to property rights in land (including, in one of the chapters, water within irrigation communities in which the two were closely connected). Needless to say, the same broad conceptual questions might be asked of property rights in virtually any kind of asset, or for that matter of any economically relevant institutions.

We imposed neither strict theoretical guidelines nor a detailed questionnaire on the authors. The broad, exploratory questions that we asked welcomed an equally broad array of perspectives, from local or regional to global history, from 'history from below' to neo-institutional approaches seeking to deal with a wider social context. The studies included in the book have addressed those questions in different ways, all aiming to avoid the preconceptions that we often hold, as heirs to the idea that property rights evolved towards perfection as an automatic response to economic progress. Our collection of essays does not reflect a geographical or historical sampling rationale, but rather the concern to present the relevance of the guiding questions in the light of a wide diversity of historical–geographical contexts and scales, from the early modern period to still evolving processes in post-socialist transition. They range from more classical inquiries on the relationships between property rights regimes and economic growth, to detailed analyses of collaboration and conflict over property institutions, and of moral judgements and cultural memories at play in disputes over entitlements to land. As a whole, they make up a wide array of cases and subjects, which allow for a discussion of the nature of changes in property rights, the social and power relations that put those rights at stake, and their local or specific appropriations; in short, of the historically contextualized and contingent nature of such rights.

The first two chapters concern large-scale and long-term adaptations in institutional templates for property, promoted by colonial or national states in response to changing circumstances and shifting power balances among social interests. José Serrão's and Eugénia Rodrigues's essay opens the debate by looking at the distance going from a government's will to impose new property rights upon social groups – in their cases, a colonialist power upon colonial societies – to the way the latter appropriate those rules. Such processes, at the core of a world history perspective, are watched through the lens of the migration and adaptation of a Portuguese template of emphyteutic property rights to colonized regions in the Portuguese *Estado da Índia*, stretching from the sixteenth to the nineteenth centuries.

The *Estado da Índia* was made up of regions in the Indian subcontinent and the island of Ceylon, and of east African colonies in Mozambique. The former included territories with long-standing agricultural and commercial traditions and well established regulations regarding the use and appropriation of resources. The Zambezi region in Mozambique, on the other hand, was peopled with semi-nomadic societies, relying on subsistence farming and with much less control over land. The time-span and the social and political diversity across the cases has allowed the authors to describe the adaptive evolution of this institutional template, which they call 'Indo-Portuguese emphyteusis', and its varying results. Such evolution resulted from the Portuguese rulers' initiatives, but above all from their interaction with varied local contexts and use by different social groups, both aboriginal and colonial, which had varying capacities to negotiate such changes, making the resulting institutions quite different both among themselves and from those that were in force in the imperial metropolis.

Mats Morell's study of Scandinavia, focusing on the case of Sweden, also deals with long-term changes in property rights. These began with the eighteenth-century liberal offensive to overturn old rights and continued down to our days, when the supposedly 'absolute' nature of liberal property was put in question by a more explicit articulation of the social nature of specific resources.

The long-term analysis may be broken down into three distinct phases. The first, from the end of the eighteenth and through much of the nineteenth centuries, marks the political endeavour to establish absolute and individual property rights in land within a predominantly agricultural economy. The second, covering the end of the nineteenth and much of the twentieth centuries, saw those rights change through the rise of industrial interests, with new rules being politically negotiated as a consequence. The most recent and, as yet, open-ended stage under analysis is that of a post-industrial society placing greater emphasis on different values, both economic and moral, on the collective appropriation of resources and the defence of the environment, and the ensuing tensions over competing appropriations. In each of these phases, the study clearly shows that property rights did not develop linearly and were continually renegotiated according to changes in land use, conflicts of interest and the balance of power. This long-term vantage point has also allowed the author to show how ancient institutional forms tended to mould new ones, not only in terms of property rights themselves, but also in the political models used to resolve disputes, explicitly introducing processes of path dependence.

The following three chapters deal with regional changes in the legal definitions of property rights and their effects on economic growth in the first and second cases, on inequality in the second, and on the practical renegotiation of customary contracts in the third. Andrea Locatelli's and Paolo Tedeschi's chapter on Lombardy largely agrees with one of the strongest tenets in new institutional economics. According to the authors, late eighteenth- and early nineteenth-century changes in property rules and records, which made property rights better defined and more enforceable, coupled with land-tax policies in a way that provided strong incentives for economic growth. This took place in a region that combined an agrarian economy able to adapt to market changes with the development of an advanced urban system and manufacturing sector. Their long-term view shows that the adoption of these changes in property not only had lasting consequences, but also in turn depended on a much lengthier process dating back several centuries and on context-specific social dynamics, resources, and attitudes. The overall growth-inducing result in Lombardy is contrasted with different reactions and effects within the region itself and with neighbouring Veneto, to show that even where the same property rules and policies were adopted, differences in contexts and timing produced quite diverse and sometimes adverse results. Yet another contrast is made with the limited success of similar intentions to reform in southern Italy, where the power of large landowners and a more closed, polarized social structure brought a comparable political momentum to a quite different outcome.

Julio Djenderedjian's and Daniel Santilli's work deals with economic growth in the wake of changes in property rights, but also, and centrally, with the issue of land-wealth distribution. The authors have studied the province of Buenos Aires, the most dynamic region leading economic and social change in Argentina in the late nineteenth and early twentieth centuries. This period witnessed a shift in the country's economy, from its colonial matrix oriented to the internal market into becoming a dynamic agro-exporting area in the world economy. In the case of Buenos Aires, this brought about a fast increase in the value of land and the endeavour of the landed elite to secure their ownership rights, which up until then had allowed a broad range of different people to access land in a variety of legal and customary forms.

The study shows that the ruling elite sought to change property rights after considerable economic growth had already taken place, which therefore was not a linear result of the aforesaid changes. In keeping with neo-institutional economic theory, little actual change was achieved in property rights before the strengthening of state authority made it gradually able to implement them, by setting up a cadastral system, and also before economic and technological conditions made physical delimitation and enforcement cost-effective. The chapter also systematically deals with the distributional consequences of the process under analysis, showing beyond a doubt that the new situation was accompanied by growing inequality in landed property. This appears to have resulted from the kind of economic growth that took place, from the particular point within the growth process at which those new property rights were put into force, and from the particular way they were allocated. As with the previous chapter, the comparison between what happened in Buenos Aires and in the neighbouring province of Santa Fe, which had experienced an altogether different story of land allocation, shows how the same kinds of market incentives and property rights might have different distributional effects according to contextual differences.

Benedita Câmara's and Rui Santos's study discusses the bearing of the nineteenth-century liberal offensive on changing property rights in a specific rural society, by analysing the history of a widely used customary sharecropping contract in the Portuguese island of Madeira. Among other basic points, the so-called *colonia* contract established that all improvements made on the owner's land became the sharecropper's property, which the landlords would have to buy back upon the former's eviction. In the course of the eighteenth century, in the context of the growing export trade in Madeira wines, the contract proved effective in leading to peasant investment in land clearance and improvements, as well as to a wide diffusion of property rights in shares of improvements, as these percolated through the egalitarian inheritance system.

The research focus here is on analysing how the different local agents, related through this contract, reacted to the top–down changes in property rules following the establishment of the liberal regime, up to and after the approval of the 1867 Civil Code. As the customary rules, which set a balance of legitimate power between landowners and sharecroppers, had to be reinterpreted within the new legal and jurisprudential framework, this opened up normative ambiguities which were played upon by the agents. This eventually contributed to the resilience of the contract and the durability of its effects on land appropriation, even after its eventual waning during the twentieth century.

A further two chapters address cases in Spain, dealing with a fundamental issue in the history of property rights, which is also discussed in the previous chapters on Scandinavia and Lombardy as part of their wider concerns – that of the management and privatization of collective rights. In the first, Samuel Garrido discusses the management of rights to water in a number of irrigation communities in eastern Spain. In most though not all of those communities, private rights to appropriate common water were tied up with property rights in the irrigated land. The chapter's main aim is to discuss in this light Elinor Ostrom's well-known principles underlying the design of institutions for effectively 'governing the commons'.

Since an important part of Ostrom's empirical evidence concerned the very same irrigation communities dealt with in this chapter, Garrido provides a critical reappraisal of the historical data and syntheses on which her theoretical inferences had relied. Backed up by abundant and detailed empirical evidence, Garrido both corroborates a number of the inferred principles, and pinpoints those about which the historical data was lacking or had been misinterpreted. A closer look at actual practice, beyond the rules and norms, shows that while fully retaining its heuristic strength as a sensitizing device, Ostrom's institutional model still portrays a somewhat idealized vision of the actual governance of common property. Not only did some observable norms and behaviour fail to comply with the principles in the model, but also, far from having disrupted these communities, such 'deviant' characteristics may indeed have contributed to their adaptability and resilience in their specific ecological and social contexts.

Iñaki Iriarte's and Jose-Miguel Lana's chapter is less concerned with property institutions themselves, dealing instead with the social processes of dispute surrounding them. It concerns the representations made by local councils and workers' associations in 1931–1934, at the request of the Spanish Second Republic's land reform agency, to revive commons and collective rights which had been privatized in the course of the liberal reforms. Property rights and their relation with inequalities regarding the appropriation of resources are at the core of the empirical research, the historical context of which in itself shows how shifts in the balance of power opened up opportunities for the social agency of disadvantaged groups to dispute the boundaries of legitimate property rights. Changes in the latter are therefore not seen as the result of inevitable processes driven by economic efficiency, but rather as a winding road expressing contingent outcomes of struggles to appropriate land.

The empirical analysis draws on a large corpus of complaints lodged by a number of Spanish villages regarding privatized commons. Against the dominant narratives of progress which had justified such privatizations, the complaints offer the claimants' own counter-narratives of illegitimacy and abuse, which are but a part of a long-drawn process of social conflict. These narratives show that as they were implemented under the liberal regime at the local scale, the reforms were far from a perfect delineation of private property rights. Instead, they were a set of rather fluid rules, definitions and procedures of which local agents availed themselves according to their unequal powers and abilities to use them.

Joyce Bromley's and Axel Wolz's chapter on East Germany also brings together the history and memories of expropriation and appropriation. The East German countryside suffered a drastic sequence of changes in property rights under the socialist regime in the post-Second World War period, moving from expropriation and redistribution to complete collectivization of land. Then, following regime change, land was reprivatized and the country was reunited in the 1990s with one of Europe's most successful capitalist economies and brought into European and global markets. Privatization had to be negotiated among competing claims to ownership by a wide range of interest groups which had been created during the overall process: formerly large landowners who had been expropriated during Soviet occupation, peasants who had been settled on expropriated land before collectivization, later-day émigrés who had fled collectivization, former peasants who had remained in agricultural cooperatives and state farms as labourers, and, last but not least, the former managers of those collectives, who endeavoured to reconstitute large scale 'industrial' farming out of scattered private ownership rights they rearranged under cooperative or corporate enterprises. The resulting agrarian structure ended up being very different from the West German model of capitalistic family farming, which had been envisaged by reunification policies.

Contending claims during these changes deployed various economic, political, social and symbolic resources. In this complex and conflictive environment, as the political arrangements surrounding reunification had denied them right of redress, expropriated large landowners or their heirs tried to buy privatized land and establish themselves 'back' as farmers in their families' 'historic homelands'. They were often perceived as a threat by established communities, entrepreneurial interests, and state organizations. Looking through the prism of their personal narratives of encounters and disputes, Bromley and Wolz show how cultural memories were deployed in social relations and discourse as (de-)legitimation resources, and suggest this was a significant factor in the micro-processes leading to the macro-structural outcome.

The book closes with a chapter of our own. Rather than a general conclusion, we have written a discussion article in which we state our theoretical assumptions and arguments, reviewing and incorporating the empirical chapters' main findings to highlight the authors' different approaches to the questions we had set out before them. It goes without saying that the authors' views do not necessarily coincide in all points with ours, and that we alone are accountable for our assessment of their findings. Nevertheless, we believe that bringing them into our general theoretical discussion will add to the compelling reading that each of them affords in their own right.

Notes

1 The reader will find a fuller account of our argument, complete with references, in our closing chapter.
2 R. Congost, 'Property rights and historical analysis: What rights? What history?', *Past and Present*, 181 (2003), pp. 74–106; R. Congost, *Tierras, Leyes, Historia: Estudios sobre la 'Gran Obra de la Propiedad'* (Barcelona: Crítica, 2007); R. Congost and R. Santos, 'From formal institutions to the social contexts of property', in R. Congost and R. Santos (eds), *Contexts of Property in Europe: The Social Embeddedness of Property Rights in Land in Historical Perspective* (Turnhout: Brepols, 2010), pp. 13–36; J. Gelman, 'Derechos de propiedad, crecimiento económico y desigualdad en la región Pampeana, Siglos XVIII y XIX', *Historia Agraria*, 37 (2005), pp. 467–88.

1 Migration and accommodation of property rights in the Portuguese Eastern Empire, sixteenth–nineteenth centuries

José Vicente Serrão and Eugénia Rodrigues

Introduction

There is currently a consensus that early modern colonization and empire-building were among the major early drivers of globalization. Notwithstanding the asymmetrical power relations on which they rested and the violence that so often accompanied them, they irrefutably promoted the interconnection of places and nations across the globe, and fostered the worldwide circulation of people, diseases, plants, commodities, religions and concepts, etc. – including, of course, institutions.

As the Europeans settled in overseas territories and began ruling them, they had to set up institutional frameworks to deal with the often closely intertwined issues of territorial powers and land property rights of both colonizers and colonized. Legal and customary templates of property rights that prevailed in the colonizing nations were then transplanted, re-created and adapted in different ways to the colonial settings, through processes of negotiation and conflict, often with long-lasting consequences for post-colonial societies.

Formally, the Portuguese overseas empire lasted from the conquest of Ceuta in 1415 to the restitution of Macao to China in 1999, and at different points and with different configurations it extended to Africa, Asia and South America.[1] It, therefore affords a privileged vantage point to look at such process of transfer and, at times reciprocal, the accommodation of European property rights in diverse parts of the world.

In this chapter, however, we will focus primarily on the early modern period and only on the eastern part of the empire, the so-called *Estado da Índia*, which encompassed a set of territories in Asia and East Africa bordering the Indian Ocean.[2] In spite of the initial lack of relevance of land related issues in this mostly maritime and commercial empire, they did become important in some territories at different points in time. This was the case with Goa, the Northern Province, Ceylon, and Mozambique. Differently from their and other Europeans' experiences in the Atlantic world, the Portuguese met there with established native polities and communities, with their own consolidated political, fiscal, and social organizations. Consequently, the colonial rule over land and its attempts to reset the system of property rights became a highly-complex and challenging endeavour involving different institutions and legal traditions, of which the Portuguese formed but one set. This is the process we wish to bring to light. Furthermore, we aim to understand how the innovations in the institutional 'rules of the game' were conditioned and appropriated by the 'players' to whom they were addressed, within their different social, political and economic contexts.

The relevance of these issues has been acknowledged in different disciplinary and sub-disciplinary fields, and in a huge body of literature that addresses them from a variety of perspectives although, surprisingly, there is little written concerning the Portuguese empire.[3] Scholars in economics and economic history have been the most prolific writers, especially since the influential work by Douglass North placed institutions high on the economists' research agenda. Some of the most interesting developments of the foundational neo-institutionalist propositions concern precisely their application to the process of colonization and empire-building, questioning the origins, quality and performance of colonial institutions in the process of economic development.

For simplicity's sake, we can sort this abundant literature according to a few main guidelines, which can be represented by the seminal contributions of La Porta *et al.*, Engerman and Sokoloff, and Acemoglu *et al.*[4] All share the thesis that the institutions created during the colonial period played a crucial role in the long-term economic performance of the formerly colonized countries, and were, thereby, a signifi-cant cause for path-dependent divergence in their comparative development. Somehow, they argue, some colonies and post-colonial countries had obtained 'good' institutions – meaning more democratic, inclusive and protective of private property rights and fair market competition – whereas others were burdened with 'bad' ones – meaning economically extractive, based on political and social inequality, and adverse to market competition. What sets the theories apart is the ways in which they explain this alleged historical bifurcation.

Briefly, La Porta and his co-authors stress the exogenous nature of colonial institutions, brought in by the colonizing powers, the diverse cultural and legal backgrounds of which led them to transpose either 'good' or 'bad' institutions – the former usually being identified as those of British, German or Scandinavian legal origin. The other authors stress instead that colonial institutions were endogenous in the sense that they were (re-)created anew in the colonized areas as a response to local conditions, which were the determinants of short-term and long-term divergence in institutional quality and efficiency. However, they differ in the sets of factors and causal mechanisms that they emphasize. While Engerman and Sokoloff refer to factor endowments such as the climate, the geography and natural resources, and the availability of land and labour, Acemoglu *et al.* focus on different disease environments and their impact on the settlers' mortality rates.

It is impossible to give a full account here of the theoretical and empirical contributions made by such institutionalism-inspired scholarship.[5] Nevertheless, this rests on debatable and biased assumptions, such as the belief in supposedly absolute and universal values as the rule of law, and well-defined, exclusive and secure property rights. This historical, and perhaps ideological, construct of the modern Western path to capitalism should not be projected back to the early modern period, let alone to the non-Western world. The overall Eurocentrism of this mainstream literature may explain some of its shortcomings, one of which being the surprisingly blind eye it turns on pre-colonial native institutions. Research on the colonial origins of comparative development is solely focused on the alleged long-term effects of *colonial* institutions, namely those that were transplanted or created during European colonization. Even the concept of *endogenous* institutions usually refers to institutions created by European settler societies as a response to local conditions, rather than to indigenous institutions.

A second shortcoming is their insensitivity to the concrete agency of individuals and their social behaviour in the appropriation of institutions, especially with regard to indigenous peoples. It is necessary to look outside the dominant literature to find some degree of attention being paid to these aspects, which, as we will see, are crucial for a proper understanding of the Portuguese imperial experience. Christopher Bayly, for instance, posits the hybridity and heterogeneity of the sources of comparative economic development, suggesting that:

> the debate about the role of institutions in the modern development might benefit from a historical investigation of how, when and why indigenous people appropriated, adapted, absorbed and often totally reconstituted European-style institutions . . .[6]

We should stress that our subject matter, broadly defined as the regulation and the exercise of rights concerning the occupation, possession and use of land in colonial contexts, is not just about the economy and economic institutions. It is closely related to a number of key issues about colonialism and empire-building and has, therefore, been addressed by multiple alleyways of scholarly inquiry, such as sovereignty, ethnicity, indigenous rights, settler colonialism, the environment, politics, spatial history, and legal history.[7] In the latter field, a special mention should be made to 'legal pluralism', a concept which proved very useful in our study, understood in at least two distinct meanings which we have used interrelatedly: as the existence of multi-layered rights over the same thing, person or community, and as the co-habitation of multiple legal and judiciary systems, namely those of the native societies and the imperial powers.[8]

Following this introduction, the first section addresses the earlier experiments in institutional rearrangements and land policies as they developed in Goa and the Northern Province in India during the sixteenth century. These experiments inspired later developments in Ceylon and Mozambique, which were the most important and extensive cases of territorialization in the Portuguese eastern empire, which are dealt with in the next two sections. Across all cases, we highlight how and why rule over land became a concern of the colonial project, which native and former imperial institutions were already in place, how these were replaced or merged with those brought in by the Portuguese, and how the multiple players, both within the colonizer and the colonized society, reacted to, or made use of institutional innovations. The concluding section presents a tentative interpretation of the whole process.

The first experiments in India: The making of an Indo–Portuguese emphyteusis in sixteenth-century Goa and the Northern Province

As the Portuguese arrived in the Indian Ocean at the turn of the sixteenth century, they had no preconceived plan to deal with land, nor was this a priority in their initial imperial strategy. Nevertheless, the need to regulate land and property rights arose as soon as they took possession of Goa in 1510 and occupied the Northern territories shortly after. These were the first two experiments in a long-term, evolving process of learning-by-doing in land policy-making, often based on trial and error as the Portuguese rulers ventured into new and unknown contexts. They were the first Europeans to engage in territorial occupation in Africa and Asia, in areas already occupied by organized societies. Aside from their military strongholds in Morocco, their former colonial experience was limited to previously uninhabited Atlantic islands. The colonization of Brazil, besides being different in nature, only actually began in the mid-sixteenth century, after or alongside the Indian endeavours.

The case of Goa takes on a special significance. Even though in the sixteenth century this was a small territory of less than 1,000 square kilometres, it was the seat of the *Estado da Índia* and it was there that, for the first time, the Portuguese had to deal with land issues in their Asian possessions.

In 1510, newly-conquered Goa was basically a Hindu society under the Muslim rule of the Bijapur Sultanate. Upon conquest, the Portuguese faced two main types of land appropriation. Firstly, there were those lands belonging to the small Muslim ruling elite that locally supported and rendered services to the sultan. Secondly, and the largest part by far, were the lands that remained in possession of the Hindu village communities, which numbered about 150 in the whole territory. As almost everywhere in India, in Goa the villages formed the basic territorial organizational units for agrarian, fiscal, judiciary, military and other purposes.[9] Goan villages were almost entirely self-governed by a council (*ganvkari*) of descendants of the founding lineages (*ganvkars*). These headmen collectively owned and administered the village land and shared the village's profits and losses. A part of the village land was assigned to the maintenance of the Hindu temples, another part was shared among the *ganvkars* and their servants, and what remained was left for public and common use. Although full individual ownership rights did not seem to exist, much land was held under long-term and hereditary tenancy rights. The *ganvkars* were also in charge of collecting the taxes due to the ruler, who thus kept a kind of fiscal-based sovereignty.[10]

In the aftermath of the conquest, the Muslim lands were confiscated and became Portuguese Crown property to be redistributed for free, mainly to Portuguese *casados*.[11] The same applied to the lands that were held by those native Hindus who had refused Portuguese sovereignty and fled to Bijapur, the difference being that these were to be redistributed among Indians who had converted to Christianity. The latter aside, village communities and their *ganvkar* elites had their property rights confirmed, as long as they remained loyal to the Portuguese government and kept paying it the taxes previously due to the sultan. The guideline for this initial land policy, largely correlated with political, fiscal and social goals, was to keep things as much unchanged as possible concerning the interests of the majority of the population. This principle, repeatedly proclaimed at the highest level including by the king, saw its finest expression in the *Foral de Mexia*, a charter of local usages dated 1526, which was an attempt to compile, codify and enact the native institutions – customary laws, practices and customs – with a special focus on land rights, inheritance rules and the revenue collection system.

This is an especially interesting document, for several reasons. Firstly, it demonstrates that right from the beginning of their colonial rule in the Indian Ocean, the Portuguese were concerned with surveying, understanding, and, to some degree, acknowledging the pre-existing native institutional framework – a concern which would later be replicated in all their other dominions through the drawing up of similar charters and *tombos* (land registers). Secondly, since the charter was drawn up in consultation and with the collaboration of native officials and informants, it certainly involved some negotiation and compromise with colonized groups. Thirdly, the *Foral* was a striking instance of legal pluralism, as part of a more general policy of indigenous populations being ruled by their own customary laws, institutions, and elites; the colonizer's law only applied to the Portuguese and the converted natives.[12]

Nevertheless, these principles were soon to be compromised, especially as religion gradually became a tool for the political rule of the colonial power, an opportunity for a part of the native population, and a focus of resistance for another. In the 1540s, Hindu temples were destroyed and had their lands confiscated by the Crown. Many Hindus abandoned those territories and entire villages rebelled against the Portuguese rule, following which the villagers' lands were confiscated as well, to be redistributed among Portuguese settlers, religious orders (mostly the Jesuits) and converted natives, often of lower caste and social rank. There was also much trading of land among these groups. This had a strong impact on the distribution of land and of property rights between the different ethnic, religious and social groups.[13] In Goa, however, institutional change only became significant after the middling decades of the sixteenth century, to which the developments of the second experience of territorial occupation in India made a significant contribution.

The Northern Province consisted of about 5,000 square kilometres in the vicinity of the Gulf of Cambay, north of Goa. Even though the region mattered to the Portuguese mostly for its strategic value and the commercial wealth of its port cities (Diu, Daman, Bassein, Chaul and Mumbai), it also contained a rich agricultural sector that generated substantial land revenue.[14] The incorporation of these territories within the Portuguese empire took place between 1534 and 1559, a little after Goa, by means of war and negotiation with the Sultanates of Gujarat and Ahmadnagar.[15] Both experiences coevolved very closely, with regard to the aspects being analysed. However, it was in the Northern Province that the innovations that would prove more decisive in the long term were first introduced.

As in Goa, the mainly Hindu population was governed by Muslim rulers, and the villages, around 750 in total, formed the basis of the territorial organization. However, they enjoyed much less autonomy and self-government. The villages were grouped in larger unities, the most important of which were the *iqtas*. The *iqta* was a common institution for provincial and district-level administration across the Islamic world, with mostly military and fiscal functions. The Muslim king granted each *iqta* to an *iqtadar*, along with a substantial part of its revenue instead of a salary. The *iqtadar* was a seigniorial-like figure who played an intermediary role between the native Hindu population and the alien Muslim ruler, acting simultaneously as landlord, district governor, military chief and revenue collector.[16] Also differing from Goa, the Northern villages had neither collective nor full ownership rights over their lands. There was instead a chain of multi-layered rights of a different nature (ownership, tenancy, fiscal and sovereignty rights), at the top of which the king sat as the territorial overlord, with the Hindu peasantry at the bottom and the *iqtadar* lords and some middling groups in between.

When this territory became part of the *Estado da Índia*, the Portuguese king presented himself as the sultan's successor in regard to lordship over the territory, in the process declaring the land as Crown property. For political and certain practical considerations as well, the Portuguese could not formally accept the pre-existing institutional framework. But they would not change it radically, either, because it proved effective for political control and the collection of land revenue. What they eventually did was to render the existing structure Portuguese-like, by transferring a set of homeland institutions to India that were as close as possible to those already in place.

The main role in this institutional grafting was played by emphyteusis, a modified version of which was put in force in the Northern Province. This was originally a legal and socio-economic system of overlapping layers of property rights with a long tradition in Portugal. Its basic principle was the splitting of a thing's ownership into two distinct domains by means of a contract: the original proprietor retained a nominal holding on the property, called 'direct' or 'eminent' domain; the taker received the 'useful' domain consisting of most remaining property rights, either for a specified number of successive lives or in perpetuity, at the cost, alongside some other duties, of an annual fee (quitrent or ground-rent) called *foro*, whereby the taker was commonly called *foreiro*; the contract itself was more often designated as *aforamento* or *prazo*.[17]

As it was adapted to the local interests and circumstances, the Portuguese emphyteusis mixed with the donation of Crown assets, as well as with some native features, into a new hybrid system. More specifically, lands, villages, rents and several types of rights in land would thereafter be granted as Crown 'gifts' (*mercês*), though not for free as previously in Goa, but rather in return for a ground rent in cash (*foro*) and some service duties, namely military; the grantees (*foreiros*) were compelled to dwell on the land and to provide a stipulated number of men and weapons in the event of war. The new legal framework and vocabulary thus turned the former *iqta* grants into *aforamentos* or *prazos*, the former *iqtadars* into *foreiros*, and the parcel of fiscal rights and whatever land revenue was formerly owed to the sultans into a *foro,* which was now to be paid to the Crown for its eminent property right.

This Indo–Portuguese emphyteusis, as we shall name it, became the main innovative feature in the institutional framework used to regulate property rights and the allocation of land in Portuguese India. To begin with, it provided a smooth transition to the Portuguese colonial rule, while ensuring that supreme lordship and the ability to reallocate lands and rents was kept in the king's hands. Moreover, it allowed the Crown to fulfil multiple goals, such as rewarding personal services, the formation of a military force to defend the territory, and the preservation of a network of tax collectors that ensured mediation between village communities and the treasury administration.

In social terms, the main consequence of these institutional changes was the replacement of the former Hindu and Muslim aristocracy of *iqtadars* and suchlike by Portuguese and Christianized Indians from Goa, as well as by some Catholic orders. Once in place, this class of *foreiros*, never numbering more than a few hundred, soon learned how to use and subvert the emphyteutical rules to their own benefit, and the Northern *prazos* became probably the largest breeding ground for the creation and reproduction of a landed aristocracy in the *Estado*. The economic impact of their settlement on the region, however, was minimal, since they were hardly involved in the real rural economy. As ever, this was left to the native peasantry, whose rights and duties were not touched by the changes described above.

As we shall see, these pioneering experiences in transfer, accommodation and change involving both Portuguese and native institutions would inspire future Portuguese policies in the East, concerning the redefinition of land grants and land rights, as well as their social appropriation.

The transfer and development of Indo–Portuguese emphyteusis in seventeenth-century Ceylon[18]

The first contact of the Portuguese with Ceylon, now Sri Lanka, dates back to 1506. However, they only acquired political rights in the island in 1597, when the last king of Kotte, the most important of the three kingdoms in the country, bequeathed his crown to the Portuguese king, who thus became *de jure* entitled to govern the Sinhalese monarchy.[19] Although they never achieved full control of the island – the Jaffna kingdom was only conquered in 1619 and that of Kandy was never subdued – the Portuguese remained in Ceylon as the main ruling power until their defeat and replacement by the Dutch East India Company (VOC) in 1658. During their short rule there, they undertook the most remarkable project of territorial occupation in the eastern empire, which included ambitious plans for land surveying and land reform with political, fiscal and economic goals.

Sri Lanka is an island with 65,000 square kilometres. At the time, Ceylon had an estimated population of between 0.75 and 1.3 million and, at the basis of social and territorial organization, some 22,000 villages.[20] The Sinhalese (about four-fifths of the population) and the Tamils formed the main ethnic groups, culturally rooted in Theravada Buddhism and Hinduism, respectively. The Portuguese inherited a fully-fledged system of governance and administration, which they could not replace or change dramatically because they had to rely on the native administration and part of the former ruling elite to implement colonial rule. On the other hand, besides having to deal with a permanent state of warfare with the native kingdoms and the Dutch throughout the period, Portugal never ceased to be seen as a foreign power, whose authority was challenged and which faced both passive and active resistance, including multiple uprisings. All this put the Portuguese under tremendous pressure and required multiple strategies for negotiating their power and alliances. Colonial rule in Ceylon involved managing a variety of often-divergent interests on both sides. On the Portuguese side, there were the governments in Lisbon, Madrid and Goa,[21] the civil and military authorities in the island, the community of *casados*, and the various missionary orders. On the Ceylonese side, there were the courtly aristocracy, the royal officials (from the provincial governors to the district, village and caste headmen), the native militias, the *goyigama* and the *pangukaraya* castes of cultivators, to mention but a few.[22]

The Portuguese never actually intended to settle extensively in Ceylon, neither did they wish to develop a plantation economy similar to those in their Atlantic areas.[23] Their main goal was to exploit the island's economic resources that were in demand in international markets (pearls, elephants, areca nuts and especially cinnamon, deemed the best in the world), which required direct control of their production and not just their trade. Moreover, the Portuguese also wished to appropriate the fiscal and other land-based revenues formerly due to the Sinhalese monarchy, on which they were relying to pay for the colonization of Ceylon, if nothing else.

This combination of economic, financial and political goals bestowed tremendous importance on land, both directly and indirectly. Directly because the island's richest economic resources, as well as most of its taxation sources, came from the rural sector.[24] Indirectly because the distribution of land and its income was perceived as the main resource for attracting and rewarding Portuguese settlers and soldiers, and to secure compliance and cooperation from the native authorities and populations.

When it came to defining a strategy to deal with land, one of the biggest challenges faced by the Portuguese was the complexity of the indigenous system of property rights, land tenure and labour organization. This system rested on two fundamental principles of the Ceylonese society, both related to the king's role as the primary source of authority and the patron of social cohesion: *bhupati,* the king's 'lordship of the lands',[25] and *rajakariya,* the 'service to the king'. According to these principles, individuals had the right to hold or enjoy a landed asset only by royal grant or authorization, and always by way of service tenure. Therefore, strictly speaking, there were no land*owners* in Ceylon, only land*holders*. The general principle was that land was not bound to particular persons, but rather to specific services, as a source of maintenance and a reward. Consequently, the concept of private ownership of land did not exist in Ceylon. What existed were limited rights in certain lands that were tied to a network of obligations.[26]

Granted these basic principles, there were important variations with regard to the specific tenurial rights and to the kinds of granted holdings. Concerning the former, the main distinction was between *paraveni* (hereditary) and *badawedili* (more precarious) tenures. The holdings ranged from simple parcels of land to entire villages. Within the complex village organization, in turn, there was significant overlapping of property rights in different kinds of land, and of correlative service and rent obligations. Moreover, the villages were not equal in status and their titles of possession. They could be grouped into three main categories: the *gabadagam* villages, of higher income or strategic value, were never granted and were kept under direct administration by the royal treasury; the *viharagam* and *devalagam* villages, which the Ceylonese kings had granted over time, respectively, to Buddhist monasteries and Hindu temples for their maintenance, fully exempt from services and rents, and lastly, the largest group was the *nindagam* villages, which the king had granted mostly to the Sinhalese nobility and bureaucracy in service tenures. The *nindagam* grantees were entitled to a combined rule over land, labour and revenues, in return for performing specified 'public' service duties.

In spite of its complexity, this native institutional system had a number of strikingly similar features to those in the Portuguese homeland and in other overseas territories, namely those in Goa and the Northern Province, such as: the village as the basic unit of property, agriculture and territorial organization; the large amount of land held directly by the Crown; the bond between land or village tenure and services rendered to the Crown; imperfect ownership and overlapping property rights; a high absentee landlord rate; and, above all, the fact that the king held the ultimate lordship over all the land and the consequent prerogative of distributing it among the vassals, which could be easily translated into the Portuguese endowment of Crown assets and the emphyteutical eminent domain.[27] As was previously the case in India, this was crucial in allowing the Portuguese Crown, acting as the new sovereign, to regulate the whole system on its own terms without clashing head on with the traditional sources of legitimacy.

The Portuguese land policy in Ceylon, the guidelines of which were more clearly set down in 1607–1608, aimed at three main goals: to gather information about the existing tenurial system; to change to its advantage the legal framework that regulated the relationship between the Crown, the grantees and their assets; and to promote the redistribution of landed resources among the Portuguese and their allies, not excluding large-scale holding transfers.[28]

The first goal was achieved by the *tombos* of Ceylon (1614, 1618, 1622, and 1645), which were books of detailed records from extensive surveys of all villages and singular land plots, stating their holders and tenure titles, agricultural uses, taxes and duties, along with copious other data.[29] As to the second and third goals, the Portuguese transplanted and adapted the same concept and formulae to Ceylon which they had tested in the Northern Province: all new grants of land and villages were thenceforth to be carried out in emphyteusis by a letter of *aforamento*, in exchange for ground-rent in cash and some stipulated obligations, military and other. Portuguese and natives were included alike in these regulations, albeit under different conditions and following a list of priorities conceived mostly to reward soldiers, attract settlers and draw in collaborative indigenous elites. All pre-existing grants might be kept in the same hands, but they had to adapt accordingly and, most importantly, they had to undergo a process of qualification and re-entitlement. Finally, assets of strategic value, namely the villages, lands, and labour more closely engaged in the production of cinnamon, were kept under the Crown's direct administration.

These seemingly radical plans for land reform and institutional change were actually rather conservative in most respects, and some of their results diverged from initial expectations. Change was rather moderate concerning the distribution of landholdings. With perhaps a few exceptions, the Portuguese did not take over land and villages from Sinhalese people. They entered into land tenure in Ceylon almost exclusively through grants of royal and temple villages, the main beneficiaries of which seem to have been those in charge of land distribution themselves and their clients: governors, commanders and other military, the Crown's local representatives, religious orders and a few *casado* settlers. In total, they did not exceed a few hundred.[30]

The thousands of *nindagam* villages were kept in Sinhalese hands, albeit not necessarily the same hands as before. Indeed, on the whole the prime beneficiaries of Portuguese land policy were indigenous elites, either by being granted new holdings from the royal estate or by extending or confirming such *nindagam* as they already held; those who took part in land reallocation decisions certainly reinforced their social and political status in the island. However, this process depended on the indigenous elites' ability to negotiate with the Portuguese and to manage their political alliances and religious confessions; as a result, not all native groups benefited from this, giving rise to discontents. Finally, we should bear in mind that whether new or old, Portuguese or Sinhalese, the grantees of village (re)allotments were not usually themselves farmers; as village or landholders, they only collected rents and made use of the native labour force. By and large, similarly to what happened in Goa and the Northern Province, the peasantry kept the land they tilled and their landholding status, complete with rent and labour dues.

Therefore, the foundations of the local system of property rights were barely scratched by Portuguese colonial rule. Neither the new institutional framework, especially the merging of the Indo-Portuguese emphyteusis with the native system, nor the redistribution of tenures and the resulting reconfiguration of the island's landed aristocracy, relabelled as *foreiros*, overhauled the traditional structure. Village holdings remained basically a rent gathering position and a way to remunerate past or present services. The new framework closely translated the indigenous institutions, reproducing the hierarchical and 'dual dominium' relationships in which the ownership of land and villages was split between the landholders and the king. Deliberately or not, the most remarkable adjustment seems to have been that of the European institutions to the colonial environment, rather than the other way round.

Arguably, some of the major changes may have resulted from the system's unintentional side-effects, such as the development of a market in *foros* and tenures of lands and villages, mainly from the 1620s on – which was a quite normal market in Portugal, and was, therefore, fostered in Ceylon by both the legal framework and the Portuguese land- and rent-holders' actions – and the imposition of quit-rents in cash on most villages, both of which sped up the monetization of Ceylon's economy. As seen from below, to the general population the innovations mostly meant additional and heavier charges and became an enduring factor of discontent.[31] To the colonial rulers, the difficulty in collecting taxes and dues, the frequent embezzlements, by both Portuguese and Ceylonese officials, and above all the huge military expenditure made this colonial endeavour a constant source of deficit, falling utterly short of the expectations that had driven the intervention in Ceylon.

Indo–Portuguese emphyteusis migrates to East Africa: The *prazos* in seventeenth- to nineteenth-century Mozambique[32]

Yet another process of colonization and large-scale territorial occupation began in the early seventeenth century in the Portuguese Captaincy of Mozambique, mainly in the Zambezi valley.

When the Portuguese first arrived in Mozambique in 1498, their major goal was to control the gold and ivory trade networks, from the plateau south of the Zambezi down to the Indian Ocean ports. During the sixteenth century, they moved towards the Zambezi valley to seize the trade routes from their sources, including the gold mines themselves. As the area was at the time occupied by several warring African polities,[33] the Portuguese intervened in those conflicts to consolidate their own territorial domains, both by conquest and alliances with African rulers. In 1607 the ruler of Monomotapa, one of the Karanga states, gave the Portuguese possession of the mining territories, and in 1629 he proclaimed his allegiance as a vassal to the Portuguese king, to whom he offered an extensive area on the right bank of the Zambezi. This eventually allowed the Portuguese to take hold of the entire right bank, as well as the Makua country north of the delta.[34]

Thus, through war and diplomacy, large tracts of land formerly under African rulers were subjected to Portuguese sovereignty and thereafter allotted and granted in emphyteusis to Portuguese settlers, following the institutional template that had been developed in India and was at the time being adapted in Ceylon. The indigenous political organization in the region consisted of at least two levels of authority, which might in turn be subject to higher Karanga or Maravi rulers. The upper of the two basic levels was that of the *amambo* (*mwini dziko*, in Maravi), whose legitimacy drew on lineage ancestry going back to the primordial inhabitants of the territory or to groups of conquerors. They held jurisdiction over the territories held by the second level, the *af'umu* (*mwini mudzi*, in Maravi), ruling them either directly or through *af'umu* village chiefs.

Regrettably, little is known of pre-colonial land ownership, tenure and use in the Zambezi valley. All evidence suggests that they were deeply connected to power relations and a social organization based on kinship networks and personal ties. As in other African societies, land tenure implied a twofold set of rights and obligations, related to group belonging, on the one hand, and on the other to the control of land as a resource.[35] The literature on Africa usually refers to collective land ownership with family or individual rights of land use, a pattern that seems to have prevailed in the Zambezi valley as well.[36] The *amambo* held the power to confirm the right of the *af'umu* lineages to occupy land, in exchange for the payment of taxes and their acknowledgement as territorial lords. Within each village, land use rights were usually distributed among kinship groups. Nevertheless, because the power and wealth of the rulers depended mostly on the number of their subjects, land rights would also be granted to newcomers, in exchange for their allegiance to *amambo* authority and the eventual creation of kinship ties.[37]

Following the acquisition of sovereignty in the Zambezi valley, the Portuguese Crown began granting land to its vassals – with the exception of mining land which, like the Ceylonese cinnamon grounds, was reserved for the Crown – according to the template that had evolved in India, that is, the mix of emphyteusis with the endowment of Crown assets that we termed the Indo-Portuguese emphyteusis. Once more, this was grafted onto the pre-existing hierarchy of domains, but this time the absence of a centralized chain of service mediated by land grants meant that there were no beneficiary indigenous elite groups to begin with. The Indo-Portuguese system was, therefore, initially superimposed on the native one, to the benefit of a purely colonial elite only.

The first formal regulation of property rights in Mozambique was enacted in Goa in 1608. It ordered the compilation of *tombos* and gave the Captain (*i.e.*, the governor) of Mozambique jurisdiction to grant land in exchange for the payment of a *foro* and the grantees' obligation to reside in the territory and to ensure its defence and administration. In exchange, they could collect such taxes and tributes as were in force in the African societies, both in kind and in labour, from the population within their territorial holdings. Land concessions varied greatly in size and could cover one or more of the districts ruled by the native *amambo*.

As before in the Northern Province and in Ceylon, these land grants combined legal and lexical features of both the emphyteusis and Crown donations. They were individually granted by letters of '*aforamento e mercê*', the Portuguese terms for emphyteutical allotment and the Crown gift or benefice, respectively. The grantees were indistinctly called *foreiros* and *mercenarios* (those who received a *mercê*). As to the territorial holdings themselves, they were initially known either as 'Crown lands' or by native denominations such as *muzinda* and *incumbe*. It was only in the early eighteenth century, and following a similar evolution in the Northern Province, that these holdings took the designation by which they are best known to this day, that of *prazos*.[38]

According to the *tombo* drawn up in 1634–1637, the grantees were mostly Catholic institutions and Portuguese soldiers who had served in Mozambique and elsewhere in the *Estado da Índia*. At first the system was geared to extraction, rather than production. Neither the *foreiros* nor the Crown aspired to establish in Mozambique the kind of plantations that were so characteristic of other colonial areas. In addition to tax income, the landholdings mainly formed the power basis for the *foreiros* to recruit slave labour for trade, prospecting and eventually mining, their core economic activities, and warfare. A rise in debt enslavement was indeed one of the main social outcomes of the spread of trade relations. Because of that and of the very power relations embodied in the *prazos*, the volume, gender profile (masculinization) and social relations of slavery were considerably reshaped under the Portuguese rule.

The *prazos* became the identifying symbol of the colonial elite, and ensured its economic and social reproduction. The fact that they were granted in terms of lives favoured the strong local rooting of this elite, who had to remain in place to ensure their right of renewal. At the same time, the principle of free succession, by which the grantees might stipulate non-kin as successors, suited them by enabling the physical and symbolical continuity of heirless houses, in an area with high mortality among Europeans.

To the Crown, the Zambezi *prazos* basically served political purposes, as a positive expression of Portuguese sovereignty in the area, a tool for territorial administration, and a stock of assets for rewarding services rendered. From the economic standpoint, the mining activities soon proved unprofitable and the quit-rents themselves were not a major source of income for the royal treasury, as compared with the tax revenues collected on trade – for which the assertion of sovereignty, territorial administration, and military and civil services to the Crown were paramount.

For the Africans in the Zambezi valley, the institution and spread of the *prazos* had significant and variable impacts, depending on their particular situations. On the one hand, as stated above, more Africans were enslaved and the profile of slavery changed. On the other, the Karanga rulers suffered a considerable loss of territory and vassals, which affected their collection of taxes and tributes. Consequently, they either fought the *foreiros* to recover former territorial borders, or forged alliances with them in an attempt to keep what power had remained to them.

At a lower level, the local chiefs established in Portuguese-ruled territory maintained their institutional and political positions. While some sought alliances with the *foreiros*, most commonly they challenged their authority and resisted paying taxes. There was fierce competition between the native rulers and the *foreiros* in this regard because besides material earnings, tax collection carried strong political symbolism.[39] When the *foreiros* attempted to widen their power, either by increasing taxation or a more intensive use of native labour, both the local leaders and the common people often resisted by revolting or migrating to other territories.[40] Nevertheless, some landholders did see their ruling power acknowledged by the Africans, by adopting, in a more or less detached way, the traditional practices incumbent on those who ruled the land, such as rain ceremonies and rites honouring the ancestors, among others.[41]

'In the course of the eighteenth century, the Karanga gradually reoccupied the Tete area on the right bank, forcing the *foreiros* into left bank Maravi country. Besides military incursions and the creation of new *prazos*, the expansion of the Portuguese territorial occupation also proceeded through private acquisition of land from local rulers. It is not clear whether or not this land trade was an innovation introduced by the Portuguese. Although the thesis of the absence of a land market in pre-colonial Africa has been most widely accepted, recent research sustains that land and land use rights were regularly traded in some regions, giving rise to a 'pseudo-market'.[42] It was indeed common among the Maravi to trade rights in land use, which the Portuguese reinterpreted as land ownership. Such land transactions became regular among colonists as well, leading to the development of a land market outside the rules for the *prazos*.[43]

The system, built during the first decades of the seventeenth century, eventually underwent important changes as a result of the Portuguese policies laid down in Lisbon, Goa or Mozambique itself, and of their appropriation by local social actors. Among the most interesting developments were the 'africanization' and feminization of the *foreiros* elite, through inheritance strategies and some unintended effects of colonial policies. As the number of European-born settlers decreased, due to high mortality, the *prazos* were gradually transferred to Afro– Indo–Portuguese mixed-race individuals and to persons of Goan origin. During the eighteenth century, a growing number of mostly mixed-race women became landholders, both as a result of family inheritance and alliance strategies, and of a policy of granting *prazos* to these women, on the hope that this would allure European men to come and settle in Mozambique as their consorts. By the end of the century, over half the *prazos* were registered to women who became known as *donas* (ladies), a designation that reflected the importance of this newly gendered (and to a large extent racialized) landholding group by associating them with the colonial elite.

In the meanwhile, the rules concerning the granting and holding of *prazos* had been reformulated since 1752, as Mozambique was severed from the *Estado da Índia* and placed directly under the central imperial government of Lisbon. In a context of legal harmonization and striving for agricultural development, the *prazos* were to some extent, and mostly in discursive terms, identified with the *sesmarias*, the land-granting model followed in the Portuguese Atlantic, primarily intended for colonization and agricultural improvement in unpopulated territories.[44] As of 1760, new regulations, inspired by the laws in force in Brazil, were but a failed attempt at a major shift in the rationale of the property rights encapsulated in the *prazos*, which were to be conditional on agricultural improvements and European settlement, rather than on services rendered. The path of the Indo–Portuguese emphyteusis we have followed up to this point would have been replaced by a new offspring of the Atlantic imperial tradition. As it happened, even though in 1760 the legislation on the *prazos* did formally incorporate some rules borrowed from the *sesmarias*, in practice the system remained fundamentally the same. In a different vein, by the end of the century, the Mozambique government set a limit on the number of *prazos* that each might hold and narrowed inheritance to family members, aiming primarily to displace a part of the existing *foreiros* to release land for new landholdings. The main beneficiary of this policy was an elite of new players: the merchants in the Mozambique Island, a recent and rising elite based on the slave trade, who acted as absentee landlords, and had the land either managed by stewards or leased out.[45]

In the mid-nineteenth century, a new generation of larger *prazos* called '*supra-prazos*' or 'secondary states' reshaped the territory – the latter name reflecting their highly political nature.[46] This was an attempt by local warlords to take advantage of the political and social instability caused by the increasing slave trade and the Nguni expansion from the South to fight the Nguni, rival *foreiros* and the Portuguese administration itself, which was being forced by international pressure to put an end to the slave trade. The government of Mozambique eventually awarded these warlords formal titles to the land that they had already occupied, along with military patents, in the hope of forging alliances to regain territorial control. However, unintended consequences followed. The landlords of these '*supra-prazos*', mostly mixed race or of Goan origin, seldom maintained their alliance with the Portuguese authorities and preferred instead to forge agreements with African chieftaincies, thus becoming an effective barrier to the expansion of the colonial government.[47] They would eventually lose their power and landholdings during the ensuing colonial occupation wars and the legal redefinition of land-granting rules.

The model of granting extensive tracts of land for development and territorial control, however, remained in place, in part to be appropriated by new players and interests. Wide areas were then assigned for economic development, along with delegated territorial sovereignty, to a chartered corporation funded with international capital, namely the *Companhia de Moçambique*, or leased to other capitalist entities.[48] The *foreiros* of the remaining *prazos* eventually rebelled in the late nineteenth century against this state of affairs, supported by their former slaves whom the capitalist companies were turning from hunters, tax collectors and private soldiers into forced labour.[49]

Conclusion

The settlement of the Portuguese and their colonial rule in the territories considered in this study differed somewhat in nature, purpose and duration. Goa, occupied by the Portuguese in 1510, was a small territory of mostly political significance, as the capital of the *Estado da Índia*. The Northern Province, under Portuguese rule between 1534 and 1739, had a wider territorial extent, as well as strategic relevance. It was a source of agricultural provisions for Goa, and it provided the European-born and Indo–Portuguese elites of the *Estado* with their best opportunity to gain a foothold in landed assets. Ceylon, formally ruled by the Portuguese from 1597 to 1658, counted mostly due to the economic importance of its agricultural products, which were in high demand in international trade. Inland Mozambique, which was incorporated in the Portuguese empire between the early seventeenth century and 1975, was a huge, scarcely populated area, the territorial occupation of which was of limited interest to begin with, mostly intended for geopolitical purposes and to control the trading routes and the gold mining sites.

The Portuguese never succeeded, nor indeed intended to settle massively in these territories on the Indian Ocean, and consequently, even counting mixed-race descendants, they made up but a minority of the total population. In all cases, the demographic imbalance between colonizer and colonized required permanent political negotiation with the native elites – however much that might differ according to the local social and political organization and to different sets of circumstances. The Portuguese exerted colonial rule there over previously organized polities and populations, with their own institutions, political structures and social hierarchies, although with different levels of complexity and sophistication – as for instance between Ceylon and Mozambique. The indigenous notions of property and territory and the pre-colonial systems of land tenure also varied widely at the outset.

Despite such variations, our set of case studies shows that land and the definition of rights concerning its occupation, possession and use not only were part of the Portuguese colonial experience in the Indian Ocean, but were also far more significant than is usually acknowledged. Regardless of the fact that the main colonial objectives lay elsewhere, the issues related to land rights ended up being of great instrumental importance for the sustainability of the eastern empire. That was so not for economic reasons alone, as was the control of the agricultural production in Ceylon and more generally the collection of tax revenue, of which land was one of the chief sources. Land rights mattered also, and probably mostly, for political and social reasons – as a resource to attract settlers, to reward services to the colonial power by both the Portuguese and the natives, and to try and keep social peace among the colonized populations, by disturbing as little as possible the land rights of the common people and drawing in a part of their elites; in a related way, they became a tool for religious policy as well. And of course, the rule over land was an intrinsic part of the physical and political occupation of the territory and therefore a key requirement for the exercise or delegation of sovereignty.

This varied set of reasons eventually compelled the Portuguese colonial authorities to implement land policies and to reformulate the institutional framework regulating land and property rights in their overseas dominions. This was an ongoing learning process across time and space, which gradually came to define a sort of *modus faciendi*, the main features of which can be summarized as follows.

Firstly, once sovereignty over a territory was acquired, the King of Portugal asserted himself as the successor to the previous ruler, in his condition as the sole 'owner' or supreme lord of all the land in the territory – a widespread notion in Asian societies, and which was not very different in East Africa.[50] This initial step conferred the Portuguese Crown full legitimacy to intervene in the system of property and fiscal rights in land.

Secondly, the Portuguese placed remarkable importance on the indigenous arrangements in place. Legal and customary institutions concerning possession, use, transfer, and inheritance of rights in land were for the most part acknowledged, in line with the overall policy of legal pluralism the Portuguese explicitly or implicitly adopted in their Eastern empire – at least to the extent that they did not directly harm Portuguese interests. Most importantly, as a rule the ordinary indigenous people were not dispossessed of their land and tenures. Usually, changes were only imposed either at the top political level, where the exercise and display of territorial sovereignty were at stake, or at the middling level in which the Portuguese and their native allies moved in to get hold of land and, above all, of rights regarding land revenue, often encroaching on the positions formerly held by dispossessed segments of the former ruling elites.

Lastly, in order to regulate these processes within the legal order of the Portuguese monarchy, it was necessary to set up a suitable legal and institutional framework. For this purpose, the Portuguese migrated some of their legal institutions overseas, namely the emphyteusis and the endowment of Crown assets – but not in their original forms. These Portuguese institutional templates were actually remixed and recreated overseas, mostly in order to adapt them as much as possible to native institutional frameworks that were already in place, even to the extent of partially 'translating' the latter into the new framework. This gave birth to the hybrid legal system we have called the 'Indo–Portuguese emphyteusis'. First created and tested in the Northern Province in India, it was later replicated and readapted in other territories to become the most distinctive feature of Portuguese property rights institutions in Asia and in East Africa.

In the latter territory, however, the evidence, as far as it goes, suggests that the incorporation of native institutions was feebler. Rather than being adapted to the institutions in place, which were more fluid and not as well defined to begin with, the institutional template which migrated from Portugal and Portuguese India was mostly overlaid on the local chieftaincies, either creating a new level of appropriation or replacing that of the former African kingdoms it had displaced. In Mozambique, from the mid-eighteenth century onwards, the Indo–Portuguese emphyteusis was also formally reinterpreted by another migrating template, that of the *sesmarias* brought in from the Atlantic experience of the Portuguese empire, but not substantially altering actual practice, which left a lasting imprint in the very name *prazos da Coroa* and which would finally evolve from the late nineteenth century into a capitalist plantation model based on Crown grants.

The incorporation of native elements into the institutional reconfiguration of property rights in colonial contexts, as resulted from the analysis of the Portuguese case, should be highlighted. As we stated in the introduction, this is a largely overlooked issue in the mainstream literature, especially in economics and economic history. As made evident by our study, the migration of metropolitan institutions, which inevitably bore the mark of their Portuguese roots, was tempered with accommodation to local circumstances, including to the pre-colonial indigenous institutions. Rather than imposing a new institutional order imported straight from Europe, the Portuguese largely adopted and translated native institutions into their own legal order. Reciprocally, they used the local institutions as the branches on which they grafted their institutional innovations, thereby infusing them with their own meanings – following what was a consciously devised conservative policy to achieve legitimacy and consent and to prevent social and political unrest, however ineffectually at times.

Our study also shows how the institutional regulations introduced by the colonial authorities could also be resisted against, undermined or reshaped by local vested interests, both native and Portuguese. This asserts the role of individual and collective agency, another element often overlooked by the current literature. Institutions are not independent variables which work by themselves; rather they are appropriated and acted upon by different social players, according to their variable interests and relative strengths.

Finally, it is important to highlight the contribution to early globalization of the Portuguese empire-building experience in the Indian Ocean, by carrying out the first contacts and the first two-way processes of transference – however unequal the reciprocity – of concepts, languages and institutions of property between Europeans, on the one side, and Asians and Africans, on the other.

Acknowledgements

This chapter is a result of the research project 'Lands over seas: Property rights in the early modern Portuguese Empire' (PTDC/HIS-HIS/113654/2009), funded by the Portuguese Foundation for Science and Technology (FCT).

Notes

1 For an overview, see F. Bethencourt and D. R. Curto (eds), *Portuguese Oceanic Expansion, 1400–1800* (Cambridge: Cambridge University Press, 2007); A. R. Disney, *A History of Portugal and the Portuguese Empire*, vol. 2 (New York: Cambridge University Press, 2009); J. P. Oliveira e Costa, J. D. Rodrigues and P. A. Oliveira, *História da Expansão e do Império Português* (Lisbon: Esfera dos Livros, 2014).
2 M. Pearson, *The Indian Ocean* (London: Routledge, 2003), pp. 118–58; S. Subrahmanyam, *The Portuguese Empire in Asia, 1500–1700: A Political and Economic History*, 2nd ed. (Malden: John Wiley & Sons, 2012).
3 The most recent exceptions are to be found in J. V. Serrão, B. Direito, E. Rodrigues and S. M. Miranda (eds), *Property Rights, Land and Territory in the European Overseas Empires* (Lisbon: CEHC-IUL, 2014), at https://repositorio.iscte-iul.pt/bitstream/10071/2718/3/proplandterrit2014-ebook.pdf [last accessed 10 March 2016].
4 D. Acemoglu, S. Johnson and J. A. Robinson, 'The colonial origins of comparative development: An empirical investigation', *American Economic Review*, 91 (2001), pp. 1369–401; S. L. Engerman and K. L. Sokoloff, 'Factor endowments, inequality, and paths of development among New World economies', *Economia*, 3:1 (2002), pp. 41–88; R. La Porta, F. Lopez de Silanes and A. Shleifer, 'The economic consequences of legal origins', *Journal of Economic Literature*, 46:2 (2008), pp. 285–332.
5 A comprehensive overview can be found in C. Menard and M. Shirley (eds), *Handbook of New Institutional Economics* (Dordrecht: Springer, 2008).
6 C. A. Bayly, 'Indigenous and colonial origins of comparative economic development: The case of colonial India and Africa', *Policy Research Working Paper* 4474 (Washington: World Bank, 2008), p. 6, at http://documents.worldbank.org/curated/en/

2008/01/8941952/indigenous-colonial-origins-comparative-economic-development-case-colonial-india-africa [last accessed 10 March 2016]. Different criticisms can be found in G. Austin, 'The reversal of fortune thesis and the compression of history: Perspectives from African and comparative economic history', *Journal of International Development*, 20:8 (2008), pp. 996–1027; P. Boomgaard, 'Labour, land, and capital markets in early modern Southeast Asia from the fifteenth to the nineteenth century', *Continuity and Change*, 24:1 (2009), pp. 55–78; M. Laborda Pemán, '"Hombres que entre las raíces": Plantation colonies, slave rebellions and land redistribution in Saint Domingue and Cuba at the late colonial period, c. 1750–c. 1860', *SEHA Working Paper*, 11–02 (2011) at http://repositori.uji.es/xmlui/bitstream/handle/10234/20697/DT%20SEHA%2011-02.pdf?sequence=1 [last accessed 10 March 2016]; S. Michalopoulos and E. Papaioannou, 'Pre-colonial ethnic institutions and contemporary African development', *Econometrica*, 81:1 (2013), pp. 113–52.

7 J. D. Amith, *The Möbius Strip: A Spatial History of Colonial Society in Guerrero, Mexico* (Palo Alto: Stanford University Press, 2005); S. Banner, *How the Indians Lost Their Land: Law and Power on the Frontier* (Cambridge, MA: Belknap Press of Harvard University, 2005); C. Boone, *Property and Political Order in Africa: Land Rights and the Structure of Politics* (New York: Cambridge University Press, 2013); S. Engerman and J. Metzer (eds), *Land Rights, Ethno-Nationality and Sovereignty in History* (London: Routledge, 2004); A. Fitzmaurice, *Sovereignty, Property and Empire, 1500–2000* (Cambridge: Cambridge University Press, 2014); C. Lloyd, J. Metzer and R. Sutch (eds), *Settler Economies in World History* (Leiden: Brill, 2013); A. Pagden, 'Law, colonization, legitimation and the European background', in M. Grossberg and C. L. Tomlins (eds), *The Cambridge History of Law in America*, vol. 1 (Cambridge: Cambridge University Press, 2008), pp. 1–31; J. F. Richards (ed.), *Land, Property, and the Environment* (Oakland: ICS Press, 2002); D. Washbrook, 'Sovereignty, property, land and labour in colonial South India', in H. Islamoglu (ed.), *Constituting Modernity: Private Property in the East and West* (London and New York: I. B. Tauris, 2004), pp. 69–97.

8 On the different interpretations of this concept, see L. Benton and R. Ross (eds), *Legal Pluralism and Empires 1500–1850* (New York: New York University Press, 2013).

9 A comparative overview of India's villages, rural life and land tenure systems prior to the colonial period can be found in B. H. Baden-Powell, *The Indian Village Community* (New Haven: HRAF Press, 1957); I. Habib, *The Agrarian System of Mughal India, 1556–1707* (New Delhi: Oxford University Press, 1999).

10 P. Axelrod and M. Fuerch, 'Portuguese orientalism and the making of the village communities of Goa', *Ethnohistory*, 45:3 (1998), pp. 439–76; R. Dias, A socio-economic history of Goa with special reference to the Communidade system, 1750–1910 (PhD dissertation, Goa University, 2004), pp. 35–94; E. Rodrigues, 'A agricultura: Entre as comunidades de aldeia e os empreendimentos estatais', in M. J. Lopes (ed.), *O Império Oriental (1660–1820)*, tome I (Lisbon: Estampa, 2006), pp. 449–510; T. R. Souza, 'Rural Economy and Corporate Life', in *Medieval Goa: A Socio-Economic History* (Goa: Goa–1556 and Broadway Book Centre, 2009), pp. 27–75; A. B. Xavier, 'Goa', in J. V. Serrão (ed.), *A Terra num Império Ultramarino* (Lisbon: Imprensa de Ciências Sociais, forthcoming).

11 *Casados* was a specific social category in the *Estado*, meaning the Portuguese men who married native women.

12 A commented English translation of the *Foral* in B. H. Baden-Powell, 'The villages of Goa in the early sixteenth century', *Journal of the Royal Asian Society of Great Britain and Ireland* (1900), pp. 261–91. See also: L. Benton, *Law and Colonial Cultures: Legal Regimes in World History, 1400–1900* (Cambridge: Cambridge University Press, 2002), p. 119; J. D. M. Derrett, 'Hindu law in Goa: A contact between natural, Roman and Hindu laws', in *Essays in Classical and Modern Hindu Law: Consequences of the Intellectual Exchange with the Foreign Powers*, vol. 2 (Leiden: Brill, 1977),

pp. 131–65; J. K. Fernandes, 'Invoking the ghost of Mexia: State and community in post-colonial Goa', *Ler História*, 58 (2010), pp. 9–25; Souza, 'Rural economy'.

13   A. B. Xavier, *A Invenção de Goa: Poder Imperial e Conversões Culturais nos Séculos XVI e XVII* (Lisbon: Imprensa de Ciências Sociais, 2008).

14   G. J. Ames, 'The Province of the North: Continuity and change in an age of decline and rebirth, c. 1571–1680', in L. M. Brochey (ed.), *Portuguese Colonial Cities in the Early Modern World* (London: Ashgate, 2008), pp. 129–48; Pearson, 'Indian Ocean'; A. Teixeira, Baçaim e o seu território: Política e economia (1534–1665), (PhD dissertation, Universidade Nova de Lisboa, 2010), at http://run.unl.pt/bitstream/10362/9389/1/tese_andreteixeira.pdf [last accessed 10 March 2016]. More specifically on our topic, the following pages owe much to S. M. Miranda, 'Property rights and social uses of land in Portuguese India: The Province of the North (1534–1739)', in Serrão *et al.*, *Property Rights,* pp. 169–80. See also L. Antunes, 'Algumas considerações sobre os prazos de Baçaim e Damão', *Anais de História de Além-Mar*, 3 (2002), 231–57; L. Ferrão, 'Tenants, rents and revenues from Daman in the late 16th century', *Mare Liberum*, 9 (1995), pp. 139–48; A. T. Matos (ed.), *O Tombo de Damão 1592* (Lisbon: Comissão Nacional para a Comemoração dos Descobrimentos Portugueses, 2001).

15   The bulk of this region remained under Portuguese rule until 1739, and some parts of it up until 1961. Here we shall focus only on the sixteenth and early seventeenth centuries.

16   On the *iqta* system, see I. M. Lapidus, *A History of Islamic Societies* (New York: Cambridge University Press, 2014), pp. 197–200. (On more general topics, see note 10.

17   A more detailed account in R. Santos and J. V. Serrão, 'Property rights, social appropriations and economic outcomes: Agrarian contracts in southern Portugal in the late-eighteenth century', in G. Béaur, P. R. Schofield, J.-M. Chevet and M. T. Pérez Picazo (eds), *Property Rights, Land Markets, and Economic Growth in the European Countryside (Thirteenth–Twentieth Centuries)* (Turnhout: Brepols), pp. 475–94, on pp. 478–9.

18   The following draws largely on J. V. Serrão, 'The Portuguese land policies in Ceylon: On the possibilities and limits of a process of territorial occupation', in Serrão *et al.*, *Property Rights*, pp. 183–95.

19   On the political history of the Portuguese in Ceylon, see Z. Biedermann, 'The Matrioshka principle and how it was overcome: Portuguese and Habsburg attitudes toward imperial authority in Sri Lanka and the responses of the Rulers of Kotte (1506–1656)', *Journal of Early Modern History*, 13:4 (2009), pp. 265–310; P. E. Pieris, *Ceylon: The Portuguese Era*, 2 vols. (Colombo: Ceylon Aphotecaries Co., 1913); A. V. Saldanha, 'O problema jurídico-político da incorporação de Ceilão na Coroa de Portugal: As doações dos reinos de Kotte, Kandy e Jaffna (1580–1633)', *Revista de Cultura (Macao)*, 13/14 (1991), pp. 233–57.

20   P. De Zwart, 'Population, labour and living standards in early modern Ceylon: An empirical contribution to the divergence debate', *Indian Economic and Social History Review*, 49 (2012), pp. 365–98.

21   The importance of the government in Madrid was due to the Portuguese and Spanish crowns being held together by the Spanish kings from 1580 to 1640. (Editors' note.)

22   On the Ceylonese society and caste system, see N. Dewasiri, *The Adaptable Peasant: Agrarian Society in Western Sri Lanka under Dutch Rule, 1740–1800* (Leiden: Brill, 2008); B. Ryan, *Caste in Modern Ceylon: The Sinhalese System in Transition* (New Brunswick: Rutgers University Press, 1953); N. Wickramasinghe, *Sri Lanka in the Modern Age: A History of Contested Identities* (Hawaii: University of Hawaii Press, 2006).

23   Differently from what the Dutch and especially the British would later do in Ceylon. A. Bandarage, *Colonialism in Sri Lanka: The Political Economy of the Kandyan Highlands, 1833–1886* (Colombo: Lake House Publishers, 2005); A. Schrikker, *Dutch and British Colonial Intervention in Sri Lanka, 1780–1815* (Leiden: Brill, 2007).

24 In 1634, this amounted to about 80 per cent of total revenue. V. M. Godinho, *Les Finances de l'État Portugais des Indes Orientales, 1517–1635* (Paris: Fundação Calouste Gulbenkian, Centro Cultural Português, 1982), pp. 105–12.

25 On the concept of *bhupati*, see Dewasiri, *Adaptable Peasant*, pp. 131–6; W. I. Siriweera, 'The theory of the king's ownership of land in ancient Ceylon: An essay in historical revision', *Ceylon Journal of Historical and Social Studies*, 1:1 (1971), pp. 48–61.

26 M. U. de Silva, 'Land tenure, caste system and the Rajakariya under foreign rule: A review of change in Sri Lanka under Western powers, 1597–1832', *Journal of The Royal Asiatic Society of Sri Lanka*, 37 (1992–93), pp. 1–57.

27 There is an extensive and often contradictory literature on this complex native system. Besides the references in the previous footnotes, see T. Abeyasinghe, *Portuguese Rule in Ceylon: 1594–1612* (Colombo: Lake House, 1966); H. W. Codrington, *Ancient Land Tenure and Revenue in Ceylon* (Colombo: Ceylon Government Press, 1938); K. Paranavitana, *Land for Money: Dutch Land Registration in Sri Lanka* (Colombo: 2001); L. Perera, 'Proprietary and tenurial rights in ancient Ceylon', *Ceylon Journal of Historical and Social Studies*, 2:1 (1959), pp. 1–36; Pieris, *Ceylon*; C. R. Silva, *The Portuguese in Ceylon, 1617–1638* (Colombo: H. W. Cave & Company, 1972). Some primary sources were published in [Anonymous], 'Tenures of land in the Kandyan Kingdom', *Asiatic Journal*, 6:24 (1831), 322–4; F. Queiroz, *The Temporal and Spiritual Conquest of Ceylon* [1692], edited by S. C. Perera, 3 vols (Colombo: A. C. Richards, 1930); J. Ribeiro, *The Historic Tragedy of the Island of Ceilão* [1685], edited by P. E. Pieris (New Delhi: Asian Edu Services, 1999); J. E. Tennent, *Ceylon: An Account of the Island* (London: Longman, Green & Roberts, 1860).

28 The main documents are a royal charter sent to the viceroy in 1607, published in *Documentos Remetidos da Índia ou Livros das Monções*, vol. 1 (Lisboa: Academia das Ciências, 1880), pp. 161–4, and the standing orders delivered to the superintendent of revenue in 1608, published in *Archivo Portuguez-Oriental*, vol. 6 (Nova Goa: Imprensa Nacional, 1876), pp. 804–9; the latter was translated into English in T. Abeyasinghe, *A Study of Portuguese Regimentos on Sri Lanka at the Goa Archives* (Colombo: Department of National Archives, 1974), pp. 37–41.

29 On the Portuguese *tombos*, see A. Caprioli (ed.), *Tombos of Ceylon (Arquivo Histórico Ultramarino)* (Lisbon: CEHU, 1979); K. Paranavitana, 'The Portuguese Tombos as a source of sixteenth- and seventeenth-century Sri Lankan history', in J. M. Flores (ed.), *Re-Exploring the Links: History and Constructed Histories between Portugal and Sri Lanka* (Wiesbaden: Harrassowitz, 2007), pp. 63–78; S. G. Perera (ed.), *The Tombo of the Two Korales (ms 2637, Fundo Geral, Bibl. Nac., Lisbon)* (Colombo: Ceylon G. Press, 1938); P. E. Pieris, *The Kingdom of Jafanapatam, 1645: Being an Account of its Administrative Organisation as Derived from the Portuguese Archives*, 2nd ed. (Colombo: Ceylan Daily News, 1944).

30 It has been estimated that in the 1640s there were 350 to 400 Portuguese *foreiros* in Kotte and about 90 in Jaffna. T. Abeyasinghe, *Jaffna Under the Portuguese* (Colombo: Lake House, 1986), p. 42.

31 On the connections between land, tax and revenue policies in this period, see Abeyasinghe, *Portuguese Rule*, pp. 134–83, and Silva, *Portuguese in Ceylon*, pp. 190–229.

32 This section draws largely on E. Rodrigues, *Portugueses e Africanos nos Rios de Sena: Os Prazos da Coroa em Moçambique nos Séculos XVII e XVIII* (Lisbon: Imprensa Nacional – Casa da Moeda, 2013).

33 These were mostly the Karanga, the Tonga, the Maravi and the Makua. D. Beach, *The Shona and the Zimbabwe 900–1850* (London: Heinemann, 1980); S. I. G. Mudenge, *A Political History of Munhumutapa c. 1400–1902* (Harare: Zimbabwe Publishing House, 1988); M. Newitt, *A History of Mozambique* (London: Hurst & Company, 1995), pp. 31–78; K. M. Phiri, O. J. Kalinga and H. H. K. Bhila, 'The Northern

Zambezia – Lake Malawi region', in B. A. Ogot (ed.), *Africa from the Sixteenth to the Eighteenth Century* (Oxford and Paris: Heinemann and UNESCO, 1992), pp. 608–39.

34   M. D. D. Newitt, *Portuguese Settlement on the Zambesi* (London: Longman, 1973), pp. 48–59; Newitt, *History of Mozambique*, pp. 79–104; Rodrigues, *Portugueses e Africanos*, pp. 41–336.

35   J.-P. Chauveau and J.-P. Colin, 'Customary transfers and land sales in Côte d'Ivoire: Revisiting the embeddedness issue', *Africa*, 80:1 (2010), pp. 81–103.

36   G. Austin, 'Sub-Saharan Africa: land rights and ethno-national consciousness in historically land-abundant economies', in Engerman and Metzer, *Land Rights*, pp. 276–93; J. Thornton, *Africa and Africans in the Making of the Atlantic World, 1400–1800* (Cambridge: Cambridge University Press, 1998), pp. 74–85. Studies discussing the land issue are mainly focused on the modern period, although some go back to the final stage of the pre-colonial period, *e.g.*, S. Berry, 'Debating the land question in Africa', *Comparative Studies in Society and History*, 44:4 (2002), pp. 638–68; Chauveau and Colin, 'Customary transfers'; P. Shipton and M. Goheen, 'Introduction: Understanding African land-holding: Power, wealth and meaning', *Africa*, 62:3 (1992), pp. 307–25.

37   A. F. Isaacman, *Mozambique: The Africanization of a European Institution: The Zambesi Prazos, 1750–1902* (Madison: University of Wisconsin Press, 1972), pp. 24–6, 43–5.

38   Rodrigues, *Portugueses e Africanos*, pp. 569–80. Concerning the *prazos*, J. Capela, *Donas, Senhores e Escravos* (Porto: Afrontamento, 1995); Isaacman, *Mozambique*; A. Lobato, *Colonização Senhorial da Zambézia e Outros Estudos* (Lisbon: Junta de Investigações do Ultramar, 1962); Newitt, *Portuguese Settlement*; Newitt, *History of Mozambique*, pp. 217–42.

39   Isaacman, *Mozambique*, pp. 30–4; Newitt, *Portuguese Settlement*, pp. 169–86; Newitt, *History of Mozambique*, pp. 232–3; Rodrigues, *Portugueses e Africanos*, pp. 805–47.

40   Isaacman, *Mozambique*, pp. 37–42; Newitt, *Portuguese Settlement*, pp. 176–8; Rodrigues, *Portugueses e Africanos*, pp. 889–915.

41   Rodrigues, *Portugueses e Africanos*, pp. 787–94, 801–5.

42   Austin, 'Sub-Saharan Africa', p. 100; R. M. Baum, *Shrines of the Slave Trade: Diola Religion and Society in Precolonial Senegambia* (Oxford: Oxford University Press, 1999).

43   Rodrigues, *Portugueses e Africanos*, pp. 513–21.

44   On the *sesmarias* in Brazil, see C. O. Alveal, 'Seigniorial identities and conflicts: Converting land into property in the Portuguese Atlantic world, 16th–18th century' (PhD dissertation, Johns Hopkins University, 2007); M. Motta, 'The law of *Sesmarias* and colonial occupation: concerning the Laws', in *Right to Land in Brazil: The Gestation of the Conflict 1795–1824* (Niterói: Editora da UFF, 2014), pp. 117–36. A comparison with Mozambique can be found in E. Rodrigues, 'Cruzamentos entre a história do Brasil e de Moçambique: Terra, lei e conflito no final do período moderno', in M. Motta, J. V. Serrão and M. Machado (eds), *Em Terras Lusas: Conflitos e Fronteiras no Império Português* (São Paulo: Editora Horizonte, 2013), pp. 291–319. (*Sesmarias* are also mentioned by Câmara and Santos in chapter five, concerning the colonization of Madeira. Editors' note.)

45   Rodrigues, *Portugueses e Africanos*, pp. 649–733.

46   Isaacman, *Mozambique*, pp. 124–53; A. F. Isaacman and B. Isaacman, *The Tradition of Resistance in Mozambique: The Zambezi Valley 1850–1921* (Berkeley and Los Angeles: University of California Press, 1976), pp. 22–48; R. Pélissier, *História de Moçambique: Formação e Oposição 1854–1918*, vol. 1 (Lisbon: Estampa, 1994) pp. 87–102, 401–74, on p. 89.

47   Isaacman, *Mozambique*, p. 128; Newitt, *Portuguese Settlement*, pp. 326–76.

48   B. Direito, 'Políticas coloniais de terras em Moçambique: O caso de Manica e Sofala sob a Companhia de Moçambique, 1892–1942', (PhD dissertation, Universidade de

Lisboa, 2013), at http://repositorio.ul.pt/handle/10451/8723 [last accessed 10 March 2016]; L. Vail and L. White, *Capitalism and Colonialism in Mozambique: A Study of Quelimane District* (London: Heinemann, 1980).

49 E. Allina, *Slavery by Any Other Name: African Life Under Company Rule in Colonial Mozambique* (Charlottesville: University of Virginia Press, 2012); J. Capela, 'Como as aringas de Moçambique se transformaram em quilombos', *Tempo*, 10:20 (2006), pp. 72–97, on p. 75, at www.scielo.br/scielo.php?script=sci_arttext&pid=S1413-77042006000100005 [last accessed 10 March 2016].

50 P. Boomgaard, 'Long-term changes in land-tenure arrangements in pre-modern and early-modern Southeast Asia: An introduction', *Journal of the Economic and Social History of the Orient*, 54:4 (2011), pp. 447–54.

2 Alternative uses of land and re-negotiation of property rights

Scandinavian examples, 1750–2000

Mats Morell

Introduction

By the mid-sixteenth century, vast areas of boreal forests in northern Sweden had been claimed as crown property. In 1635, Carl Bonde, a government official, wrote that 'It is hoped here, that by the help of God it shall be the West India of the realm'.[1] Later, in order to promote colonization, increase tax revenues and population, the crown began privatizing forest areas, through donations and sales. Land ownership was granted to settlers who set up new farmsteads and cleared land, along with temporary tax exemption.[2] Settler activities clashed with the Sami reindeer economy, which involved transhumance into the eastern lowland forest in winter, using vast areas intermittently for pastures. Settlers and farmers, backed by the crown, usually won legal cases against the Sami. The crown taxed the latter heavily and they were only granted *usage rights* for extensive grazing, whereas they claimed land *ownership*, based on ancient occupation and land use in certain mountain areas.[3] As recently as 1981, the Supreme Court denied Sami ownership claims, stating that the Sami's usage rights in these areas were just as protective as ownership. Yet the Sami have lost most recent conflicts against individual farmers, forest owners or mining companies.[4]

The perennial conflict between state-supported Swedish settlers and Sami reindeer herders illustrates the connection between land use and property rights arrangements, and potential clashes over property rights once competing land uses come into conflict. The 'solutions' to such clashes illustrate that property rights are underpinned by power relations.

In this chapter I will discuss the implications of the emergence of alternative land uses on the functioning and formulation of property rights. The overarching point of departure is that property rights are not relations between humans and assets, but rather sanctioned, socially acknowledged and changeable human-to-human relations allowing certain actions with regards to assets to certain persons, while excluding other actions and persons.[5]

A second point of departure is that the functioning of institutionalized property rights is the result of social action in efforts to adapt to and appropriate them. Such actions may lead to their reformulation. The rights are recurrently renegotiated and their composition, formulation and normalized use are determined by the relative strengths of the social actors involved. Both the formal manifestations of property rights and their actual empirical content thus represent power relations.[6]

A third point of departure is the nowadays commonplace notion of the multifunctionality of land. There have always been several ways to use land. Potentially different uses and users open a door both for contesting rights in land and to the fragmentation and overlay of the rights to use any given piece of land. Overall social and economic development tends to determine which new demands are placed upon land (and nature), and which power relations will be dominant and result in newly prioritized land use. Re-negotiated property rights develop because of new claims to land use, which may trigger conflict among social actors involved in or aspiring to such new uses, and with representatives of 'old' uses who stick to their hitherto acknowledged rights. Power relations exert influence, the outcome of which can be empirically studied. Dialectically, such new, either formal or informal, but generally acknowledged and sanctioned rules as may develop as the outcome of the struggle will, in turn, enter as parameters into renewed claims and re-negotiations of property rights.

A fourth point is the expectation of a strong element of path dependence concerning the direction of the action of social entities and, thus, of changes in property rights. Solutions to property rights conflicts that developed along a certain path will tend to exclude later solutions, which are not on the same path.

The rest of the chapter will exemplify these hypothetical statements using Scandinavian evidence. I will start by comparing the outcomes of the emergence of 'absolute' property rights in land in Denmark and Sweden, as part of an elite agenda to develop farming. I will go on to discuss property rights within the rise of modern forestry in nineteenth-century northern Sweden. I will then turn to the property rights implications of the intensified and more widespread recreational use of land in the first half of the twentieth century, and finally to the efforts by the end of the twentieth century to curb negative environmental externalities and to safeguard and restore public goods, for example, biodiversity and landscape heritage.

The rise of 'absolute' ownership and the owner–occupier farmer: Sweden and Denmark compared

In Scandinavia, as in Europe at large, early modern property rights were fragmented in ways reflecting power relations between the state, landowners, tenants, and village communities. Early eighteenth-century Sweden peasant freeholders held roughly one third of the country's land. They could sell and buy land, and pass it over to their heirs, but they could not legally subdivide it. They paid land taxes to the state (theoretically equating to the surpluses above simple reproduction needs). Repeated failure to pay taxes implied a risk of eviction and the loss of the farmstead.[7] Moreover, the crown enjoyed pre-emption rights when a farm was sold. Thus, the state had *de facto* eminent ownership in freehold land. Lineage rights ensured the influence of family, as relatives also enjoyed pre-emption rights.

The crown directly owned another third of the land. Tenants paid rents to the crown and tenure was secure for life. Some categories of crown tenants could pass their tenancy to heirs. A third category of land was owned by nobles and divided into demesnes and tenant farms. This land was tax-exempt and lords retained the entire rent. Tenants on such manorial land enjoyed no particular security of tenancy. Importantly, a peasant estate represented freeholders and crown tenants in the Swedish parliament.[8]

Most farms were organized in village communities. Arable land was privately held in open fields, while pastures, forestland, and sometimes meadows were held in common.[9] Arable fields and meadows were protected from grazing cattle by common fences, but were opened for grazing after harvest. The villagers cooperated in the expensive and laborious fencing work and there were bylaws aimed at protecting land from overexploitation by common use.

The situation was similar in Denmark, yet with some considerable differences. By the mid-eighteenth century, there were practically no freeholders there and differences between crown tenants and tenants of the nobility (who made up the majority) were negligible. Tenants were heavily burdened by *corvée* labour in demesnes and *stavnsbåndet*, instituted to secure the supply of soldiers, forbade villagers from leaving their lots.[10] Peasants lacked constitutional access to political influence.

Anglophile currents emerged in both countries in the eighteenth century.[11] In 1727 Jacob Serenius, legation preacher at the Swedish church in London, presented the English enclosures in a book written in Swedish. Twenty years later Jacob Faggot, the director of the Swedish land surveying authority, wrote the first pamphlet promoting enclosures in Sweden, in line with views that circulated on the continent for individualized ownership, privatization of commons and large-scale farming.[12] He explicitly referred to:

> the English statute, which several years ago was passed concerning the commons, which as long as they were used collectively were infertile land of little use, but have been transformed into fertile and fruitful land once they were assigned and handed over to specific owners.[13]

He also claimed that commons, rather than private ownership, led to the overexploitation of forest.[14] However, his focus was on farming, not forestry, and his efforts were in line with the perceived need to reduce regular grain imports, which according to mercantilist doctrines were detrimental to the balance of trade and to population growth.[15]

In order to enhance agricultural development, the political elite adopted contemporary ideas promoting 'absolute' property rights. In 1789, the crown's pre-emption right on freeholds was abolished, freeholder ownership was secured, peasants were allowed to buy tax-exempt 'noble land', and crown tenants were formally able to secure hereditary tenancy and the exclusive right to purchase their holdings. Grain trade had been liberalized somewhat earlier. Together with a gradual fall in the real value of land taxes, these institutional reforms helped transform freeholders and crown tenants into entrepreneurs who produced surpluses for the market. Lineage rights were successively downplayed as well, as was the legal prohibition to subdivide farms.[16] The nobility's tenants enjoyed none of these improvements in relation to their landlords. Their rights in land were not secured and, in the nineteenth century, evictions were common.[17]

Most importantly, landholding and land ownership were privatized as the influence of the village community upon land use ceased. A succession of national enclosure acts were passed from 1749 to 1827, which stipulated how village land should be redistributed into a structure of consolidated individual holdings. The later and more radical acts gave each landowner or crown tenant within a village the right to demand enclosure and redistribution of land, including commons, according to the principles laid down in the acts. This empowered them to force such changes upon fellow villagers.[18] From the government side, the aim of the enclosure movement was to develop agriculture and to create opportunities for farmers to produce more grain. Accordingly, the motivation for 'progressive' farmers to demand enclosure was to profit from rising grain prices and obtain better control over possibilities to grow more grain. This was definitely true for Scania in Southern Sweden, where much freehold land had been enclosed by the first decade of the nineteenth century, following the high grain prices during the Napoleonic wars. Enclosures in Scania were also related to the advancement of new and more complex crop rotations.[19]

Legal instruments such as the 1803 Scanian *enskifte* act and the 1827 *laga skifte* act do not convey the full implications of institutional change. Enclosures in mid-Sweden, often occurring up to fifty years later, were not obviously related to the same factors as those in Scania, and it remains uncertain as to what purpose farmers in these districts made use of the law to enclose and consolidate their land.[20] In many cases in northern and mid-Sweden, where animal husbandry was of major importance, the most significant aspect of the nineteenth-century enclosure was the parcelling out of forest commons. Peasants in the parish of Leksand in Dalarna county reacted to the enclosures by locally pooling their privatized forest to carry on using it in common for grazing: the enclosure acts merely made the collective management more cumbersome and costly, as more local rules were needed when ownership became private while usage remained common.[21] Thus, the outcomes were a question of who had the will and the strength to appropriate or adapt to the new rights, in what way and for which purposes.[22]

Danish development in this regard was quicker and produced more radical results. Peasant mobility was restored by reforms from above in the 1760s, which aimed at creating a prosperous and efficient class of farmers. As there were no freeholders in Denmark, efforts were directed towards gradually reinforcing tenants' land use rights into full ownership. Tenants were granted hereditary tenure, evictions were banned, and demesnes were not to be enlarged at their cost. *Corvée* labour was abolished, though not for the large and growing group of small cotters and tenants. Landowners were encouraged to sell off farms to their tenants. Finally, in 1919 the few remaining tenants were granted the unconditional right to buy their farms in freehold.

As land ownership was still very concentrated when enclosure acts were promulgated in the late eighteenth century, enclosures and farm consolidations swiftly followed. The emerging stratum of viable owner–occupiers became the leading actors in the transformation of Denmark into a major exporter of corn and later of dairy products. This class was also politically emancipated, and economic processes were connected to cultural and educational progress. Bottom-up farmers' unions and later, strong producer cooperatives were created. In brief, due to the absence of freeholders in Denmark, the will of the enlightened elites to establish a class of thrifty owner-occupiers in Denmark could only take place via the tenants.[23]

In contrast, reforms in Sweden secured ownership status only for freeholders. They did not restrict the nobility's grip on land and crown tenants alone had their property status improved. No land reform, in the conventional meaning of the term, was ever carried out, and, consequently, noble land ownership remained substantial by European standards. Large landowners played a distinctively more important role in agricultural organizations (even cooperatives) in Sweden. It is but a mild exaggeration to state that while in Denmark the establishment of full ownership rights made tenants into landowners, in Sweden it deprived most of them of any access to land ownership.

This can be explained by the representation of freeholders and crown tenants in the Swedish Parliament. The peasant estate strove above all to reduce land taxes, which brought no advantage to the nobility's tenants who paid rent to the noble landowners for tax-free land. Therefore, it was suspicious of the nobility's tenants and did not act on their behalf.[24]

The reforms, which started in the mid-eighteenth century in both countries, were part of elite-led programmes to transform farming in order to fulfil their ideals of national strength, in line with contemporary ideas of the virtues of 'absolute ownership'. However, similar institutional changes produced divergent results depending on the political and social structure at the outset of the reform. Moreover, local adaptations to the reforms and the appropriations from the resulting property rights could vary greatly, not least in accordance with the local social structure and balances of power, market conditions and types of land use.

Forestry versus farming

The privatization process and the fixing of borders between crown land and private land in the northern forest districts of Sweden were intensified from the 1820s onwards, following new legislation along with the enclosure movement. In the early nineteenth century, individual freeholders were endowed with vast areas of boreal forest, sometimes amounting to several hundred hectares per farmstead.[25] The rationale was that 'you employ more economy and thrift when you use what you own yourself compared to when you use property belonging to someone else'.[26] Forest endowments were expected to stimulate land clearance and active farming. The forest areas were to provide peasants with pastures, winter fodder, firewood and material for buildings, tools and fences. Peasants could also fell, saw and sell timber.

By the mid-nineteenth century a new competitor entered the scene. Large sawmill companies emerged as the value of timber and forestland increased sharply, following an export boom related to West European industrialization and the introduction of free trade. Export sawmills, operating on a wholly different scale than peasant sawmills, were established along the Baltic coast.

Sawmill companies were not interested in either the cultivation of farmsteads or land clearance. Instead, they needed timber and labour. Therefore, they bought felling contracts from peasant landowners, which were legally valid for up to fifty years. However, due to a growing fear of deforestation, in 1889 the duration of the felling contracts was restricted to twenty years, and then to five years in 1903. However, by then companies had begun purchasing entire farmsteads with forest holdings. Previous owners and farmers were turned into tenants doubling as forestry workers. In the debate that followed, critics argued that peasants were not fully informed of the potential value of the forestland. They also claimed that access to high wages for felling and transportation work had reduced the peasants' inclination for farming, that the state of agriculture had deteriorated, and that the free peasantry in the north was threatened. Following considerable indignation in the press and parliamentary committee work, in 1906 sales of agricultural and forestry land to corporate bodies and to persons who were not local residents were prohibited in northern Sweden.[27]

In modern terms, the critics of the sawmill companies argued that information asymmetries had led to market failure, as forests had been evaluated too lowly and had, therefore, been over-felled for immediate gain. However, this conflict was also a struggle between competing ways of using land and promoting the nation, namely through agriculture or through industry.

Those who favoured the prohibition law claimed that farmers needed forests to make their farms viable. This side was partly influenced by conservative nationalistic ideas, viewing industrialization and proletarianization as threats to social order. They idealized the free peasantry as the backbone of the nation, the guarantee of a defensive readiness and a reservoir of fresh blood, without which the growing urban populations would degenerate. Accordingly, the importance of protecting the peasant class from extinction was beyond economic arguments. However, on top of this conservative critique, radical liberal and socialist strands were recognizable. Some were related to a Georgist land reform movement arguing for 'land for everyone', a single tax hitting only land ownership, and opposing all kinds of land ownership by corporate bodies. Some spoke of the nationalization of land and favourable leasing arrangements for smallholders. Unifying these disparate currents was the belief and confidence in the prospect of expanding agriculture in the north. Inasmuch as these thoughts were not outrightly anti-modernist, they envisaged a modernization project built on rurality, agriculture and small-scale entities rather than large corporate industries and urban growth.[28]

The industrialist side argued that the nation's natural endowments – forests, waterfalls and ore deposits – should be used rationally in a grand modernization project. It was argued that agriculture and forestry had to be divided, as the peasants' agricultural use of the forest, namely for grazing goats and cattle, destroyed its value. Only corporate owners could carry out scientifically based forestry that took care and made full use of such resources. The pro-industrialists defended *laissez faire* principles, absolute ownership and the right for private parties to make binding contracts without public involvement. Conversely, the conservative and radical critics defended governmental interference if it was for the good of the nation (the conservatives) or of individuals (the radical liberals). Thus, they *de facto* referred to a higher common good to advocate that the exclusive right of land ownership, including the right to freely make binding contracts, should be restricted.[29] The so-called 'Norrland question' boiled down to a conflict about the legitimate control over land use, i.e., to an issue of property rights in land.[30]

The 1906 prohibition law was a strong breach in the trend towards increasing corporate land ownership in the North. However, earlier expectations that such a law might be passed had led to a rally in the northern real estate market, and the companies had strongly increased their share of land. Further south, around the Bergslagen mining area of central Sweden where the law was not valid, forest companies and ironworks depending on tenants for charcoal and transportation services intensified land purchases after 1906. This development was halted in 1925, when the prohibition law was applied to the entire realm.[31] Agricultural land remained overwhelmingly owned by individuals or families. Forest ownership was a different matter, though. By 1937, the state and other public bodies owned 25 per cent of the forest area (mostly in the north); another 25 per cent was held by corporate bodies and the remaining half was privately owned by individuals or families associated with agricultural farms.[32]

One alternative considered in the debate was passing a 'social tenancy' legislation, which would regulate the conditions under which tenants doubling as forestry workers leased farmstead and paid for it with work for a forest company.[33] Formally, these agreements were leasing contracts and tenants who failed to pay their rent risked eviction. However, they could also be viewed as disguised labour contracts, in which the transferred rights to use the land of the small plots were part of the wages paid by the company.[34]

Social researchers agreed that the tenant–worker system was socially favourable as compared with 'pure' wage labour systems, since it offered the workers a possibility to better their conditions by diligent labour on their leased plots. However, they also claimed that reformed tenancy legislation was required in order to develop this potential. They argued for written contracts, regulated workloads and compensation to tenants for investments in land improvements. It should not be possible to sign away regulations. Given such legislation, it was suggested, even small tenant–workers could make a substantial contribution to the national agricultural output. However, large landowners, who dominated the upper house of parliament, resisted such a law, claiming that it would violate ownership rights and the right to make binding contracts.[35]

The general tenancy law enacted in 1907 was a rather modest, but much more forceful, law concerning the forested northern counties and was eventually passed in 1909, together with a land-use supervisory law. Written contracts became mandatory, workloads were to be regulated and evaluated, and tenants were given the right to compensation for land clearance work, as well as to use company forests for household purposes. The minimum length of leases was set at fifteen years. Provisions were included in the supervisory law to stop corporate landowners from leaving farmsteads uncultivated, if they found the tenancy law made it unfavourable to lease them out.[36] The supervisory law was later made more widely applicable, but it did not become as important as a similar law in Norway that was part of a legislation package designed to secure more land for smallholders.[37]

Besides saving northern farming and ensuring reasonable conditions for tenant–workers, another factor underlying the legislation was the fear of de-forestation and of forest misuse, as timber reserves sank to a national all-time low at the turn of the century. The growing cadre of university educated forestry experts turned against the peasants, who they claimed regarded forests as obstacles to expanding farming and who felled trees when wood prices were favourable, without considering regeneration.[38] Even though the fifty years of massive exploitation by sawmill companies and other industrial concerns were more to blame for the depletion of timber reserves,[39] the promoters of scientific forest management sided with the large companies, assuming these were able to use the forest rationally. The starting point for regulation was the 1903 silviculture act, which stipulated mandatory regeneration of forest in proportion to felling, and the creation of governmental county forestry boards in 1904–1905 reporting directly to the ministry of agriculture.[40]

Gradually, legislation became more intricate with increasingly detailed rules concerning the protection of trees according to age, obligatory notifications regarding clearance felling, and replanting where the old forest was growing thin. Finally, in 1983 this extended to obligatory thinning of young forest, cutting of certain proportions of older forests, and drawing up a forestry plan by each private owner. Such legislation was developed in order to secure the supply of wood for sawmills and the pulp industry, which afforded the country large export earnings. Forest ownership by a mass of small owners using it as a life- and business-cycle buffer or to fund farm operations could not guarantee the supply flow. Therefore, governments of varying political colours from 1903 to 1983 heavily restricted the dispositional rights attached to forest ownership.

While large forestry companies had few problems with these legislative instruments, matters were made worse for many small-scale owners who combined forestry with farming. Following technical and institutional developments, small-scale owners increasingly joined as shareholders into management associations, which handled their operations. For many of them, the forest continued to function as a reserve fund to which they resorted when heirs had to be bought out, or when larger investments had to be financed for farm machinery or buildings. Therefore, they strongly opposed the legislation and the most recent and far-reaching laws were eventually repealed in 1993.[41]

In this way the state steered a course involving a series of compromises among competing interests. The government implicitly argued that market failures necessitated regulation. While private ownership was still certainly sacred, it seems as though the governing majorities driving through the Norrland legislation, the tenancy legislation and the silviculture legislation adhered to or developed a view according to which the content of property rights was not a given, but rather negotiable and in the last resort determined by political aims. It had the character of a social contract and as such it could be renegotiated when dominant political forces found that advantageous for the nation. This *de facto* social contract view of property right smoothed the way for the interventionist state.[42]

The welfare state and the rise of the recreational use of land

Land has long been used for recreational purposes, such as tourism and sports. However, up until recently countryside activities have mostly been reserved for the upper classes. In Sweden, freeholders achieved hunting rights in 1789 and hunting remained economically important to smallholders, but sports hunting was often restricted to specific strata.[43]

Private incomes rose with industrialization. Since expenditure on recreation is highly income-elastic, its share of total private expenditure grew disproportionately: in Sweden, it almost doubled between 1931 and 1960.[44] Recreational spending is a wide-ranging basket containing travel services and hotel stays, as well as a growing diversity of material goods. As some recreational activities require access to land or 'nature', the recreational use of land increased.

Wildlife tourism first developed to a certain scale in Britain, and early British tourists went to Alpine regions in Central Europe and to Norway, where they wandered in the mountains, hunted, and fished in fiords and rivers. In the second half of the nineteenth century, national parks were founded in the USA and Alpinism became popular on the European continent. A tourist association was founded in Norway in 1868, followed by a Swedish one in 1886, both initially focused on mountain tourism.[45]

Nature became important in late nineteenth-century nationalist discourse in Sweden, as in many other countries. Klas Sandell identifies four unifying trends related to nature and wildlife in Sweden at that time: the interest among the upper strata for 'national consolidation', and the 'creation of a new spatial and social identity to replace the vanishing rural village society'; a strong geographical zeal for exploration; an aspiration for natural protection in the wake of the emerging industrial society; and an increasing interest in the recreational use of natural landscape, coloured by a national romantic ideal.[46] Sverker Sörlin speaks of a 'new patriotism' and a 'canonization of a new Swedish conception of nature . . . nature was brought into focus and became somewhat of a leitmotif in the arts, discussions of industrial policy and the lively *fin de siècle* debate on national character and racial character'.[47] Just as industrialization and urbanization gained pace, a consensus view developed of healthy rural, natural life contrasted with the coal smoke and over-crowded multifamily houses in the city.[48] This national romantic nature current remained forceful far into the post-Second World War era.

The early tourists in the Scandinavian wilderness were too few for their activities to be considered problematic, whether or not land was privately owned.

However, expanding railroad networks soon placed the north-western mountain areas within the reach of tourists from urban centres. Propaganda in the yearbook of the Swedish Tourist Association contributed to spreading wild life tourism among broader layers of well-off *burghers*. Tourist stations, commercial exploitation and mapping further increased accessibility. An association specifically for the promotion of skiing and outdoor life – *friluftsliv*, literally 'open air life' – was founded in 1892. This type of nature-related holiday was perceived as a calming, healing balm for people stressed in urban environments.[49]

During the interwar period other social strata adopted such activities, including working-class households. The tourist association made efforts to democratize its outlook and started to encourage domestic tourism in more accessible agricultural areas.[50] Shortening the working week around 1920 and legislation in 1938 that granted two-week paid holidays provided time for people to engage in recreational activities and created a boom in camping and bicycle tourism. Scenic natural areas not too far from home ranked high amongst budget tourist targets in those decades.[51] In the 1950s and 1960s the spread of mass motoring and successively extended vacations strengthened this trend, and although coach trips and airborne charter flights were on the rise, the number of recreation hours per inhabitant spent in domestic natural surroundings increased. One important aspect of the increased recreational use of land was the rapid rise in summerhouses and second homes from the 1950s onwards. While in 1950 there were fifty Swedes per summerhouse, the ratio dropped to only nineteen in 2001.[52]

Thus, as the divide between working and leisure time became more definitive with urbanization and maturing Fordist industrialization, and the desire for a recreational outdoor life took firm root across the social spectrum, it became an issue for political parties to render it possible for their urban constituents to partake in this new use of land and nature.

In 1936 a social democratic parliamentary bill demanded an official investigation to ascertain the possibilities for non-landowners to enjoy *friluftsliv*. The proponents wanted to reserve certain areas for public recreational activities and natural protection, claiming that landowners in the vicinity of towns were trying to prohibit the public from wandering in forests, and that rich urban residents had acquired and closed off beach areas around lakes and along the coast. A government appointed committee published a report in 1937 proposing to restrict the building of residential houses along beaches, which however did not result in legislation at the time.

A second report in 1940 concerned the creation of recreational public reserve areas attached to towns, which the state was supposed to purchase from private landowners. This report contained an attachment by Gunnar Carlesjö, which was to become of paramount importance. He claimed that there was no valid reason for barring individuals' access to private land, if no economic loss was inflicted on the landowner through their presence:

> As is well known, it is allowed for anyone to roam and remain to some length on another's land without the consent of the owner, to use water in lakes and

rivers for boating, bathing, washing etc., and to use certain natural goods from other persons' land such as wild berries, flowers, herbs and mushrooms.[53]

From the viewpoint of outdoor recreational life, these may well be the most important rights, to be found under the label 'every person's right' or 'the right of the public'.

This involved no special public reserves and, therefore, no public funds were needed for buying up such land. Instead, government and civil society should propagate a responsible use of nature for recreation, anywhere nature might be found. Herein was born the modern *allemansrätt*, or public access to uncultivated private land.

The legal foundation of the *allemansrätt* had been set down since the turn of the twentieth century. A proposal for a new land law in 1909 claimed that some restrictions on landowners' rights to dispose of the land in the nation were needed for the common good. Different individual estates together formed the land on which the people should live their lives, and it should not be left to the discretion of individual landowners to dispose of their land in such ways as might jeopardize the good of the whole body.[54] This proposal was designed at about the same time as the previously-mentioned forestry and tenancy legislation, which similarly traded landowners' absolute rights of disposal for another kind of common good.

Prior to this, Adolf Åström, a juridical authority who wrote some booklets for the Georgist land reform league, had pointed out that the doctrine of absolute land ownership originating in Roman civil law was not positively stated in Swedish law. He disputed absolute ownership, claiming that private ownership granted by the state was subordinated to eminent ownership, rooted in old Germanic tribal law. He also claimed that non-privatized land, the remaining countryside commons, was the joint property of 'all men', and that the multitude of productive functions of land and water necessitated restrictions upon private property rights.[55] His rebuttal of a 'natural right of absolute property' recalls early twentieth-century American legal realists and economic institutionalists.[56] Moreover, he referred to the Swedish criminal law of 1864, which listed what a person might not take from somebody else's land without committing an offence; Åström's interpretation was that these statements should be understood literally and that whatever was not listed could be taken.[57]

Like mushrooms, wild berries were not listed. However, lingonberries, which had been much used in peasant households, had become significant with improved transportation facilities and access to cheap sugar for making jam. By the end of the nineteenth century, lingonberries had become a domestic and even an export commodity. People with no affinity to the forest were said to pick berries for commercial purposes, depriving landowners of the berries for their own use or to derive income from them. Even radicals sided with the landowners, complaining that poor smallholders' widows' assets had been handed over to urban commercial interests. Several parliamentary bills requested some kind of landowner protection for the berries. However, no such law was ever enacted and since the *allemansrätt* was defined as a customary rule in 1940, the public right to pick berries on private land remained in place.[58]

The fundamental part of public access rights was the freedom to visit and to walk across privately owned uncultivated land. While permanent camps were not allowed, people might camp for a couple of days on the same spot. The limits of *allemansrätt* were negatively defined in reference to other legislation: one was not allowed to use the land in a way that hurt the landowner economically (by destroying the physical qualities of the area or by removing growing or non-growing valuables from it); one could not intrude close to someone else's house or garden. Successively from the 1950s to the 1990s, the right was made more precise, with rules prohibiting the landowner from unduly fencing off areas. Propaganda and information disseminated through various organizations and schools ensured that the *allemansrätt* became common knowledge. Still only negatively defined, it was included in the natural protection law of 1974. In 1993 it was included in the constitution, alongside the right to private ownership.[59]

If a landowner built residential houses in an area, the integrity rule implied that the area around them was no longer to be publicly accessed. In certain areas, notably the archipelago east of Stockholm, summerhouses were increasingly built along beaches. The answer was the revival of a suggestion dating back to 1937, which aimed at protecting beaches from being exploited. In 1950 a temporary law, made permanent without much debate in 1952, forbade the setting up of buildings within 300 metres of a beach, except for professional fishing or farming purposes. Since the 1990s this legislation has been liberalized and the governmental county boards have had a freer hand to make exceptions, for the benefit of economic development in remote areas.[60]

Carlesjö, following Åström, vaguely derived the *allemansrätt* from customary principles including freedom for the public to move across land owned by others, to rest, to make a fire, to pick wild fruits of little value to eat, etc.[61] But this view is largely anachronistic, as in pre-modern society there was really no 'public' in the modern sense and the rights to use a commons were restricted to those who jointly owned it.[62] The *allemansrätt* was in fact a distinctly modern product of political and juridical choices made in the early twentieth century. It was formulated as *one* specific solution for the emerging social problem of access by the urban masses to land for recreational purposes, which had hardly materialized at all in any considerable sense before the interwar era.[63]

It has been suggested that the Scandinavian solution to the common recreational land use problem – versions of public access rights – contrasted with the solutions chosen in Britain and in the British colonies, and that this reflected different legal traditions.[64] In reality, however, loopholes allowing commoners to move around commons and uncultivated land probably existed in pre-enclosure Britain to a similar extent as in pre-enclosure Sweden, the real difference lying in the proportions of outlying forested land to arable land.[65]

Still, when the *allemansrätt* was formulated in Sweden, referring to some kind of ancient customary legacy obviously played a role in the rhetorical legitimation of the right to public access, not least since it connected to a nationalist romantic view of nature-loving Swedes – or Scandinavians, for that matter. Similar rules for recreational use of land actually emerged in the rest of Scandinavia, and in the Norwegian case the right of public access was more clearly, albeit more narrowly defined in law in 1957. In Denmark, the smaller proportion of uncultivated land meant that less land was available for public access.[66] However, the beach protection act passed in Sweden was modelled after Danish interwar legislation protecting the extensive Danish seaside.[67]

In Switzerland and in parts of Germany, free access to uncultivated land exists in ways similar to Scandinavian cases.[68] In the common law regions solutions varied. Former British colonies like the USA and New Zealand draw on:

> a 'new world' land-management context dominated by large tracts of public land, contested indigenous rights and a frontier or pioneer ethos. Both countries have a history of managing landscapes based on a 'pristine myth' that presumes some pre-European standard for the ecological integrity of the landscape ... In Britain (and Scandinavia) human history does not afford as sharp a distinction between the cultural and natural landscape.[69]

Thus, in the nations formed from Anglo-Saxon settler colonies the problem of modern public access to uncultivated land has been solved by the government purchasing or keeping in public ownership wide areas of uncultivated land and setting up large national parks, which can be responsibly accessed by the public. Private landowners, in turn, are fully entitled to block public access to their land, while remaining free to invite the public in for commercial purposes.[70]

Post-enclosure England, on the other hand, was a country of concentrated land ownership, in which recreational land use was heavily class-specific. Landowners were intensively engaged in outdoor sports, not least hunting, while walking became the main plebeian countryside recreation in the early twentieth century. Walkers were allowed by default to follow demarcated footpaths, located so that hunting parties would not be disturbed, but walking organizations could negotiate access with private landowners and they lobbied for increased general access. They received the right to wander on common land within urban districts in 1925, but the 1939 Access to the Mountain Act still forced wanderers to negotiate access on a case-by-case basis.

The Labour government passed a National Parks and Access to the Countryside Act in 1949.[71] The results proved disappointing. The growing municipalities that had bought land to use as catching grounds for urban water supplies did not enter into the access agreements, alleging concerns at the risk of contamination, but probably just as concerned at the loss of income from leasing out licences for shooting grouse.[72]

The neoliberal turn around 1980 strengthened the landowners' side and reduced public access.[73] What remained of default access rights after the 1981 Wildlife and Countryside Act were discontinued, loopholes were tightened, and historically open footpaths were physically blocked. Minor trespass offences, which would formerly be overlooked, were increasingly prosecuted.[74] In 2000, the Labour

Countryside and Rights of Way Act again delivered measures to improve public access to the open uncultivated countryside and registered commons.[75]

While the former was valid for England and Wales, the Scottish Land Reform Act of 2003 granted much wider public access to the Highlands for recreational and educational purposes and even 'for the purposes of carrying on, commercially or for profit, an activity, which the person exercising the right could carry on otherwise than commercially or for profit'.[76]

The rules for public access to uncultivated land in Scandinavia thus represent one specific set of solutions to handle the rising demand for some kind of access to land for recreational uses, as nations get richer, urbanized and increasingly inhabited by people without any direct affinity to rural land, let alone owning it. It drew on previous ways of handling conflicts over property rights arising from new land uses through the political composition of interests. In that sense there was an element of path dependence in the shaping of the solution. It has been suggested that the peculiar solution in Scandinavia draws on specific legal traditions, distinctly different to those in both France and the common law countries. However, the actual ruling mix of property rights is ultimately the outcome of struggle or negotiation between actors with conflicting interests and draws on competing sources of legitimacy. This is evident as Britain (particularly Scotland), with legal traditions different to Scandinavia, recently enacted access rules similar to the Scandinavian ones.

Post-Fordist challenges: Post-productivism or new commodities?

At the height of the Fordist era in western Europe, during the third quarter of the twentieth century, industrial employment peaked and so did levels of GDP increase in many countries, not least in Sweden. Mass consumption of standardized goods and services evolved. A productivist line ruled agriculture: Swedish farms were geared towards producing higher quantities of homogeneous products, for negotiated output prices between producer and consumer representatives and the government, while tariffs guaranteed sustained prices. Likewise in the CAP area, intervention prices and border protection maintained prices and farmers' incomes. Such measures were largely introduced because the farm sector was under pressure, as low income-elasticity of food products implied that in a free market context, farming could not expand at a similar rate to household incomes. Demand had turned to industrial goods, ever cheaper in real terms due to productivity gains, to welfare services and to various forms of recreation.

When Fordist economic mechanisms ran into trouble in the 1970s and the traditional industrial sectors started to slim down in many countries, breakthroughs in and the establishment of new core technologies – automation, biotechnology and ICT – laid the ground for more flexible labour markets, instant capital flows and a new wave of globalization.[77]

Consumption patterns also changed. In richer countries, they became much more individualistic, with a stress on distinction. Increased importance of design and branding went hand in hand with many consumers' concerns over how goods are produced, raw materials, origins, and ethical and ecological principles. More people were prepared to pay a premium for goods that met their environmental concerns, thus transforming them into effective demand.

This had a threefold effect on the food and farming sector. Firstly, new demand patterns energized alternative production niches such as certified organic production, quality on-farm processed products and regional specialities. Secondly, the consumption of leisure services increased and was reconstituted. Lifestyle concerns led to a growing interest in rural dwelling, and, during the last few decades, many secondary homes in areas close to urban centres were turned into permanent dwellings, thus making a closer relation to nature a more permanent part of life.[78] New recreational patterns opened up business opportunities for many farmers: agritourism developed in many countries, horse-related leisure provided demand for fodder and leases of pasture and stable boxes,[79] as did hunting for leases of hunting grounds. Around 1990, rules were repealed that had forbidden the purchase of farmland for non-agricultural uses and had excluded corporate bodies from buying farmland, easing investment to take advantage of recreational demand.

Thirdly, significant public demand emerged for nature conservation, protecting or restoring biodiversity and cultural heritage. Governments in Europe and the USA promoted policies, legitimized by market failure arguments, to secure environmentally safer agricultural practices. This implied impinging on the farmers' land use rights. In the USA, this largely amounted to restricting farming practices to reduce negative externalities, such as erosion and pesticide abuse. In Europe, alongside such restrictions, the EU also promotes positive externalities by paying farmers for services such as landscape restoration.[80]

Activities using land to produce other values than those directly related to food and fibres have been summarized under the commonplace term 'post-productive'.[81] 'Pre-modern' agricultural methods had tended to create landscape values that are longed for nowadays, and which now have to be deliberately produced and paid for. To (re)produce such landscape elements has become a secondary occupation for farmers. 'Landscape beauty' has become a new product or, as Howard Newby put it, a new 'crop'.[82] Therefore, the term 'post-productive' is misleading. This is indeed production of new commodities or services, for which demand – partly channelled through the state – has risen in some rich countries in comparison to the demand for bulk food and fibres, which are more cheaply produced overseas with affluent supplies of land and labour.

A range of utilities summarized as 'Nature' have thus become (re)produced commodities. Access to these peculiar utilities is harder to disentangle and their categorization as commodities needs conceptual clarification, as well as how property rights are affected by their creation.

A resource is subtractable if appropriation from it 'by one owner or stakeholder diminishes the amount available for another'. Where exclusion of any potential appropriator or consumer of subtractable resources is feasible, the good or resource in question may be private. Where this is not the case, we talk of common pool resources. In such cases, some kind of institutional arrangement is needed to avoid overexploitation. If goods are non-subtractable and exclusion is feasible, they are 'toll' or 'club' goods: you are excluded from visiting the natural park unless you pay for it, but once you have paid, your consumption of the landscape does not diminish the experience of other paying members of the public.[83] Finally, where there is no subtractability and exclusion is not feasible, we talk of public goods.[84]

Fibre and food produced by conventional agriculture are clearly private goods. Public access regimes imply that resources such as lingonberries, which are subtractable and can be picked by anyone, belong to a common pool. Some of the 'new' or 'alternative' products related to recreational use of land are toll or club goods, since once strict private ownership in land is maintained, the owner can give access to non-subtractable recreational uses (such as wandering, skiing, sightseeing, etc.) for those paying a fee.

According to Berge, who endeavoured to adapt the theory of commons to landscape and environmental goods and services, 'the club aspect of a good tells us that the utility of the good cannot be exported. To enjoy the good a person has to be within the landscape area'.[85] However, non-exportability only makes for a club good if exclusion is possible. If there is a sanctioned public access right allowing people to visit privately owned land, exclusion is unlawful (and in a sense costly).

Exportable non-subtractable goods, on the other hand, are pure public goods:

> [T]he wilderness character of an area is meant to capture the existence values of nature and ecosystems. This is a public good. Anywhere in the world the certainty can be enjoyed that the mountains and ecosystems of Geiranger-Herdalen (a landscape in Norway) exist in their pristine form.[86]

Private landowners cannot exclude anyone from consuming that good. Therefore, the social regulation of the management of such resources is the only way to secure that they will not be 'under-produced', a textbook case of market failure. The willingness of people in a given society to 'consume' such goods might imply changes in the rights of land use within the bundle of property rights. Stretching the argument somewhat, the 'national' or 'common' utility invoked to justify enclosures, the regulation of owners' rights in connection with the expansion of forestry, tenancy and the silviculture legislation, may just as well be perceived as a public good. The same goes for the national health and social equality targets lying behind the efforts to ease outdoor recreational life in the 1930s and 1940s.

While all societies have tried to some extent to regulate markets in order to avoid market failures in the provision of public goods, differences in the readiness and scope of such attempts may reflect a certain amount of path dependence, as past solutions to conflicting property claims seem to mould later solutions to different problems. But it is no less clear that such path dependence in turn stems from power relations, which by formulating what is 'normal' have determined in most instances the effective outcome of political negotiations over property rights.

Conclusion: Multifunctional land use and property rights conflicts

The chapter started with the notion that property rights are socially sanctioned and changeable human-to-human relations allowing for certain actions concerning assets. It has been held that property rights originate from social action, that innovations in land use tend to lead to conflicts concerning property rights, that the solutions negotiated tend to be moulded on solutions tried out in earlier conflicts, and that their outcomes rest on the balance of power among involved interests. Sometimes the formulation of property rights has excluded certain uses, sometimes property rights have in fact been divided up according to the different functions of land.

'Absolute' land ownership implies that the owner is in full control of all usage rights (except for pure public utilities as discussed above) and is able to sell or lease out any rights to potential users. The establishment of such 'absolute' rights involved dispossessing some other users of some of *their* rights and in turn has created externalities, with which social actors, including governments, have tried to find ways to restrict the dispositional rights of owners, thus changing the sanctioned bundle of rights.

As new land uses appear, the question arises of the compatibility of different kinds of use rights organized in various ways. This caused the fight over disposal rights in forestland 120 years ago, and homologous problems and solutions have kept popping up until the present day.

Not much conflict can be detected between conventional farming and recreational use of land, as even public access regimes concern somewhat *uncultivated* land. However, forests have normally been less intensively cultivated and conflicts between forestry management and recreational use have repeatedly been placed on the agenda. In the 1970s, the wide use of pesticides by Swedish forest companies led to confrontations with berry pickers and people making use of the right to public access for recreational purposes.

It is also easy to perceive a conflict between extended public access to land and sports hunting, which generates income for landowners. The remaining, albeit weakened, restrictions to building on privately owned beaches remind us that it is not self-evident that private ownership is favoured over public access rights to certain land uses.

Two conflicts involving the appropriation of property rights currently stand out in Sweden. One concerns the couple of hundred wolves remaining within Swedish borders. Their existence is strongly resented by sheep farmers, reindeer herders and hunters. There is, however, strong public interest in securing the population of wolves for biodiversity reasons. The struggle has taken the shape of parliamentary debates, court procedures, negotiations with EU lawyers, and widespread poaching. There are buy-out solutions, but the conflict remains unsolved. For the hunters and herders, wolves threaten both private and common pool resources, while for the public defending the very survival of the wolves this is seen as a public good in itself.

The second conflict concerns the commercial use of public access rights, in situations where the landowner could feasibly act as a gatekeeper of a club resource, which is instead appropriated by non-landowning members of the 'public'. Public access rights are increasingly used for commercial purposes: riding schools and horse tourist firms, which use land extensively for riding tours, cash in on the use of public rights, as do adventure tourist entrepreneurs organizing rafting expeditions. Some entrepreneurs in Sweden take advantage of relaxed labour immigration laws to import temporary labour to pick berries for sweatshop wages. They thus use free public access to private land to appropriate resources to their own private profit, besides those of staffing companies and ultimately the canning industry. Other private interests, such as day-care centres offering outdoor activities and wildlife tourism organizations, profit from gatekeeping for club goods that they produce on land they do not own.

Legal procedures have so far tended to allow such commercial use of public access, as long as it does not harm the landowner's assets, in which case it comes under the heading of a criminal offence. The leading farmers' organization (LRF) opposes this and has requested restrictions on the *allemansrätt*, which has put it under some pressure. The case is on the political agenda and it seems a fair guess that some renegotiations of property rights will ensue, along the lines followed earlier.

Notes

1 Quoted by S. Sörlin, *Framtidslandet: Debatten om Norrland och Naturresurserna under det Industriella Genombrottet* (Stockholm: Carlssons, 1988), p. 30.
2 T. Wiklund, *Det Tillgjorda Landskapet: En Undersökning av Förutsättningarna för Urban Kultur i Norden* (Göteborg: Bokförlaget Korpen, 1995), p. 95.
3 C.-J. Gadd, *Den Agrara Revolutionen 1700–1870: Det Svenska Jordbrukets Historia 3* (Stockholm: Natur och Kultur/LT, 2000) pp. 239–41; L. Lundmark, *Så Länge Vi Har Marker: Samerna och Staten under Sexhundra År* (Stockholm: Rabén Prisma, 1998); J. Myrdal, *Jordbruket under Feodalismen 1000–1700: Det Svenska Jordbrukets Historia 2* (Stockholm: Natur och Kultur/LT, 1999), pp. 227–8.
4 I. Flygare and M. Isacson, *Jordbruket i Välfärdssamhället: Det Svenska Jordbrukets Historia 5* (Stockholm: Natur och Kultur/LT, 2003), pp. 35–7; T. Hahn, *Property Right, Ethics and Conflict Resolution: Foundations of the Sami Economy in Sweden* (Stockholm: Stockholm University, 2000).
5 A. A. Alchian and H. Demsetz, 'The property rights paradigm', *Journal of Economic History*, 33 (1973), pp. 16–27; R. H. Coase, 'The problem of social cost', in R. H. Coase, *The Firm, the Market and the Law* (Chicago and London: University of Chicago Press, 1990), pp. 95–156; R. Congost and R. Santos, 'From formal institutions to the social contexts of property', in R. Congost and R. Santos (eds), *Contexts of Property in Europe: The Social Embeddedness of Property Rights in Land in Historical Perspective* (Turnhout: Brepols, 2010), pp. 15–38.
6 Congost and Santos, 'From formal institutions', pp. 19–20.
7 A. Åström, *Om Svensk Jordäganderätt* (Stockholm: Nordstedts, 1897).
8 M. Morell, 'Property rights and growth in Swedish agriculture in the late eighteenth and early nineteenth centuries', in G. Béaur, P. R. Schofield, J.-M. Chevet and M. T. Pérez Picazo (eds), *Property Rights, Land Markets and Economic Growth in the European Countryside (Thirteenth–Twentieth Centuries)* (Turnhout: Brepols, 2013), pp. 495–514.

9   B. Ericsson, 'Central power and the local right to dispose over the forest common in eighteenth-century Sweden: A micro study of the decision making process during Sweden's age of freedom', *Scandinavian Journal of History*, 5 (1980), pp. 75–92; U. Lovén and H. Lovén, *Häradsallmänningarna: Från Medeltida Kulturarv till Modern Samverkan* (Björklinge: Norunda Häradsallmänning, 2003).

10 L. Dombernowsky, 'Ca. 1720–1810', in C. Bjørn and T. Dahlerup (eds), *Det Danske Landbrugs Historie II 1536–1810* (Odense: Landbohistorisk Selskab, 2010), pp. 211–393.

11 C. Porskrog Rasmussen, 'An English or a continental way? The great agrarian reforms in Denmark and Schleswig-Holstein in the eighteenth century', in R. Congost and R. Santos (eds), *Contexts of Property*, pp. 125–44.

12 M. Morell, 'Cultivation: Swedish agriculture in the cosmopolitan 18th century', in G. Rydén, (ed.) *Sweden in the Eighteenth-Century World: Provincial Cosmopolitans* (Farnham: Ashgate 2013), pp. 69–92.

13 Quoted by G. Utterström, *Jordbrukets Arbetare*, 1 (Stockholm: Tiden, 1957), p. 250.

14 B. Hanssen, 'Jacob Faggots memorial av År 1755', *Ekonomisk Tidskrift*, 58 (1946), pp. 275–89.

15 Morell, 'Cultivation'.

16 Morell, 'Property rights'.

17 M. Olsson, *Skatta dig Lycklig: Jordränta och Jordbruk i Skåne 1600–1900* (Hedemora: Gidlunds, 2005), pp. 176–7.

18 C.-J. Gadd, 'The agricultural revolution in Sweden 1700–1870', in J. Myrdal and M. Morell (eds), *The Agrarian History of Sweden 4000 BC–AD 2000* (Lund: Nordic Academic Press, 2011), pp. 118–64.

19 Olsson, *Skatta dig Lycklig*.

20 M. Morell, 'Ecological constraints and property rights in Swedish agriculture c. 1750–1850', in B. J. P. van Bavel and E. Thoen (eds), *Rural Societies and Environments at Risk: Ecology, Property Rights and Social Organisation in Fragile Areas (Middle Ages–Twentieth Century)* (Turnhout: Brepols, 2013), pp. 41–84.

21 J. Larsson, 'Boundaries and property rights: The transformation of a common-pool resource', *Agricultural History Review*, 62:1 (2014), pp. 40–60.

22 A. Locatelli and P. Tedeschi, in chapter three, and I. Iriarte and J. M. Lana, in chapter seven, also address the privatization of common lands. (Editors' note.)

23 M. Morell and M. Olsson, 'Scandinavia 1750–2000', in B. J. P. van Bavel and R. Hoyle (eds), *Social Relations, Property and Power: Rural Economy and Society in North-Western Europe, 500–2000* (Brepols: Turnhout, 2010), pp. 315–47; Porskrog Rasmussen, 'An English or a continental way'.

24 M. Morell and M. Olsson, 'Scandinavia 1750–2000'; M. Olsson, 'Varför har Sverige saknat en jordreform?', in A. Wästfelt, *Att Bruka Men Inte Äga: Arrende och Annan Nyttjanderätt till Mark i Svenskt Jordbruk från Medeltid till Idag* (Stockholm: KSLA 2014), pp. 74–83.

25 S. Carlsson, *Bonden i Svensk Historia 3* (Stockholm: LT, 1956), pp. 173–6; Gadd, *Agrara Revolutionen*, pp. 303–4.

26 Hanssen, 'Jacob Faggots Memorial'.

27 Carlsson, *Bonden*, pp. 362–6; Sörlin, *Framtidslandet*, pp. 187–88; O. Gerard, 'The Norrland question 2: Studier i regeringens och riksdagens behandling av Norrlandsfrågan med särskild hänsyn till förbudslagstiftningen 1901–1906', *Economy and History*, 16:supplement (1973); G. Prawitz, *Jordfrågan: Jord-och Fastighetsbildningspolitiken på den Svenska Landsbygden under Förra Hälften av 1900-talet* (Stockholm: Sveriges Lantmätareförening, 1951).

28 N. Edling, *Det Fosterländska Hemmet: Egnahemspolitik, Småbruk och Hemideologi kring Sekelskiftet 1900* (Stockholm: Carlssons, 1996); Sörlin, *Framtidslandet*, pp. 206–50.

29 Sörlin, *Framtidslandet*, pp. 161–79.

30 Carlsson, *Bonden*, pp. 363–71; Prawitz, *Jordfrågan*; Sörlin, *Framtidslandet*; S. Sörlin, 'Sveriges moderna miljöhistoria', in K. V. Abrahamsson, J.-E. Hällgren, T. Sundström and S. Sörlin (eds), *Humanekologi: Naturens Resurser och Människans Försörjning* (Stockholm: Carlssons, 2001), pp. 381–440.
31 Carlsson, *Bonden*, pp. 363, 371–2.
32 *Historical Statistics of Sweden 2*, (Stockholm: SCB, 1957), p. 80.
33 Carlsson, *Bonden*, p. 371; M. Morell, 'Det svenska jordbruket och det tidiga 1900-talets arrendelagstiftning', in Wästfelt, *Att Bruka*, pp. 151–92.
34 SOU 1922:48, Jordkommissionens betänkanden 5, F. Sandberg, *Redogörelse för Resultatet av Vissa av Jordkommissionen Företagna Enquâter i Jordfrågan* (Stockholm, 1922); Morell, 'Det svenska jordbruket'.
35 Morell, 'Det Svenska Jordbruket'.
36 SOU 1968:57, *Jordbruksarrende: Arrendelagsutredningens Slutbetänkande* (Stockholm, 1968), pp. 84–9.
37 R. Almås, *Norges Landbrukshistorie IV, 1920–2000: Frå Bondesamfunn till Bioindustri* (Oslo: Det Norske Samlaget, 2002), pp. 60–2.
38 Carlsson, *Bonden*, pp. 361–2; Sörlin, *Framtidslandet*, pp. 145–6.
39 R. Pettersson, 'Economics in the forest' in Ulf Jansson (ed.), *Agriculture and Forestry in Sweden since 1900: A Cartographic Description* (Stockholm: Royal Swedish Academy of Agriculture and Forestry, 2011), pp. 116–18.
40 P. Eliasson, 'The state-owned forests: Silviculture, mechanization and institutional change', in H. Antonson and U. Jansson (eds), *Agriculture and Forestry in Sweden since 1900: Geographical and Historical Studies* (Stockholm: The Royal Swedish Academy of Agriculture and Forestry, 2011), pp. 390–405; K.-G. Enander, 'Forestry policy in the twentieth century', in Jansson, *Agriculture and Forestry*, pp. 118–22; S. Lundell, 'Family forestry in transition: Times of freedom, responsibility and better knowledge', in Antonson and Jansson, *Agriculture and Forestry*, pp. 406–22; Sörlin, *Framtidslandet*, pp. 145–6.
41 Enander, 'Forestry policy'; Lundell, 'Family forestry'.
42 T. W. Merrill and H. E. Smith, 'What happened to property in Law and Economics?', *Yale Law Journal*, 111 (2001), pp. 357–98.
43 J. Broad, 'Whigs and deer-stealers and other guises: A return to the origins of the Black Act', *Past and Present*, 119 (1988), pp. 56–72; G. Broberg 'Jaktens förvandlingar', in J. Christensen (ed.), *Signums Svenska Kulturhistoria, Karl-Johantiden* (Stockholm: Signum, 2008), pp. 387–429; E. P. Thompson, *Whigs and Hunters: The Origins of the Black Act* (London: Allen Lane, 1975).
44 C.-J. Dahlman and A. Klevmarken, *Den Privata Konsumtionen 1931–1975* (Stockholm: Almqvist & Wiksell, 1971), pp. 13–14.
45 L. Eskilsson, 'Svenska Turistföreningen från fjäll till friluftsliv: Från den vetenskaplige vildmarksmannen till den cyklande husmodern', *Historisk Tidskrift*, 116 (1996), pp. 257–82.
46 K. Sandell, 'Naturkontrakt och allemansrätt: Om friluftslivets naturmöte och friluftslandskapets tillgänglighet i Sverige 1880–2000', *Swedish Geographical Yearbook*, 73 (1997), pp. 31–65.
47 Sörlin, 'Sveriges moderna miljöhistoria' p. 386.
48 Edling, *Fosterländska Hemmet*, pp. 336–43; B. Sundin, 'Ljus och jord! Natur och kultur på Storgården', in T. Frängsmyr (ed.), *Paradiset och Vildmarken: Studier Kring Synen på Naturen och Naturresurserna* (Stockholm: Naturförlag, 1984).
49 O. Löfgren, 'Känslans förvandling: Tiden, naturen och hemmet i den borgerliga kulturen', in J. Frykman and O. Löfgren (eds), *Den Kultiverade Människan* (Malmö: Gleerups, 1979), pp. 21–127; Sörlin, *Framtidslandet*, pp. 82–92; S. Sörlin, 'Upptäckten av friluftslandskapet' in K. Sandell and S. Sörlin (eds), *Friluftshistoria: Från 'Härdande Friluftslif' till Ekoturism och Miljöpedagogik* (Stockholm: Carlsson Bokförlag, 2000), pp. 16–26; Sörlin, 'Sveriges moderna miljöhistoria', pp. 387–9.

50   Eskilsson, 'Svenska Turistföreningen'.
51   A. Lewen, 'Det var en lyckad semester! Semesterfirande svenskars preferenser år 1938–1959' (licentiate thesis, Stockholm University, 2011).
52   D. K. Müller, 'Second homes in the Nordic countries: Between common heritage and exclusive commodity', *Scandinavian Journal of Hospitality and Tourism*, 7 (2007), pp. 193–201; Sörlin, 'Upptäckten av friluftslandskapet'; Sörlin, 'Sveriges moderna miljöhistoria', pp. 381–440.
53   Wiklund, *Tillgjorda Landskapet*; G. Wiktorsson, *Den Grundlagsskyddade Myten: Om Allemansrättens Lansering i Sverige* (Stockholm: City University Press, 1996), pp. 114–54. Quote from SOU 1940:12, *Betänkande med Utredning och Förslag Angående Inrättande av Fritidsreservat för Städernas och de Tättbebyggda Samhällenas Befolkning Avgivet av Fritidsutredningen* (Stockholm, 1940), p. 268.
54   Lagberedningen, *Lagberedningens Förslag till Jordabalk*, 3, *Förslag till Jordabalk M. M.* (Stockholm, 1909), p. 105.
55   Åström, *Om Svensk Jordäganderätt*; Wiktorsson, *Grundlagsskyddade Myten*, pp. 73–90.
56   Merrill and Smith, 'What happened to property', p. 365.
57   Wiktorsson, *Grundlagsskyddade Myten*, pp. 44–67.
58   Sandell, 'Naturkontrakt', pp. 40–1; Wiklund, *Tillgjorda Landskapet*, pp. 105–7; Wiktorsson, *Grundlagsskyddade Myten*, pp. 91–110.
59   J. Campion and J. Stephenson, 'The "right to roam": Lessons for New Zealand from Sweden's *allemansrätt*', *Australasian Journal of Environmental Management*, 17 (2010), pp. 18–26; K. T. Colby, 'Public access to private land: *Allemansrätt* in Sweden', *Landscape and Urban Planning*, 15 (1987), pp. 253–64; A. Dahlberg, R. Rodhe and K. Sandell, 'National parks and environmental justice: Comparing access rights and ideological legacies in three countries', *Conservation and Society*, 8 (2010), pp. 209–24; P. Donnelly, 'The right to wander: Issues in the leisure use of the countryside and wilderness areas', *International Review for the Sociology of Sport*, 28 (1993), pp. 187–201; B. P. Kaltenborn, H. Haaland and K. Sandell, 'The public right to access: Some challenges to sustainable tourism development in Scandinavia', *Journal of Sustainable Tourism*, 9 (2001), pp. 417–33; B. Segrell, 'Accessing the attractive coast: Conflict and co-operation in the Swedish coastal landscape during the twentieth century', in C. Watkins (ed.), *Rights of Way: Policy, Culture and Management* (London: Pinter, 1996), pp. 142–61; K. Sandell and M. Svenning, *Allemansrätten och dess framtid* (Stockholm: Naturvårdsverket, 2011); Wiktorsson, *Grundlagsskyddade Myten*.
60   E. Berge, 'Protected areas and traditional commons: Values and institutions', *Norwegian Journal of Geography*, 60 (2006), pp. 65–76; Segrell, 'Accessing the attractive coast', pp. 149–59.
61   SOU 1940:12 p. 268; Sandell, 'Naturkontrakt'; Wiklund, *Tillgjorda Landskapet*, pp. 103–14; Wiktorsson, *Grundlagsskyddade Myten*, pp. 73–87, 143–54.
62   Wiktorsson, *Grundlagsskyddade Myten*, p. 220.
63   Sandell, 'Naturkontrakt'.
64   D. R. Williams, 'Sustainability and public access to nature: Contesting the right to roam', *Journal of Sustainable Tourism*, 9 (2001), pp. 361–71.
65   Donnelly, 'The right to wander'; N. Ravenscroft, 'New access initiatives: The extension of recreation opportunities or the diminution of citizen rights?', in Watkins, *Rights of Way*, pp. 35–48.
66   Wiktorsson, *Grundlagsskyddade Myten*, pp. 231–8.
67   Segrell 'Accessing the Attractive Coast'.
68   M. Shoard, 'Robbers v. revolutionaries: What the battle for access is really all about', in Watkins, *Rights of Way*, pp. 11–23.
69   Williams, 'Sustainability', p. 362.
70   Campion and Stephenson, 'Right to roam'; Dahlberg, Rodhe and Sandell, 'National parks'; J. J. Pigram, 'Outdoor recreation and access to the countryside: Focus on the

Australian experience', *Natural Resources Journal*, 107 (1981), pp. 107–23; Williams, 'Sustainability'.
71 R. W. Hoyle, 'Securing access to England's upland: Or how the 1945 revolution petered out', in Congost and Santos, *Contexts of Property*, pp. 187–209; Shoard, 'Robbers v. revolutionaries'.
72 Hoyle, 'Securing access'.
73 Ravenscroft, 'New access initiatives'.
74 P. Donnelly, 'Right to wander'; Ravenscroft, 'New access initiatives'; Shoard, 'Robbers v. revolutionaries'.
75 Hoyle, 'Securing Access'; D. H. Sellar, 'The great land debate and the land reform (Scotland) Act 2003', *Norwegian Journal of Geography*, 60 (2006), pp. 100–9.
76 Sellar, 'Great land debate', quote from p. 106.
77 L. Schön, *Sweden's Road to Modernity: An Economic History* (Stockholm: SNS 2010), pp. 18–32.
78 U. Sporrong (ed.), *Stockholm-Mälarregionen* (Stockholm: Sveriges Nationalatlas, 2008), p. 15.
79 L. Garkovich, K. Brown and J. N. Zimmerman, '"We're not horsing around": Conceptualizing the Kentucky horse industry as an economic cluster', *Community and Development*, 39 (2008), pp. 93–113; S. Hedenborg and M. Morell, 'A vehicle in the army, a lumber jack companion or a friend in the family: The horse and the countryside in 20th-century Sweden' (Paper presented to *The ESSH Conference*, Lisbon, 2008).
80 K. Baylis, S. Peplow, G. Rausser and L. Simon, 'Agri-environmental policies in the EU and United States: A comparison', *Ecological Economics*, 17 (2005), pp. 753–64.
81 For example, G. A. Wilson, 'From productivism to post-productivism . . . and back again? Exploring the (un)changed natural and mental landscapes of European agriculture', *Transactions of the Institute of British Geographers*, 26 (2000), pp. 77–102.
82 J. Myrdal, *Den Nya Produktionen – det Nya Uppdraget: Jordbrukets Framtid i ett Historiskt Perspektiv* (Stockholm: Jordbruksdepartementet, Ds. 2001); H. Newby, *Green and Pleasant Land? Social Change in Rural England* (London: Hutchinson, 1979); E.-L. Päiviö, *Det Agrara Landskapet på Vinst och Förlust: Biologiska och Historiska Värden inom Lantbrukets Nya Uppdrag* (Uppsala: SLU, 2008).
83 Berge, 'Protected areas', quote on p. 68.
84 E. Ostrom, 'Coping with tragedies of the commons', *Annual Review of Political Science*, 2 (1999), pp. 493–535; V. Ostrom and E. Ostrom, 'Public goods and public choices', in E. S. Savas (ed.), *Alternatives for Delivering Public Services: Toward Improved Performance* (Boulder: Westview, 1979), pp. 7–49. The theory of club goods was originally stated in J. Buchanan, 'An economic theory of clubs', *Economica*, 32 (1965), pp. 1–14. (S. Garrido discusses the collective management of common pool resources in the light of Ostrom's theory in chapter six. Editors' note.)
85 Berge, 'Protected areas', p. 70.
86 Berge, 'Protected areas', p. 70.

3 Innovation in property rights and economic development in Lombardy, eighteenth– twentieth centuries

Andrea M. Locatelli and Paolo Tedeschi

Introduction

This chapter deals with the contribution of state led institutional reforms in property rights since the second half of the eighteenth century to changing Lombard agriculture and to accelerating economic development, which made this one of the most dynamic and productive regions in contemporary Europe. More specifically, our focus will be on a succession of reforms which began in eighteenth-century western Lombardy, as a province in the Austrian empire, and which were then pursued under Napoleonic rule in the early nineteenth century and later, again under Austrian rule, generalized to the other areas of Lombardy.

Those reforms involved the drawing up and the successive extension and updating of a land cadastre, which made the allocation of landed property more precise and produced a quantitative assessment of its economic potential for tax purposes; the privatization of common land and collective rights; and correlative fiscal policies which had built-in incentives for landowners to either invest or sell the land to those willing to do so.

We will briefly describe the gist of the reforms and explore their impact on the performance of Lombard agriculture and the region's economic system as a whole. Rather than positing a linear causal nexus between the two, we will stress the contingent historical conditions within Lombard agriculture, economy, and society that facilitated their virtuous relationship. In order to do that, we will contrast this success case with other regions in Italy, from the neighbouring Veneto to southern Italy, and with the 'inner failure' of the privatization of the commons in the Lombard Alpine areas.

Following this introduction, the essay is organized into five sections. The first presents the region's main traits and the historical setting in which the reforms operated. The second provides a descriptive synthesis of the successive cadastral reforms and their main impacts on Lombard agriculture. The third presents the aforementioned contrasted cases. The fourth attempts a systematization of the historical, social and cultural factors that mediated the concrete appropriation of the property reforms and which help explain their economic effectiveness. The fifth and final section presents our concluding remarks.

A long history of regional dynamism

Before the Napoleonic invasion, the centre and west of Lombardy belonged to the Habsburg Empire, the east to the Republic of Venice, some Alpine valleys to the Swiss state of the Grisons and the south-east to the Duchy of Mantua. In spite of the absence of political unity and stable political and administrative boundaries for part of its early modern history, as a region Lombardy had a lengthy cultural and civic tradition that created a distinct Lombard society. Its economic system too had a specific identity even during French and Austrian domination, which was easily distinguishable from both the Piedmont, characterized by the Turin polarity, and the Venetian area, in which the relationships between Venice and the surrounding towns and rural territories were less well structured than the Lombard highly-urbanized regional system.[1]

This urban system was an integrative factor within a very diverse countryside, from the highly productive, irrigated plains in the River Po Valley to the less fertile, non-irrigated plains and hilly areas and the poor lands in the Alpine valleys, all with very different productive capacities, agrarian structures, and agricultural landscapes.

Lombardy has been said to have gone through an 'agricultural revolution' in the fourteenth and fifteenth centuries[2] – an expression that may appear exaggerated, but which does convey the strong dynamism that agricultural and economic historians are unanimous in attributing to the region. At its core were the irrigated plains in the Po Valley, which were at the European forefront of agrarian individualism, and the rise and expansion of a market in short-term lease contracts. Throughout the early modern period, the agricultural landscapes were reshaped by innovations in cultivated plants, husbandry systems and field layout, sustained by an irrigation system that took advantage of the vast network of canals that the Dukes of Milan had developed since the fourteenth century, for defence and navigation purposes as well as irrigation.

On the whole, notwithstanding the persistence of a variety of farm types and sizes throughout the early modern period, agriculture in the irrigated plains consistently moved towards the domination of large-scale capitalistic farming, driven by response to market demand, through the concentration of farm ownership and leases and the substitution of hired labour for traditional share-cropping agreements.[3] One should, however, note the resilience of perpetual leases, at least up to the sixteenth and seventeenth centuries and in land owned by religious institutions. Such perpetual leases had actually played a significant part in an earlier phase of the process. They had evolved in previous centuries from earlier short-term leases, as a result of the legal obligation of the lessor to pay for the lessee's capital investments in land improvements on contract termination. As religious institutions, and some of the nobility as well, could or would not meet this requirement after their tenants had invested heavily in improvements, they settled for perpetual leases for next to nominal amounts of rent, in relation to the accrued output. In this way, proto-capitalist 'nearly landowners' progressively displaced the traditional peasant tenantry.[4]

In the less fertile dry plains and especially in the hills, in contrast, the peasants' access to the land was based on sharecropping contracts, with lower productivity to labour and a large part of the produce being destined for the subsistence of peasant households. Nevertheless, its most dynamic production was market-oriented, particularly that of mulberry growing and silkworm raising for the silk industry – mostly to the advantage of the landlords, who in the eighteenth century responded to expanding demand by splitting up the former farms into smaller plots, sized to the sharecropping households' subsistence needs in grains, and collected their main rent income in silkworm cocoons. In some areas, the contractual form changed from pure sharecropping to a mixed contract with fixed rent in wheat and share rent in cocoons.[5]

In the Alpine valleys, arable land was scarce and generally afforded low yields. A large part of the land was devoted to forestry, which provided timber for urban needs, and to pastures for grazing local and transhumant livestock. Large tracts of the land there were the property of the village communities, where collective rights applied, even though plots might be allotted and leased for arable uses – a point on which we will elaborate further. Privately owned land in the valleys could be farmed by peasant landowners or let out under a variety of contracts, including leases and, in some wine producing areas, a form of long-term emphyteutic contract.[6]

All these areas provided goods for urban demand. The Lombard irrigated plain produced important amounts of wheat and maize, and it provided rich pasture and forage for cattle as well, catering for the rising urban consumption of meat and dairy. The non-irrigated plains and the hilly areas produced cereals, fruits, and wine, besides the aforementioned silkworm cocoons. The valleys provided wood, as well as pasture for transhumant cattle coming in from the plains. As a result, the varied rural areas in Lombardy interacted intensely through the backbone of large cities such as Como, Bergamo and Brescia and the regional capital, Milan, which was the core of a highly synergic relationship among the Lombard urban centres.[7] In spite of early industrialization, up until the first decades of the twentieth century, the agricultural sector still produced the most wealth in Lombardy, largely because of its ability to adapt to changing economic circumstances.[8] The different functions of the Lombard towns complemented themselves and induced spatial division of labour through economic relations with their hinterlands and with outside regions. Thus, for instance, when silk manufactures were established in the towns in the second half of the nineteenth century, they took advantage of the long established mulberry cultivation, silkworm breeding and silk thread processing in the countryside.[9]

In the irrigated plains, farmers enhanced productivity with advanced rotation practices, alternating staple cereals and nitrogen-rich crops such as clover, which doubled as soil fertilizer and forage for cattle.[10] The development of this agro-system and of the related commercial produce, together with incentives to invest built into the lease contracts, facilitated social attitudes favouring the widespread adoption of the most productive use of land and labour, as well as the inclination to trade outside regional borders. This long-term attitude of accepting rural entrepreneurship within the social order was crucial to the rate of innovation in Lombardy and its subsequent economic vitality.

The Austrian and French cadastres, land taxation, and incentives to growth

The implementation of the Habsburgs' land-tax cadastre in western Lombardy in the second half of the eighteenth century was a significant event in the history of the region's economic development. Besides a clearer demarcation and better securitization of property in land through a uniform registry system certified by the state, it introduced changes in the distribution of the fiscal burden on land revenue and in the incentives to invest in agriculture.[11] The Lombard nobility and urban elite interest groups, which represented most of the rentier landlords, opposed this tax reform and secured a long delay, from a failed start of the process in 1718 and its re-launch in 1749 to it finally entering in force in 1760. Nevertheless, the new cadastre was eventually imposed on them, albeit in a somewhat mitigated form through concessions made by the state in order to temper the protest.[12]

The tax burden was placed on the landowners, even when they were not farming the land themselves, and the cadastre removed some of the exemptions that had favoured the nobility and Church institutions. The cadastre and the correlative fiscal policy were also designed to enforce a social norm of 'profitable property'. To that effect, it introduced an analytical recording system that involved describing and measuring the entire area, assessing the quality of land and its average crops, and estimating the overall property value based on potential income. The total land taxation rate increased, but the real level of taxation on smallholders was lowered and specific reductions were made adjusting for soil quality and the nature of crops. A sliding scale of taxation rates was applied, decreasing in proportion to increases in production, and the taxation band was fixed for twenty-five years, during which all production above the estimated levels was exempted from tax. The fact that production increases would not be taxed in the short run led landowners to invest and have their tenants invest in land and technological improvements, which in turn increased the aggregated agricultural output. The state was able to recover the loss of fiscal revenue on landed property by collecting more sales tax on the increased agricultural output.

The French rule (1797–1814) kept the structure of the Habsburg cadastre in force in western Lombardy, with a few updates. The Napoleonic Census Office engineers released new estimates based on previous experience, mainly updating old land records to eliminate tax avoidance and to register privatized municipal assets. This Office also introduced differentiation of the estimated tax value of staple crops according to the districts, as well as tax deductions for expenses and damages, which again encouraged investment.[13]

By 1815, when the kingdom of Lombardy–Veneto was created following Napoleon's defeat, the tax estimates of the mid-eighteenth century Habsburg cadastre remained much the same in western Lombardy. This had favoured investing landowners, who had much to gain during the previous decades from improvements in agriculture, cattle and silkworm breeding, and who, therefore, paid lower taxes relative to their increased income. Conversely, rentier land-owners who had failed to invest to raise output and rents, faced a relatively higher tax burden. This also gave the former investing landowners an initial advantage when the cadastre and the land tax were subsequently generalized to eastern Lombardy and the Venetian lands in 1846, as we will point out. In the eastern Lombard lands, however, in spite of that initial disadvantage, the process eventually developed along similar lines and with identical effects to that in the western territories.[14]

Given that, if no investment had been made to improve soil fertility, the estimated tax applied even in the event of a poor harvest, rentier nobles and ecclesiastic institutions eventually opted or were forced to sell their property to urban merchant and professional groups and to wealthy farmers who were prepared to make capital investments. During the nineteenth century, all across Lombardy, new landowners and capitalist tenants took advantage of their acquired or extended foothold in land, under the market rules laid down by the French governments, to invest heavily in their farms and diversify production.[15] In the irrigated plains, besides cereals, they intensified forage growing in order to increase cattle and dairy produce; in some areas, this eventually became a specialization when cereal prices fell later in the century, demanding further capital inputs in stabling and dairy industry infrastructure. In the dry plains, landowners invested, or had lease tenants and sharecroppers invest in new vines, mulberry orchards, and silkworm breeding.

The land cadastre also contributed to increasing the mobility of property rights in land by making it easier for prospective purchasers to assess land quality, thereby reducing information asymmetries and transaction costs in land and lease markets, and allowing for better choice of investments. Highly profitable and valued land set in a mercantile and urbanized environment facilitated an active credit market, which in turn favoured risk taking and investment. As the reforms reinforced this trend by further securing property rights, fiscal incentives to investment were met by more ready access to capital. The long-term nature of the levy made it easier for landowners and tenants to estimate the profitability of farms and the amortization of capital costs over time, and therefore to assess the usefulness of getting loans for investment. At the other end of the credit relationship, the cadastre helped lenders assess credit risk and collaterals. This lowered transaction costs in the credit market as well, and eased the creation of rural banks later in the nineteenth century, together with the government's encouragement to the leading depositary bank in the province, the *Cassa di Risparmio delle Province Lombarde*, to finance agriculture in order to meet growing investment needs in machinery and infrastructure.

More investment in land and infrastructure by the landowners, coupled with higher taxation, led to an upward trend in lease rents, forcing tenants to improve land management and to take full advantage of those improvements. Upon lease termination, the tenants were entitled to compensation for their investments in land improvements, provided that the landlord had agreed to them. However, the high capital value of the irrigation infrastructure, on which land productivity depended, gave the landlords a significant weighting in the contractual relationships and extensive power in respect to the farmers' investment decisions, which curtailed the entrepreneurial autonomy of the tenant farmers. This eventually led to tensions during the 1880s as, in the midst of the agricultural crisis, the capitalist farmers' search for a way out through diversification and further investments met with the resistance of some landlords who worried about increased expenditure and, possibly, about losing some of their hold over the land, if they allowed themselves to become liable for high compensations.[16]

We must not assume an unqualified propensity to innovate among the landowners, or indeed the tenant farmers. In the first half of the nineteenth century, the farmers' distrust and/or ignorance of new technologies underpinned their conservative attitude. Even though new agrarian journals diffused information about the related advantages in production and productivity, only a few landowners were interested in them.[17] Some large rentiers and small landowners delayed adopting technological innovations up until the 'great agrarian crisis' of the 1880s, which dramatically led to plunging crop prices and eventually forced a renewal of farming practices. Landowners were especially selective when it came to substituting machinery for labour. Small farmers and landowners lacked capital, while many of the larger ones preferred to employ more farm hands rather than invest in technology. Labour-saving innovations were adopted only when their price was lower than the perceived costs of hired labour and social unrest due to peasant unemployment. Therefore, many technological innovations were not widely introduced until after urban manufacture began to absorb jobless peasants and to drive up agricultural wages.

Eventually, increased labour costs prompted new investments in the mechanization of agrarian activities such as ploughing, planting, harvesting and threshing, taking advantage of local credit institutions, while skilled agricultural labourers earned better wages in activities where innovations involved specialized production techniques, such as in viticulture, mulberry cultivation, cattle breeding and dairy farming. Landowners and tenants invested in new machinery, chemical fertilizers and hybrid seeds, modern cowsheds and dairy equipment, which led to higher profits and rents, even where it was impossible to reduce the cost of labour or to increase the shares paid by sharecroppers.[18]

Contrasting cases

In this section, we will address three contrasting cases: in southern Italy, in the neighbouring area of the Venetian lands, and within Lombardy itself. The first and more extreme case will highlight the impact of social and power structures on the actual possibilities for institutional reform. The second, that of Veneto and eastern Lombardy, will show how those structures, along with the timing of institutional reforms, caused similar institutions to experience divergent effects. The third case, that of the Lombard Alpine areas, will illustrate the divergent effects of institutional reforms that defined and secured private land ownership, in a particular area where communal land and collective rights had hitherto been an important component of the agrosystem.

Southern Italy provides the most strikingly contrasting case, in which roughly contemporaneous attempts at reform, along similar lines to those followed by the Habsburgs in Lombardy, ultimately failed. Charles of Bourbon's announcement in 1740, as king of Naples, of his intention to launch a new cadastre in the kingdom and to reform the tax system to increase taxation and distribute it more fairly met with insurmountable political resistance from the vested interests of the feudal barons entrenched in their fiefs' jurisdictional and fiscal privileges which largely removed them from the Crown's authority. As with previous attempts at reform targeting feudal rights, the plan for the new cadastre eventually came to nothing.

Later legislation aiming to suppress feudal rights, which was eventually passed under Napoleonic rule in 1799 and in 1806, was also unable to curb the power of the barons, who resisted with tactics that ranged from using their power over the peasant households and the local officials to prevent the enforcement of the law, forging documents and testimonies, to engaging in dilatory lawsuits which lasted throughout the century. As a result, they managed to keep their weighting in the structure of land ownership and income largely unchecked.

Moreover, resistance to land redistribution was not one-sided. It was socially more complex, as in some cases it was also carried out by peasants who saw their communal lands and collective rights threatened in the process, leading to new conflicts within peasant societies. Where some land redistribution did take place in the early nineteenth century, it soon proved unsuccessful. Only after Unification did the more proactive supporting policies of the new Italian state make it possible for small peasant holdings to take root in some areas in southern Italy.

As a consequence, in the late nineteenth century the aristocracy and Church institutions still reaped about 60 per cent of the total income produced (as compared to Lombardy, where the same social orders held a minority interest of 25 per cent), and they were able to hamper all extensive attempts at reform up until the second half of the twentieth century. In spite of policy attempts along the same lines as those that had taken place in Lombardy, the social power structure prevented important changes in property rights and agrarian relations, playing a major role in the widening of the economic gap between the North and the South, which came to be known as Italy's 'economic dualism'.

The dominant form of agriculture in southern Italy remained large grain farms, employing day labourers in extensive agriculture. The landowners were able to go on relying on their ability to extract rent from their oligopolistic hold over land, and to avail themselves of a large and cheap peasant labour force with few employment alternatives. There was little manufacturing in southern Italy and emigration – mostly taking the costly transatlantic route to North and South America – was virtually the sole alternative to day labour for most peasants. Therefore, in spite of yields per hectare that were less than one-third those in Lombardy, the large landlords had no incentive to invest in technological innovation. Even though the internal market widened immensely and domestic consumption increased in the course of the nineteenth century, the southern agrosystem remained ineffective, causing the region's agricultural exports to fall. While differences in geographical and climatic endowments doubtlessly played an important part in this north–south contrast, that must not obscure the lack of landowner investment due to the skewed land ownership structure and the exploitive agrarian contracts through which small farmers accessed the land, as well as the flawed government policies marked by the unwillingness or the inability to invest in infrastructure.[19]

As we said, the second case is closer to home, and also more nuanced in its contrast. When, following Napoleon's defeat, Lombardy became a part of the kingdom of Lombardo–Veneto in 1815, within the Austrian empire, the Habsburg cadastre was extended to Veneto and Eastern Lombardy, causing an immediate increase of the land tax rate in force. Even though the agricultural landscape was not uniform across the Venetian lands, many Venetian farms had displayed yield levels in the Renaissance period that rivalled those in England and France, and neared those in the Netherlands. Overall, agriculture in the Veneto had reached self-sufficiency in cereals during the sixteenth century, by resorting to land reclamation and the massive cultivation of marginal areas. For the following two centuries, however, there was no important increase in productivity in cereals, because of the lack of investment in efficient irrigation systems.[20] This points to a negative attitude of landowners concerning investment.

Venetian landowners and tenants forcefully opposed the introduction of the Habsburg cadastre. The high increase in the land tax brought about by the introduction of the Austrian cadastre in the Venetian lands, along with the auction of Church and state assets, were major sources of social discontent. Besides the overall increase in tax rates, which was higher than it had been in western Lombardy, the cadastre also brought about significant qualitative changes. On the one hand, the land and the property rights ceased to be differentiated primarily according to the landowners' status and wealth. On the other hand, the landlords' control over land taxation was severely curtailed, as land taxes ceased to be managed through co-operative agreements between the landlords and the state, replaced with a direct relationship between the bureaucracy of fiscal administration and the realm's subjects, deemed to be fiscally equal. Political opposition grew amongst the powerful Venetian elite, whose resistance involved slowing down the implementation of land registration with court appeals and judicial filibustering in the representative bodies of the nobility, the provincial congregations.

Venetian landlords and tenants also protested iniquity, challenging the Habsburg government for not having updated the long-standing 'Milan cadastre' as well. The fact that the cadastral data in Austrian Lombardy had not been updated by the beginning of nineteenth century represented a fiscal benefit for the Lombardy taxpayers. The argument also had to do with differences in the timing and the antecedents of the cadastre and fiscal reform. Criticism claimed that because the fiscal rules allowed the taxpayers to deduce the improvements they had made during the previous decades, when the fiscal rules favouring investment had already been in effect in Austrian Lombardy and not in the Venetian lands, the equal land tax objectively penalized the Venetian taxpayers, as compared with those in the former region. The Austrian government, however, paid no heed to this, arguing that the rate of investment depreciation was for the government to decide and was not open for discussion. After long negotiations between the central government and provincial delegations, the new cadastre finally came into force in 1846, resulting, however, in a low rate of innovation.[21]

Eastern Lombardy, which up to 1797 had belonged to the Venetian Republic, experienced an increase in taxation similar to that in Venice. In the eastern Lombard lands of Brescia, Bergamo and Crema, as in Venice, the sharp increase in the tax burden, especially for noble property, and the fact that the new cadastre combined with the new civil administration regime to severely limit upperclass privileges, aggravated the tensions between the landowners and the tax administration. The land tax base was also widened to include previously exempt assets such as forestland, marshland, and commons. Moreover, in eastern Lombardy the timing of the increase in land taxes coincided with an outbreak of silkworm diseases that reduced the production of raw silk, the most value-adding produce in the agrarian sector during the first half of the nineteenth century, which also certainly contributed to fuelling social discontent. Nevertheless, the impact of the Austrian cadastre and land tax differed from that in Venice because of the different reactions of the regional elites: contrary to their Venetian counterparts, landowners and large tenants in eastern Lombardy responded by increasing investments, as had happened before in western Lombardy.[22] One later upshot of this generalization of the cadastre was that, when a national Italian cadastre eventually came into force in the early twentieth century, once again changing the structure of land and crop taxation, its impact on the income of Lombard farms was buffered by their previous earnings, and the only landowners and tenants who suffered were those either unwilling or unable to invest further.[23]

Our third contrasting case involves the privatization of common land and the expropriation of collective rights in the Lombard Alpine valleys. The new cadastre increased taxation in the Alpine valleys as well, where, except for restricted areas in the lower valleys, there was little room for improvement in farming produce quality and yields. Most landholdings were too small to guarantee the peasant households' self-sufficiency, and there was little capital available for investment. More fundamentally, the land property laws passed by the French and Austrian governments in the first half of the nineteenth century confronted the residents of the Alpine valleys with the privatization of common lands and the expropriation of existing collective rights. This changed the traditional pattern of agriculture and livestock breeding in the high Alpine valleys, causing severe disruption to the livelihood of the local populations.[24]

Privatization was not entirely a novelty. Up until the beginning of the eighteenth century, the Republic of Venice had regularly sold common land in the eastern Lombard Alps to balance its budget. Nevertheless, on the whole governments favoured the maintenance of the commons, which were given in usufruct to the municipalities, particularly in the woodlands which provided timber for Venice's arsenal and for defence purposes. Once the Venetian government suspended all sales of common land in 1727, the respective villages retained important amounts of common land, which they managed to the advantage of the peasant households. Poor villagers enjoyed such rights as the *erbatico* to pick wild grass, healing herbs and sods; the *legnatico* to collect shrubs, firewood and waste timber useless for charcoal; and the *pascolo* to graze cattle and sheep, the latter under some restraints. Villagers also enjoyed rights to collect leaves for their cattle's beddings and stones for building, and to forage wild vegetables and fruits, as long as they did not harm the shrubs and the trees.

The municipalities sometimes allotted and leased out plots of common land for farming. The effects would sometimes be harmful, since as their options and potential gains were limited, the tenants of the municipalities often chose to over-exploit the allotments rather than to invest in them. Even then, villagers were collectively entitled to a part of the produce and to the *spigolatura*, the right to glean the grain remaining on those fields after the harvest was through. Several cases are known of villages where people demonstrated against attempts to block out collective access to the commons, which reveals the latent tensions involved in the management and appropriation of common land.[25]

Both the French and Austrian governments (1797–1814 and 1814–1859, respectively) favoured the privatization and sale of common land. In 1806, Napoleonic law abolished all *Ancien Régime* privileges and changed the juridical status of common land property, from the villagers' collective ownership to that of real estate owned by the municipality, which inevitably led to much dispute between the municipalities and their inhabitants. The Napoleonic code also promoted the sale of common land that had become too expensive for the municipalities to manage, a condition which was, in turn, enhanced by the fiscal reforms, since the French and later the Austrian fiscal cadastres led to a significant increase in the taxes the municipalities had to pay on their land. When the burden overcame the income the municipal councils opted to sell the former commons.

In 1839, a new Austrian law brought about a further important decrease in the share of common land, by forcing the municipalities to sell all the unculti-vated land they owned. This reduced the income of those inhabitants who had traditionally relied upon common resources to survive. In some villages where there were riots, the municipalities decided to sell only a part of the common land and lease the rest out to the villagers. The Austrian law also allowed the municipalities to let the land out in emphyteusis instead of selling it, which provided long-term access to peasants who could not afford to buy, conditional on making improvements. During the first half of the nineteenth century, this option amounted to as much as one half of the recorded deeds. In some municipalities, the Austrian government forced them to secure free private access to some plots of land.

In their belief that privatization was the best way to stimulate investment in those lands in order to increase agricultural production, the authorities grossly underestimated the impact of poor soils and the lack of sunshine on fertility, as well as the investment required of the new landowners to make effective improve-ments, even where those were possible. Moreover, the Austrian governments did not reduce the tax rate on those lands. Ultimately, the hope of creating or attracting a new class of tenants who would make more efficient use of the land met with only limited success. The yields soon decreased, and many among the municipalities' tenants could not afford to go on paying their rents. In the absence of new tenants interested in taking the common land in lease, the municipalities ended up having to sell out the land. Quite often, the new landowners were not able to increase output either, and occasionally, in their attempts to quickly recoup their investment, they caused environmental damage through excessive deforestation and general over-exploitation.

Another major issue was that the sale of common land, which had for centuries facilitated the survival of poor households, caused dramatic demographic change, particularly in the highest valleys in eastern Lombardy. Once those households lost all collective rights as the land was sold or rented, their earnings fell below subsistence level and many had to migrate to the low valleys, to the plains near the towns, to other European countries, or to the Americas. Up until the mid-nineteenth century, the emigration of Lombard labour had been largely seasonal, for example, to the farms of the Lombard plain for the cereal and grape harvests, or to the towns to work in the building sector. Longer-term migration took place only for some well paid jobs, such as iron craftsman work in the regions' forges and longshoremen employed in the docks of Genoa and Venice. In the following decades, however, more emigration became permanent, leading to a significant fall in the population of the high Alpine valleys. This migratory process was essential for the survival of many Alpine families, while at the same time it played a part in the industrialization of Lombardy.

On the upside, the resulting increase in the rents the transhumant cattle breeders paid for summer pastures up in the Alpine valleys stimulated innovation in the regional agrosystem. Transhumance was gradually replaced with sedentary cattle raising, with increasing investments to create modern cowsheds in the farms on the plains. Stabling proved better than transhumance, and this concurred with rising demand for quality produce to create large-scale specialized dairy farms producing high quality cheese, milk and other products, which came to be a viable adaptive response to the decline in cereal prices in the late nineteenth century.[26]

Making property rights work

Institutions in general, and specifically property institutions, do not work by themselves. The results depend on how they, as well as their consequences, are dealt with in their historical contexts. In this section, we review those axial characteristics in Lombard culture and society that contributed to the aforementioned institutional changes having become a factor of economic development.

First and foremost, we must keep in mind the pre-existent long-term economic trends that we sketched above in the first section, and which we will not have to go into here in any detail. Suffice to recall that long before the property reforms, a dynamic market for foodstuffs and raw materials, driven by the dense urban trade network and industry, provided stimuli for sub-regional specialization, investment, intensification, and agronomical innovation. The centuries-old accumulation of capital literally embedded in the soils of the Po Valley, in the form of an irrigation infrastructure, provided a highly productive environment in that sub-region. The political and economic weight of the privileged orders was comparatively small, and there was a wealthy business class eager to invest capital in commercial agriculture. A competitive lease market was already in place, along with other forms of land tenancy, and even traditional contracts often portrayed as 'feudal' had been used since the late Middle Ages to transfer wider property rights from the Church and the aristocracy into the hands of business-oriented tenants. Clearly, the land property and land tax reforms were grafted, as it were, on a steadily developing tree and mostly played to the region's strengths by feeding into its most dynamic sectors.

On cultural grounds, the 'humanistic civilization' had taken root in Lombardy in both its economic and civic forms. 'Economic humanism' fostered behaviour according to an ethos of self-realization and status acquisition through productive work and successful business. The civic ethos, on the other hand, encouraged collective interest organization and strong associational density.[27] The former had long-lasting effects in promoting an entrepreneurial attitude in agriculture, whenever it proved a profitable investment, which in turn contributed to adaptive and innovative responses to changing institutional rules and market stimuli. The latter's emphasis on social cohesion and organized collective action helped give voice to different social interests and to achieve change through political struggle, compromise, and state intervention.

That was particularly important to channel the effects of peasant proletarianization and the hardships of heavily burdened sharecroppers into institutionalized political struggle, somewhat countervailing the structural power imbalance in favour of the landowners and large tenants. This made class conflict effective in offsetting the direst consequences of agricultural modernization and moderating the effects of land wealth inequality. Rural trade unions, of catholic or socialist inspiration, developed in the late nineteenth century grouping peasants, sharecroppers and small tenants, fighting for higher wages and better working conditions and contractual terms. Following the promulgation of Zanardelli's Penal Code in 1890, the legal status of strikes was changed from that of crime to breach of contract. This meant that while strikers might be fired, they could no longer be arrested. The reduction in the individual costs of collective action increased the trade union's bargaining power, which reached its highest point just after the First World War.

Trade unions obviously had to face the opposition of landowners and large tenants, but they were nevertheless able to obtain better conditions for peasants and sharecroppers, because farmers could not dismiss all the labourers on strike and they were, therefore, forced to make concessions. Besides increasing the labourers' wages, the trade unions also achieved material benefits for peasant workers, such as the right to harvest all the fruits on a specific plot of land, and an improvement in the sharecroppers' share in the harvest by removing the contractual clauses that afforded higher shares to the landowners or large tenants. Small tenants who only employed family labour also benefitted from reductions in leases and took advantage of the development of cooperatives linked to the trade unions.

Even though this process was halted during the First World War, those who remained on the farms had their labour contracts regulated by the public authorities, who automatically renewed them and allowed the workers to keep a large part of their real wages. At the end of the war, rural trade unions again strove to secure better contracts for labourers, also as a strategy to increase labour costs and force landlords to sell the land to those who actually worked in the fields. New laws enacted during the economic downturn following the end of the war, during a period of intense industrial action, established coercive employment rules, the *imponibile di manodopera*, which forced farmers to employ quotas of labourers in relation to the size of the cultivated land. This met with fierce resistance by landowners and large farmers, who complained that those measures harmed their property rights, since the obligation to create jobs impacted on their freedom to determine land allocation and cultivation methods.

More importantly, the class of small peasant landowners had risen in numbers since before the war, partly because the unions' success enabled many small tenants and sharecroppers to save and buy land. The political pro-labour measures, along with the more structural divergence concerning the Socialist Party's and the Peasant Leagues' programme for socializing rather than redistributing land, breached the tense convergence of interests that had so far been maintained between landless labourers, on the one hand, and the small landowners and tenants, on the other. This eventually pushed the latter into the social support basis of Fascism in the region's countryside. However, even under the ensuing fascist rule and in tandem with the violent repression of the labour movement, fascist rural trade unions played on the regime's need to keep social peace, managing to curb reductions in real wages and to gain some additional benefits in kind for peasant labourers.[28]

Industrialization provided another key moderating factor for the social costs of agricultural modernization. This was in fact a two-way process, since investment in new manufacturing was itself fuelled by capital accumulation in agriculture. Factories provided an alternative outlet for the investment of farming profits and land rent, especially after the mid-1850s outbreaks of silkworm and mulberry diseases and of oidium, which affected two of the most valuable agricultural products. Agrarian-based growth therefore formed a base for regional economic development. Besides the investment inflow and the low cost of unskilled labour, the growth of manufacturing profited from the increasing demand for industrial farming materials, such as agrarian machinery and fertilizers, as well as from the increased peasants' spending on manufactured consumption goods like clothing and household ware. As a result, between the mid-eighteenth century and the late nineteenth century, the 'economic relational networks' in Lombardy experienced a transition from an economy relying on export-based agriculture to a new production system based on industrialization in the textile and the iron and steel sectors.[29]

New factories and the related urban development increased labour demand for specialized workers, such as carpenters and sawyers, and for unskilled labour, especially in the building industry. This promoted a continuing emigration of young peasants to earn better wages in the industrial areas. As we said previously, industrialization also provided an outlet for the migrant workforce from those poor households that had been deprived of a crucial part of their livelihood, after the privatization of the commons lands and the expropriation of collective rights in the Alpine valleys in eastern Lombardy.

More generally, the decreased labour pool in the countryside encouraged large farmers to invest further in labour-saving machinery, from which they had held back before, as we stated earlier. Conversely, once investment in machinery expanded and mechanization reduced farming labour needs, much of the rural workforce that was made redundant was eventually absorbed by the growing labour demand for factory labour. Therefore, the remaining skilled labourers and tenants retained their bargaining power, which also helps explain the relative success of the organized labour struggles. Some, such as specialized irrigation workers, cattle stockmen who controlled breeding and milking, vinedressers and winemakers, were able to substantially increase their wages.

The accumulation of human capital was also a prominent factor in the agricultural growth process. Rural workers, small tenants and sharecroppers profited from the increase in skill requirements, due to improvements in formal knowledge provision, which enhanced the rural economy's absorptive capacity for innovation and helped its diffusion. Publicly funded agricultural schools were implemented in rural areas during the final decades of the nineteenth century, and rural extension programmes were carried out from the turn of the twentieth century through the implementation of the *Cattedre Ambulanti di Agricoltura* (literally, 'itinerant agricultural lectorships').

Those were public organizations funded by the provincial administration, agricultural societies, and country banks. Their aim was to help coordinate the activities of farmers and breeders and to promote the diffusion of good practice in order to increase productivity. The *Cattedre* relied on agronomists trained in the universities and agricultural schools, who combined sound updated knowledge of agronomics and veterinary science with an understanding of the practical needs of the regional farming systems, including those of the smaller farms. Besides lectures, courses and technical training, they organized itinerant offices where farmers and breeders could obtain practical advice. Itinerant agronomists visited the province's farms and cattle holdings, down to even the most isolated villages. Both commercial farmers and peasants accepted their advice because it was usually handed to them in their own dialect and in ways that made sense to their actual practice. Along with advice, the *Cattedre* also provided free samples of new implements and fertilizers.[30] The improvement of agronomical know-how in the rural areas and the use of new technology in the farms also contributed to enhancing the contractual power of those labourers and tenants who possessed such new skills. Technological innovation and increased technical skills impacted heavily on productivity. Cattle breeding, dairy production and winemaking improved in both quantity and quality.[31] Harvests increased, while the average prices of agricultural products decreased. The result was an overall gain in real wages, both in the farms and in the factories.

Concluding remarks

The economic development of Lombardy was positively impacted upon by the legal changes in property rights, which had taken place since the eighteenth-century Austrian government reforms. The creation of a land property cadastre, the fiscal incentives embedded in land taxation, and the privatization and sale of common lands, all had effects on Lombard agriculture and on the wider society. They were the final step in the progressive dismantling of the old feudal system, in favour of new and more dynamic markets in land, labour, capital, and products.

Landowners, tenants, sharecroppers and peasant workers appropriated the new rules to develop a diversified market-oriented Lombard agriculture, using new farming techniques and technology to obtain high quality products, thereby increasing the value of the agrarian sector. Most changes then introduced in property rights stimulated the growth of Lombard agricultural production, which eventually provided capital to invest in manufacture and in turn increased demand for the region's production of both capital and consumption goods.

On the downside, long-term farm consolidation and the spread of capitalist farming led to a growing proletarianization of peasant households and to hardened sharecropping conditions, and the sales of common land did nothing to improve productivity in the mountainous areas. Indeed, besides pauperizing sectors of their peasant population, the private appropriation of land eventually caused significant environmental damage.

All these developments undeniably played a central part in shaping Lombardy's agrosystem, and its economic system as a whole, into one of the most dynamic regional economies in Italy and in Europe, in stark contrast to that which happened in the South, where the plans to build up a cadastre were checked by political resistance from the seigniorial elite, and where the extractive power over people and resources provided large landowners with little incentive to invest and innovate in agriculture.

This narrative of Lombard success should not lead us to conclude that there was an unqualified effect of the institutionalization of more perfect property rights on agricultural and economic development. The process was far less linear. Indeed, the role of state induced changes in property rights in energizing a 'virtuous cycle' of capitalist development was contingent on a specific set of historical conditions. These included long-term trends, social and economic structures already in place, and long established cultural norms, institutions and social practices that set a favourable foundation for the productive appropriation of the institutional reforms, pushing landowners and capitalist lease tenants to make the most of institutional change through productive investment and innovation.

Cultural values stemming from late medieval and early modern 'economic humanism' legitimized social behaviour based on self-realization through entrepreneurship, labour, and learning. This helped investment, market-oriented entrepreneurial agriculture, growth in human capital and a smooth adoption of agronomics and technological innovation. The visible success of the region's agrosystem fed back into those attitudes, further encouraging them. They shaped the landowners' and peasants' response to public policies, which often supported investment to increase the quantity and improve the quality of agricultural output.

The results ultimately improved rural welfare in the course of the nineteenth century, as the overall increase in output in Lombard farms lowered food prices, improving the diet of the population as a whole, and a majority of rural stakeholders were able to take advantage of gains in agricultural productivity. The region's long-standing civic culture and associational density was an important factor in that outcome, as rural trade unions were able to mobilize and engage in collective action and, according to the political conjunctures, obtain improvements in hiring conditions, wages and farming contracts.

The way the regional economic development unfolded during the nineteenth and the early twentieth centuries also played a major part in offsetting some of the negative distributional consequences for the less advantaged groups. Manufacture, including a growing dairy industry, and gradual urbanization absorbed much redundant peasant labour and a large part of the landless population. For all the innovative dynamics, and in spite of early initiators, before industrialization began pulling labour out of agriculture in the last decades of the nineteenth century, the substitution of technology for labour had not been widely spread throughout the rural society. Once industrialization set in, however, a growing number of technologically advanced and more productive farms eventually provided their reduced and more specialized agricultural labour force higher wages than those that were paid in factory jobs.

Finally, it is in the context of all these trends and inter-relationships that the effects of the institutionalization of modern property rights have to be understood, as part of a long-term process that had paved the way for their assimilation, and of the evolving and often contradictory social relations which carried out their appropriation by social agents and groups. Innovative and growth-inducing practices in agriculture and agroindustry would go on, in tandem with industrialization and urbanization, during the twentieth century, particularly after the Second Word War under the European Economic Community's agricultural and trade policies, which further supported investment, innovation and access to foreign markets.[32]

Notes

1 E. Demo, 'Manifattura vs. agricoltura: La difficile gestione delle acque nella pedemontana veneta della prima età moderna', in L. Mocarelli (ed.), *Quando Manca il Pane: Origini e Cause della Scarsità delle Risorse Alimentari in Età Moderna e Contemporanea* (Bologna: Mulino, 2013), pp. 19–34.
2 D. F. Dowd, 'The economic expansion of Lombardy, 1300–1500: A study in political stimuli to economic change', *Journal of Economic History*, 21:2 (1961), pp. 143–60.

3   B. van Bavel, 'The organization and rise of land and lease markets in northwestern Europe and Italy, c. 1000–1800', *Continuity and Change*, 23:1 (2008), pp. 13–53; G. Biagioli, 'Les contrats dans l'historiographie italienne de la période contemporaine', in G. Béaur, M. Arnoux and A. Varet-Vitu (eds), *Exploiter la Terre: Les Contrats Agraires de l'Antiquité à nos Jours: Actes du Coloque de Caen (10–13 Septembre 1997)* (Rennes: Association d'Histoire des Sociétés Rurales, 2003), pp. 63–84, on pp. 77–8; L. Cafagna, *Dualismo e Sviluppo nella Storia d'Italia* (Venice: Marsilio Editori, 1990), pp. 68–9; E. Sereni, *Storia del Paesaggio Agrario Italiano* (Bari: Laterza, 1991), pp. 239–40, 264–78; L. Faccini, 'L'Agricoltura della bassa Lombardia occidentale fra XVII e XVIII secolo: Un approccio aziendale', in G. Coppola (ed.), *Agricoltura e Aziende Agrarie nell'Italia Centro-Settentrionale (Secoli XVI–XIX)* (Milan: FrancoAngeli), pp. 59–78; G. Piluso, 'Terra e credito nell'Italia settentrionale del Settecento: Mercati, istituzioni e strumenti in una prospettiva comparativa', in S. Cavaciocchi (ed.), *Il Mercato della Terra: Secc. XIII–XVIII* (Florence: Le Monnier, [2004]), pp. 743–64.

4   Biagioli, 'Les Contrats', p. 79; Dowd, 'Economic expansion', p. 154. (Câmara and Santos, in chapter five, address a similar rule concerning improvements in a radically different context. Editor's note.)

5   Cafagna, *Dualismo e Sviluppo*, pp. 93–4, 98–109; D. M. Klang, 'The problem of leasefarming in eighteenth-century Piedmont and Lombardy', *Agricultural History*, 76:3 (2002), pp. 578–603, on p. 601.

6   L. Lorenzetti, 'Property relations, socio-economic change and the state: The Valtellina in the nineteenth century', in G. Béaur, P. R. Schofield, J.-M. Chevet and M. T. Pérez Picazo (eds), *Property Rights, Land Markets, and Economic Growth in the European Countryside (Thirteenth–Twentieth Centuries)* (Turnhout: Brepols, 2013), pp. 179–94, on p. 181; P. Tedeschi, 'Common land in eastern Lombardy during the nineteenth century', *Historia Agraria*, 55:4 (2011), pp. 75–100.

7   A. Carera, 'Gli spazi dello scambio sulle Terre del Lago', in S. Zaninelli (ed.), *Da un Sistema Agricolo ad un Sistema Industriale: Il Comasco dal Settecento al Novecento*, vol. 1, *Il Difficile Equilibrio Agricolo Manifatturiero (1750–1814)* (Como: CCIA, 1987), pp. 267–365; A. Carera, *I Confini dello Sviluppo: La Regione Economica Lombarda come Questione Storiografica* (Milan: EDUCatt, 2000), pp. 45, 56–61.

8   On the region's economic history, M. Berg and P. Hudson, 'Rehabilitating the Industrial Revolution', *Economic History Review*, 45:1 (1992), pp. 24–50; P. Hudson, 'The Regional perspective', in P. Hudson (ed.), *Regions and Industries: A Perspective on the Industrial Revolution in Britain* (Cambridge: Cambridge University Press, 1989), pp. 5–40; L. Mocarelli (ed.), *Lo Sviluppo Economico Regionale in Prospettiva Storica* (Milan: Cuesp, 1996); R. Pichler, 'Economic policy and development in Austrian Lombardy 1815–1859', *Modern Italy*, 6:1 (2001), pp. 35–58; M. Prak, 'Regions in early modern Europe', in P. Subacchi (ed.), *Eleventh International Economic History Congress: Debates and Controversies in Economic History* (Milan: Università Bocconi, 1994), pp. 19–55.

9   A. Moioli, *La Gelsibachicoltura nelle Campagne Lombarde dal Seicento alla Prima Metà dell'Ottocento* (Trento: Università di Trento, 1981), pp. 201–86; P. Tedeschi, *I Frutti Negati: Assetti Fondiari, Modelli Organizzativi, Produzioni e Mercati Agricoli nel Bresciano durante l'Età della Restaurazione (1814–1859)* (Brescia: Fondazione Civiltà Bresciana, 2006), pp. 300–6, 345–58.

10   Tedeschi, *Frutti Negati*, pp. 41–102.

11   J. Djenderedian and D. Santilli also discuss the effects of a land cadastre and taxation in chapter four. (Editors' note.)

12   D. Carpanetto and G. Ricuperati, *Italy in the Age of Reason: 1685–1789* (London: Longman), pp. 161–3.

13   A. Cova, 'Proprietà ecclesiastica, proprietà nobiliare, proprietà borghese: I cambiamenti tra il 1796 e il 1814', in S. Zaninelli (ed.), *La Proprietà Fondiaria in Lombardia dal*

Catasto Teresiano all'Età Napoleonica, vol. 2 (Milan: Vita e Pensiero, 1986), pp. 147–263; R. Zangheri, *Catasti e Storia della Proprietà Terriera* (Turin: Einaudi, 1980).

14 A. M. Locatelli, *Riforma Fiscale e Identità Regionale: Il Catasto per il Lombardo–Veneto (1815–1853)* (Milan: Vita e Pensiero, 2003); A. M. Locatelli and P. Tedeschi, 'Entre réforme fiscale et développement économique: Les cadastres en Lombardie aux 18ème et 19ème siècles', in F. Bourillon and N. Vivier (eds), *La Mesure Cadastrale: Estimer la Valeur du Foncier* (Rennes: Presses Universitaires de Rennes, 2012), pp. 19–39.

15 A. Cova, *Aspetti dell'Economia Agricola Lombarda dal 1796 al 1814: Il Valore dei Terreni, la Produzione, il Mercato* (Milan: Vita e Pensiero, 1997), pp. 17–72, 148–232.

16 Cafagna, *Dualismo e Sviluppo*, pp. 70–1; M. Malatesta, 'Les fermiers de la Lombardie (XIXe et XXe Siècles)', in Béaur, Arnoux and Varet-Vitu (eds), *Exploiter la Terre*, pp. 485–96.

17 A. M. Locatelli and P. Tedeschi, 'A new common knowledge in agronomics: The network of the agrarian reviews and congresses in Europe during the first half of the 19th century', in S. Aprile, C. Cassina, P. Darriulat and R. Leboutte (eds), *Une Europe de Papier: Projets Européens au XIXe Siècle* (Villeneuve d'Ascq: Presses Universitaires du Septentrion, 2015), pp. 187–203.

18 G. Fumi, 'Il consolidamento di un'agricoltura d'eccellenza', in G. Rumi, G. Mezzanotte and A. Cova (eds), *Cremona e il suo Territorio* (Milan: Cariplo, 1998), pp. 295–327; Tedeschi, *Frutti Negati*, pp. 183–6.

19 Carpanetto and Ricuperati, *Italy in the Age of Reason*, p. 186; J. Cohen and G. Federico, *The Growth of Italian Economy 1820–1960* (Cambridge: Cambridge University Press, 2001); V. Zamagni, *The Economic History of Italy 1860–1990* (Oxford: Clarendon Press, 1993); E. Felice, 'Regional value added in Italy 1891–2001 and the foundation of a long-term picture', *Economic History Review*, 64:3 (2011), pp. 929–50; P. Nardone, 'From barons to peasant farmers: The privatisation of feudal lands in southern Italy in the nineteenth century', in L. Lorenzetti, M. Barbot and Luca Mocarelli (eds), *Property Rights and Their Violations: Expropriations and Confiscations, 16th–20th centuries* (Bern: Peter Lang, 2012), pp. 185–203.

20 M. Knapton, 'Le campagne trevigiane: I frutti di una ricerca', *Società e Storia*, 33:130 (2010), pp. 780–9; L. Pezzolo, 'La storia agraria veneta: Risultati, ipotesi, prospettive', *Archivio Veneto*, 142:1 (2011), pp. 79–110; A. Zannini, 'Sempre più agricola, sempre più regionale: L'economia della Repubblica di Venezia da Agnadello al Lombardo-Veneto (1509–1817)', *Ateneo Veneto*, 197 (2010), pp. 137–71.

21 M. Berengo, *L'Agricoltura Veneta dalla Caduta della Repubblica all'Unità* (Milan: Banca Commerciale Italiana, 1963), pp. 123–42; A. Bernardello, *Venezia nel Regno Lombardo-Veneto: Un Caso Atipico (1815–1886)* (Milan: FrancoAngeli, 2015), pp. 67–9; A. Bernardello, *Veneti sotto l'Austria: Ceti Popolari e Tensioni Sociali* (Venice: Filippi, 1997), pp. 89–92.

22 Locatelli, *Riforma Fiscale*; Locatelli and Tedeschi, 'Entre réforme fiscale et développement économique'.

23 M. Romani, *Un Secolo di Vita Agricola in Lombardia (1861–1961)* (Milan: Giuffré, 1963), pp. 77–133; P. Tedeschi, 'Marché foncier et systèmes de production agricoles dans l'Italie du nord au XIX siècle: Le cas de la Lombardie orientale', *European Review of History*, 15:5 (2008), pp. 459–77.

24 On the impact of the privatization of common land in Lombardy, Tedeschi, 'Common land'. On the connection between property rights and economic growth, Béaur *et al.* (eds), *Property Rights*; D. Grigg, *The Dynamics of Agricultural Change: The Historical Experience* (New York: Saint Martin's Press, 1983).

25 Tedeschi, 'Common land'. On the socioeconomic conditions in the Lombard Alpine valleys, P. Tedeschi, 'Marché foncier, crédit et activités manufacturières dans les Alpes: Le cas des vallées de la Lombardie orientale (XVIIIe–XIXe siècles)', *Histoire des Alpes*, 12 (2007), pp. 247–59; P. Tedeschi, 'Economie rurale et pluriactivité dans

les vallées Alpines Lombardes (XVIIIe–XIXe siècles)', *Histoire des Alpes*, 20 (2015), pp. 209–22.

26 P. Battilani and G. Bigatti (eds), *Oro Bianco: Il Settore Lattiero-Caseario in Val Padana tra Otto e Novecento* (Lodi: Giona, 2002); C. Besana, *Tra Agricoltura e Industria: Il Settore Caseario nella Lombardia dell'Ottocento* (Milan: Vita e Pensiero, 2012); P. Tedeschi and S. Stranieri, 'L'evoluzione del settore lattiero-caseario Lombardo dall'Ottocento al duemila', in G. Archetti and A. Baronio (eds), *La Civiltà del Latte: Fonti, Simboli e Prodotti dal Tardoantico al Novecento* (Brescia: Fondazione Civiltà Bresciana, 2011), pp. 691–716.

27 J. McGovern, 'The rise of new economic attitudes – economic humanism, economic nationalism – during the later Middle Ages and the Renaissance, A.D. 1200–1550', *Traditio*, 26 (1970), pp. 217–53; R. D. Putnam *et al.*, *Making Democracy Work: Civic Traditions in Modern Italy* (Princeton: Princeton University Press, 1994).

28 *Agricoltura e Forze Sociali in Lombardia nella Crisi degli Anni Trenta* (Milan: FrancoAngeli, 1983); Romani, *Un Secolo*, pp. 133–53; F. M. Snowden, 'On the social origins of agrarian Fascism in Italy', *European Journal of Sociology*, 13:2 (1972), pp. 268–95; P. Tedeschi, *Economia e Sindacato nel Bresciano tra Primo Dopoguerra e Fascismo: Le Unioni del Lavoro (1918–1926)* (Milan: FrancoAngeli, 1999), pp. 190–228, 283–315, 341–50; P. Tedeschi, 'Contratti agrari e produttività del fattore lavoro nei primi decenni del '900 nelle province della Lombardia orientale', in S. Zaninelli and M. Taccolini (eds), *Il Lavoro come Fattore Produttivo e come Risorsa nella Storia Economica Italiana* (Milan: Vita e Pensiero, 2002), pp. 555–72.

29 A. Moioli, 'Assetti manifatturieri nella Lombardia politicamente divisa della seconda metà del settecento', in S. Zaninelli (ed.), *Storia dell'Industria Lombarda*, vol. I, *Un Sistema Manifatturiero Aperto al Mercato: Dal Settecento all'Unità Politica* (Milan: Il Polifilo, 1988), pp. 3–102. For an overall picture of the regional framework, B. Caizzi, *L'Economia Lombarda durante la Restaurazione* (Milan: Banca Commerciale Italiana, 1972); F. Della Peruta (ed.), *La Proprietà Fondiaria e le Popolazioni Agricole in Lombardia: Studi Economici di S. Jacini* (Milan: Ed. La Storia, 1996); K. R. Greenfield, *Economia e Liberalismo nel Risorgimento: Il Movimento Nazionale in Lombardia dal 1814 al 1848* (Bari: Laterza, 1964), pp. 67–76; M. Romani, *L'Agricoltura in Lombardia dal Periodo delle Riforme al 1859: Struttura, Organizzazione Sociale e Tecnica* (Milan: Vita e Pensiero, 1957).

30 G. Bigatti, 'Dalla cattedra alla scuola: L'istruzione agraria in Lombardia (1803–1870)', *Storia in Lombardia*, 15:3 (1996), pp. 41–82; O. Failla and G. Fumi (eds), *Gli Agronomi nella Storia dell'Agricoltura Lombarda: Dalle Cattedre Ambulanti ai Nostri Giorni* (Milan: FrancoAngeli, 2006); G. Fumi, 'Gli Sviluppi dell'agronomia nell'Italia settentrionale durante la prima metà dell'Ottocento', in S. Zaninelli (ed.), *Le Conoscenze Agrarie e la Loro Diffusione in Italia nell'Ottocento* (Turin: Giappichelli, 1990), pp. 177–239; R. Pazzagli, *Il Sapere dell'Agricoltura: Istruzione, Cultura, Economia nell'Italia dell'Ottocento* (Milan: Angeli, 2008); R. Pazzagli, 'From private initiative to sate intervention: The origins of public agricultural education in Italy', in N. Vivier (ed.), *The State and Rural Societies: Policy and Education in Europe, 1750–2000* (Turnhout: Brepols, 2008), pp. 231–46; Pichler, 'Economic policy', pp. 47–58; *Regio Istituto Tecnico Agrario G. Pastori* (Brescia: Geroldi, 1940).

31 C. Besana, 'Alpeggi, allevamento e attività casearie nelle Alpi Lombarde del primo Novecento', in P. Cafaro and G. Scaramellini (eds), *Mondo Alpino: Identità Locali e Forme d'Integrazione nello Sviluppo Economico Secoli XVIII–XX* (Milan: FrancoAngeli, 2003), pp. 205–34; P. Tedeschi, 'Il rinnovamento colturale: Aspetti della viticoltura bresciana fra Ottocento e Novecento', in G. Archetti (ed.), *La Civiltà del Vino: Fonti, Temi e Produzioni Vitivinicole dal Medioevo al Novecento* (Brescia: Centro Culturale Artistico di Franciacorta e del Sebino, 2003), pp. 805–9.

32 On the impact of the Common Agricultural Policy on European agriculture, A. C. Knudsen, *Farmers on Welfare: The Making of Europe's Common Agricultural Policy*

(Ithaca NY: Cornell University Press, 2009); A. Ledent and P. Burny, *La Politique Agricole Commune des Origines au 3e Millenaire* (Gembloux: Presses Agronomiques de Gembloux, 2002); K. K. Patel (ed.), *Fertile Ground for Europe? The History of European Integration and the Common Agricultural Policy since 1945* (Baden: Nomos Verlag, 2009); M. Spoerer, '"Fortress Europe" in long-term perspective: Agricultural protection in the European Community, 1957–2003', *Journal of European Integration History*, 16:2 (2010), pp. 143–55; P. Tedeschi, 'La politique agraire commune ou le grand cartel agricole communautaire', in M. Müller, H. R. Schmidt and L. Tissot (eds), *Regulierte Märkte: Zünfte und Kartelle/Marchés Régulés: Corporations et Cartels* (Zürich: Cronos Verlag, 2011), pp. 243–59.

4 The shift to 'modern' and its consequences

Changes in property rights and land wealth inequality in Buenos Aires, 1839–1914

Julio Djenderedjian and Daniel Santilli

Introduction

In recent years, there has been a breakthrough in historical research into the inequality of wealth distribution in Argentina.[1] What is more, there is a wide array of research published in the last two decades on changes in land property rights, which has challenged a large set of previously held assumptions and provided a different and richer outlook on the subject.[2] However, there are as yet no studies connecting both threads, in order to assess whether and in what way changes in property rights impacted on inequality.

This chapter analyses how the inequality in the distribution of landed wealth evolved in the Pergamino district in the province of Buenos Aires during the nineteenth century, and more specifically the effects of state intervention in the system of property rights during the last third of that century, which aimed to introduce more exclusive and near-absolute property rights. Besides the legal privatization of public domains – which legally covered all land not formally granted by the state in private property – this involved the institutionalization of land property records owned and warranted by the state. This was reinforced by technological change that supplied affordable wire fencing, which was a critical development in the physical control over land assets.

Such changes in the system of property rights disrupted traditional forms of access to land, even though some were acknowledged within the new framework. New property rights based on legal security and physical delimitation had to gain the acceptance, or at least the compliance, of a wide range of stakeholders, whose conceptions of 'legality', 'justice' and 'rights' where not necessarily the same.[3]

This shift to 'modern' property rights in Buenos Aires encompassed a long period of population growth during the second half of the nineteenth century. A consistent wave of European immigration literally upended its demographic profile, both by increasing population growth rates and by overtaking pre-existent indigenous and creole peoples. Throughout the same period, driven by the first wave of globalization, a growing portion of farming produce was earmarked for the world market, and the price of land rose steeply in relation to the other factors involved in agricultural production. This suggests that the rise in land prices was a consequence of an increasingly competitive and productive economy, but at least at certain points in the process it was probably also affected by changes in property rights. It is therefore interesting to attempt to assess the role such changes played, both in the upward trend of land prices and in the ensuing distribution of land wealth. While open range cattle herders are mainly concerned with property rights in livestock, farmers' concerns reside mainly in land.[4] An economic transformation from extensive pastoralism to sheep farming and commercial crops increasingly created pressure for change in the definition of real property rights, following earlier phases of settlement, land occupation and state-building that had combined to create huge landholdings in the hands of a social elite.

We will argue that rather than just being a by-product of capital investment, as it is commonly understood, the inequality of wealth distribution was also affected by changes in property rights due to state intervention and to administrative and technological improvements. More specifically, we will maintain that changes in property rights that happened prior to 1880 and preceded major changes in capital investment had a significant role in establishing a highly concentrated land ownership structure, which strongly determined wealth distribution in the long term. Obviously, conclusions drawn from our case study are not to be generalized, but they can help us understand what happened in a key area of the pampas throughout this crucial growth period in its history.

The case study: Pergamino in the context of the agrarian expansion of the pampas

In the nineteenth century, the Argentine pampas experienced a radical transformation. Having around forty towns and cities in 1820, by 1900 there were more than one thousand urban centres interconnected by railways and roads, each with its own theatre, church, school and mutual aid society. The province of Buenos Aires played the most prominent role in that transformation, including its agricultural foundations. By 1820, the area under cereal cultivation was 11,000 hectares; in 1914, it spread over five million hectares after growing at an average annual rate of almost 7 per cent, double the population growth rate.[5] Up to about 1835, the main activity was cattle ranching. From then on, sheep farming increased and by the middle of the century it prevailed, with ratios of some 150 to 160 sheep per 100 cattle.[6] This was quite different to traditional creole sheep ranching, particularly in scale, with flocks five to ten times larger. Investments in breeding stock, high performance feeding, baths to prevent scabies, fences, a wide-ranging infrastructure of sheds and yards, skilled labour and improved tools had resulted in a completely new layout of the ranches.[7] Fast agricultural growth took off by the end of the nineteenth century. Change was continuous throughout the whole period towards ever more intensive forms of husbandry.

For a more in-depth consideration of our questions we have selected the case of Pergamino, a northern district that up to the early nineteenth century was a borderland area. A little village of thirty inhabitants had settled in 1750, but demographic expansion had been very slow before the early nineteenth century.

From then onwards, its population grew constantly, but the economic occupation of land had not been completed by 1850. Pergamino was a strategic post located at roughly equal distances from the cities of Buenos Aires and Santa Fe near the Paraná River, which was the main communication channel in the River Plate region. The size of its district was first set down in 1784 at about 300,000 hectares. The whole district had become located within occupied borders by 1833, which however did not prevent Indian raids from taking place in 1838 and 1841. Its boundaries were formally delineated in 1865, by then encompassing 323,900 hectares. They were redrawn down to 299,178 hectares in 1892, when a small part seceded to form a new district.[8]

The landscape is plain, with very gentle hills and hollows; some streams and small lagoons make it an amenable environment for human occupation and livestock, and the whole land is suitable for agricultural use. There are no forests except for those created by man; rains are regular, allowing for dry farming. Mean temperatures range between 21°C and 26°C in summer, and between 6°C and 10°C in winter.

Table 4.1 shows that as far as land use was concerned, Pergamino was quite similar to the rest of the province of Buenos Aires until the end of the nineteenth century. The percentage of cultivated area was quite similar, as were the numbers of cows and sheep per hectare. However, a gap developed from 1895 onwards. Maize quickly gained prominence in Pergamino and became the main crop, allowing for a full use of the attributes of its rich soil; nowadays, Pergamino is part of the core area of the pampas, the main crop region in Argentina and one among the richest of the world. In 1906, a journalist reported maize yields of 4,900 to 5,700 kilos per hectare.[9]

In 1912, the Ministry of Agriculture founded an experimental station in Pergamino to carry out research into crop rotation, 'ultimately devoted to maize, trying to make . . . a permanent selection of maize seed varieties, both naturalized and commercially suitable in the area'.[10] The station also owned a pig herd for experimental research into fodder.

The first railway station was opened on 30 August 1882, connecting the district with the seaports of Buenos Aires and Rosario and from there to the global market for agricultural produce. By 1923, the district boasted twenty railway stations on three different lines.[11] Therefore it is no wonder that rural wealth increased at a fast pace, as shown by the inventory values in Table 4.1.

First of all, we should highlight the steep rise in the inventory value of land, particularly between 1866 and 1881. As we shall see below, this was the period during which the district's land was fully privatized. While in 1854 land accounted for only 10 per cent of the total rural inventory, in 1881 it amounted to 65 per cent.

Fences accounted for similar proportions of the total inventory value in 1866 and 1881, but their absolute value grew more than threefold. Back in 1854, fences were scarce and mainly took the form of ditches or rows of trees to keep cattle safe at night. Fencing around a property could only be carried out by means of wooden pales, in a landscape virtually void of forests. Expensive wood would have to be imported and carried long distances, and fencing round a large plot

Table 4.1 Rural economy data, Buenos Aires and Pergamino, 1854–1914[12]

	1854		1866		1881		1888		1914	
	P	BA	P	BA	P	BA	P	BA	P	BA

Land use, Pergamino district (P) and Province of Buenos Aires (BA)

	P	BA	P	BA	P	BA	P	BA	P	BA
% cultivated[13]	0.25	0.46	0.28	0.31	1	0.15	9	4	45	18
Cattle, heads/ha.[14]	1.07	0.38	0.65	0.25	0.35		0.16	0.26	0.52	0.36
Sheep, heads/ha.[15]	1.06	0.62	3.36	1.44	4.95	1.86	1.79	1.78	0.55	0.74

Land price (in gold pesos) and value of rural inventory at current prices (in thousand gold pesos), Pergamino district

	1854	1866	1881	1888	1914
Price of land/ha.	0.87	4.81	35.09	44.69	104.73
Total inventory	1,198.9	4,651.3	16,588.5	19,676.1	48,389.7
Land	115.3	1,003.6	10,932.4	12,609.5	31,331.7
Fences	21.3	49.6	170.5	455.3	2,961.5
Buildings	68.6	151.8	1,092.4	821.0	658.7
Permanent crops	0.8	13.2	194.4	694.7	87.7
Cattle	349.4	334.8	1,367.9	2,085.4	4,299.5
Sheep	173.9	2,819.5	2,721.9	1,742.2	558.2
Other livestock[16]	459.4	245.9	30.1	236.6	1,739.5
Operating equipment	7.3	19.8	24.7	191.6	1,438.6
Cereals, linseed	2.8	13.1	54.1	839.8	5,314.3

Value of production factors and total farming output at current prices in thousand gold pesos, Pergamino district[17]

	1854	1866	1881	1888	1914
Land	115.3	1,003.6	10,932.4	12,609.5	31,331.6
Capital	1,080.9	6,634.6	5,602.0	6,226.8	11,743.7
Labour	86.1	229.9	572.0	1,165.5	3,646.7
Output	133.3	488.4	1,427.6	2,125.2	7,534.7

would involve huge labour costs. By 1860, the first wire fences entered the scene but they were still too costly and ineffective. As the technology improved, wire fences almost completely replaced traditional ones in a relatively short time and fencing became widespread. By 1881, wire accounted for 96 per cent of the total linear extension of fences in Pergamino, a very high proportion when compared with the 61 per cent for the whole province of Buenos Aires, and the inventory value of fences kept growing at a fast pace until the early twentieth century.

The value of cereal crops increased from 0.33 per cent of total inventory in 1881 to 4 per cent in 1888, and then to 11 per cent in 1914. That of sheep rose sharply between 1854 and 1866, declining in both relative and absolute value from then onwards. The growing value of horses, which made up the bulge of the 'other livestock' in Table 4.1, is a consequence of their use in sheep farming and later as draught power for agricultural machinery, such as improved ploughs, reapers, and threshers. Yet between 1866 and 1881, the relative value of all livestock went down from 73 per cent of total inventory to only about 25 per cent. The value of operating equipment followed that of cereals and linseed. The part of buildings and permanent crops grew until 1888, falling from then on as they were replaced by larger but cheaper buildings for cattle and large-scale cereal fields, respectively.

The growth in land value up until 1881 partially remains to be explained, since neither cattle, sheep, crops nor credit seem to fully account for this.[18] Historians have highlighted the role of a speculative cycle that took place in 1886–1888, which prevented many immigrants from purchasing land in the expansive agricultural context of the pampas. Those studies argued that landowners had preferred to keep hold of their land, expecting to obtain even higher prices later on.[19] More recent research, however, found that prices collapsed after a peak in 1888, reaching only 50 per cent of the levels of that year in 1894.[20] Their conclusions indicate that a near-perfect land market was operative in those years, allowing for a significant amount of land to be offered. As a strategy, most landowners did not hold on to their property, except for a few who had purchased their land for high prices during the speculative cycle and opted to wait for prices to recover to avoid major loss.[21]

According to our data, land prices in Pergamino had risen consistently even before the speculative cycle of 1886–1888, while the years ending in 1888 seem not to have been quite as active in that respect, with a roughly 20 per cent increase in land value. As we will see, in Pergamino, as probably in other northern parts of the province of Buenos Aires, previous progress in the frontier and changes in property rights seem to have had a fundamental role in making land become a major part of total rural wealth by 1881. Integration in world markets had been advancing since the early nineteenth century, partially filling the wide price gap between both sides of the Atlantic, and the resulting economic growth must certainly have played a key role in the increase in rural inventory and land value. But as we shall argue, the implementation of more exclusive property rights – no doubt itself responding to the incentives created by growing wealth – must have played no lesser a role in translating the new economic opportunities into higher land value and how it was socially distributed.

Long-term growth, factor productivity and land value

We assume that growth in land value at a higher rate than the overall economic efficiency of farming inputs indicates that land itself is becoming a core component of wealth, in that part of the increase in its value is due to other causes than the sheer productive capacity it affords. This is key to understanding how much changes in wealth distribution were directly affected by the land property structure. We have used total factor productivity as a measure of overall economic efficiency, to allow us to identify historical turning points in that process, which may be related to changes in property rights.

We have estimated the annual growth rate of total factor productivity broken down by periods from 1854 to 1914, using the growth rates of the factors involved in agricultural production and aggregated agricultural output (Table 4.2). Total factor productivity had negative growth from 1854 to 1881, and a moderately positive one from 1881 to 1914. The main explanation seems to lie in the steep increase in the value of land until 1881, at an average annual rate of 20 per cent in 1854–1866 and 17 per cent in 1866–1881, which was far greater than those of the other inputs and, crucially, of the overall agricultural output.

The turning point took place around 1881. From then on, land value increased at a very low rate, barely higher than capital and lower than output, and total productivity growth was positive at a high rate, when compared to its previous evolution. Thus, it is the uncommon growth of land value until 1881 that needs to be explained. The sheer extension of land put to use cannot account for the whole growth, since from 1867 to 1881, when it encompassed virtually all of the district, the surface of fully occupied land grew at the average pace of no more than 3 per cent a year, a very low figure when compared with that of the aggregated land value.[22] We believe the large part remaining to be explained was the consequence of the interplay between changes in property rights and the regional incorporation in the global markets for agricultural produce.

Table 4.2 Annual growth rates (%) in the value of production factors, output, and total factor productivity, Pergamino, 1854–1914

	1854 1866	1866 1881	1881 1888	1888 1914	1854 1881	1881 1914
Land	19.76	17.30	1.98	3.57	18.35	3.24
Capital	0.64	2.93	1.52	2.47	6.29	2.28
Labour	8.53	6.27	10.70	4.49	7.27	5.77
Factors (tot.)	11.76	8.74	2.26	3.32	10.07	3.10
Output	11.43	7.40	5.87	4.99	9.18	5.16
TFP	−0.33	−1.34	3.61	1.67	−0.89	2.07

Sources: Table 4.1

The implementation of new property rights

Taxation was a major factor in the redefinition of ownership by the state. Besides providing resources to the treasury, the government met three targets by taxing the land: firstly, to sustain the whole system of legal certainty in land ownership. Secondly, to provide equity in the face of common obligations: whoever owned larger or more valuable land would pay more tax as a consequence. Finally, by establishing and maintaining cadastral records the state came to know its own property, and therefore was able to sell or lease it out. Table 4.3 shows the progress of the area in officially recognized private property, as included in tax records and in information systems owned and guaranteed by the state.

Table 4.3 Total district area and land under private ownership according to tax and land recordings, Pergamino, 1855–1914 (thousands of hectares)[25]

	1855	1863	1867	1890	1914
Total area (A)	330.0	323.9	323.9	299.2	299.2
Privately owned (B)[26]	132.5	175.7	208.6	282.1	300.9
B/A (%)	40	54	64	90	100

Since the colonial era when the creole militia had conquered it from the Indians, most land was in theory under public ownership and only a few private persons were granted legal titles. Land occupation had progressed steadily, though not without periods of stagnation and even breakdowns, and up to about 1870 it covered a rather wide array of situations, beginning very sparsely with extensive cattle ranching and becoming denser as sheep farming and crops were introduced. In areas where productive activities were not considered intensive enough to generate considerable earnings, or that were threatened by frontier insecurity, land-holdings were simply not taxed or recorded, although such areas were certainly inhabited and some livestock was raised there.

To begin with, most farmers held precarious land use rights issued by local authorities, based on social acknowledgement and old colonial customary rights that were legal under consuetudinary law but not actually granted by the state as the ultimate legal owner. In 1821, the Buenos Aires government granted public land in temporary emphyteusis at very low rents to private individuals and societies.[23] The full domain in those lands was later put on sale, but because of political unrest only a few of the tenants were eventually able to buy into full ownership. In 1839 and 1840, the provincial government of Juan Manuel de Rosas foreclosed on its political opponents' land and in the following years granted it in usufruct to Rosas's political supporters. Rosas's ousting in 1852 resulted in a revision of all tenures, in order both to sort out the juridical mess and to redress the abuses and inequities of previous years – at least such abuses as were alleged by Rosas's victorious foes.

The final aim was to set up a homogeneous and full system of private ownership inspired by the liberal concept of property,[24] and the implementation of this new set of property rights rested on the expropriation of previously institutionalized ones; from the new legal standpoint, only a small fraction of the owners held unimpeachable titles to their lands. While this process made for some conflicts, in the long run the changes were broadly accepted, partly because the district and its surroundings still enjoyed a relative plenitude of useable land. The state made a thorough revision of entitlements, paying little consideration to rights that had been held under traditional land use practices. However, it did acknowledge rights derived from long-standing occupation and managed to define them as absolute land use rights, subject to the Castilian rules of inheritance, perpetuating the succession of owners. All land in questionable ownership reverted to the state and was offered for rent, awaiting the settlement of a final regulatory framework for definitive land sales.

The first land sales act was passed in 1864. In 1876, the state lease system was terminated so that the land could be sold off, and in 1878, a new land act was issued to complete the rules for the transfer of public land to private hands. This act granted right of purchase to the occupants of up to 8,000 hectares who had continuously kept at least 300 head of cattle or 1,000 sheep during the preceding year.[27] The Cadastre was concomitantly improved. By 1880, all the new legal and administrative instruments to rearrange land ownership were either fully in force or had been put in place to be implemented.[28]

Besides the legal redefinition of real rights and a new system of records to secure and enforce legal ownership on a wide scale, the new set of exclusive property rights was also – and most importantly – implemented in practice by progress in physical delimitation and control over land. As improved technology made wire fences more affordable and increasing land values made them more appealing, fences played a key role in enforcing the new exclusive property rights with physical limits. Traditionally, the lack of effective fences had caused waste because a large part of the estates, particularly along their borders, was left empty to create buffer areas between the cattle herds of the different owners. Such loosely appropriated areas often resulted in contested property boundaries. To enclose land effectively became a main concern both for the government and for private individuals intent on implementing the new legal framework. In Pergamino, as shown in the inventory values in Table 4.1, the use of wire fences by private owners increased exponentially. They were also encouraged by the state, since effective fencing was a key instrument for the delimitation of both private and state-owned land.

Pergamino experienced quite substantial changes in land ownership. In 1859–1876, state tenants held a total of 53,783 hectares, and overall the sales of public land encompassed a total of 87,761 hectares.[29] The 1878 land act concluded the process, allowing most public land in the district to be sold off to private owners. Only a few peri-urban areas remained in commons, and these were finally sold in 1887. These land sales were explicitly aimed at spreading small and medium farms; the 1878 law even threatened large landowners in such areas with expropriation, if they would not divide their estates and put a part on sale of their own accord.[30] However, from 1854 to 1881, the value of Pergamino land had grown substantially compared with the actual performance of its rural economy.

Even more importantly, the growth in land value preceded significant investment-demanding changes in the productive system, namely the substitution of cash crops for cattle and sheep. When investment in more intensive activities started to flow into Pergamino, land prices had already reached a point that implied spending a considerable amount per hectare just to buy the land, a very high price relative to the other factors of production. This placed a high economic burden on new entrants in the real estate market and favoured the incumbent large landowners.

The distribution of land wealth

The implementation and timing of such broad changes in the system of property rights are key to understanding how wealth distribution evolved in later years. Table 4.4 shows the evolution of the Gini indexes for the distribution of land wealth, both among all households and only landowning households.

After decreasing between 1839 and 1855, inequality grew from 1855 to 1890. We can hypothesize that as long as there was land still available, control over it remained relatively loose and 'traditional' property arrangements prevailed, inequality actually decreased in spite of soaring land prices and inventory values. However, as the new property regime and a stronger control over land were implemented, inequality increased steeply. Even though we do not have full data on the value of land in 1890, from what we know it may be assumed that the evolution was parallel to that of land extension. From 1890 to 1914, both Gini indexes decreased marginally, but then the starting point was substantially higher than those in the previous periods.

The available information does not allow us to set precise date limits, but it is likely that that this process took place mostly from the early 1860s, around the time the first wire fences were introduced, to the late 1870s with the final settling

Table 4.4 Inequality in land ownership, Pergamino, 1839–1914[31]

	1839	1855	1867	1890	1914
Total population	2,751	4,466	7,337	23,945	47,460
Rural population			4,496	14,405	23,757
Total owners	72	122	198		
Rural owners			129	489	878
% annual increase		3.4	4.1	6.0	2.5
% on total population	2.8	2.7	2.6		
% on rural population			2.9	3.4	3.7
Gini index on land value					
among landowners	0.558	0.456	0.603		0.779
among all households	0.918	0.901	0.933		0.946
Gini index on the amount of land					
among landowners			0.600	0.803	0.784
among all households			0.924	0.952	0.947

Note: Years for population data are 1838, 1854, 1869, 1895 and 1914.

of changes in legal property rights and the measures aimed at the division of the largest landholdings. The legal change was paralleled by the implement-ation of more secure and exclusive property rights, both through technological improvements and more effective policies concerning land records and taxation. The increase in inequality may have hit a ceiling by the early 1880s, but this is impossible to ascertain for want of quantitative data. At any rate, the established levels of inequality proved to be very resilient, notwithstanding policy efforts to subdivide lots following the 1878 land act.

Why then, in spite of such attempts, was there not consistent enough progress in land subdivision to make inequality decline substantially? The land market was not blocked and landowners did sell their properties – only a handful of the 1867 landlords remained in 1890, and again only a handful remained from 1890 to 1914. However, many sold their estates whole and in turn the new owners were able to hold on to them, so that little division of these holdings actually took place. Despite a substantial increase in the number of landowners, which from the 1890s onwards grew at a faster rate than the rural population (Table 4.4), inequality among them remained very high.

The answer seems to lie in the period of strong capital investment and techno-logical change that followed the peak of inequality, arguably reached in the early 1880s. In a society where wealth was highly concentrated to begin with, growing demands on capital layouts combined with high land prices would keep most people away from buying land in any significant scale, while they encouraged a small number of landowners to invest in land wholesale and lease it out to farmers with operating capital. Actually, throughout the whole period, about half of the farms in the province were managed by lease tenants.

Therefore, income inequality would certainly be less than land wealth in-equality, since part of the property rights – namely, those of use – and the income they afforded was temporarily reassigned to others in exchange for rent. Moreover, as agriculture intensified, labour was in high demand and relatively well paid, causing hordes of poor migrants to come to Pergamino in search of better wages than they could obtain in Europe and in other rural parts of Argentina. However, aside from income, inequality in land wealth was a problem in itself that concerned a significant group of politicians who sought ways to secure massive access to land, particularly in order to settle immigrants. The 1895 and 1914 Censuses pointed to that goal by collecting data on the nationality of landowners.

However, Pergamino, the agricultural advantages of which were highlighted by substantial increases in cash crops during those years, had a concentrated land property pattern to begin with, and the changes in the system of property rights were laid over an agrarian structure fashioned by extensive cattle ranching and sheep farming. When absolute property titles were issued, tenures were adequately sized for extensive husbandry at a much lower technological level than would be the case from the 1880s onwards. While 3,000 hectares in extensive cattle-ranching would barely support a family back in 1840,[32] four or five decades later the same amount of land would generate a huge income in cash crops, provided the owner was able to lay out the initial capital for farm conversion – a condition that the high mortgage value of land helped to meet, since credit shortage was overcome by 1882 as a result of better economic perspectives and more abundant capital inflows from Europe.[33]

The proportion of the area of cultivated land in Pergamino rose from less than 1 per cent in 1881 to 9 per cent in 1895 and 45 per cent in 1914, parallel to the decrease in the flock and the diffusion of genetically improved cross-bred cattle. We believe that for the reasons outlined above, this agricultural intensification did not cause the inequality in land property to decrease. The result might have been different, had not the shift to modern property rights granted by the state overridden most customary tenures, without simultaneously encouraging the division of holdings under the new ones. As it happened, the changes were appropriated by a landowning elite that had amassed vast holdings during the previous period of lower land prices and political turmoil, and the authorities' later attempts to impose limits on landholding size ultimately lacked the power to secure their division.

As a term of comparison to help us make this point, let us briefly examine the evolution of agricultural colonies in the neighbouring province of Santa Fe. The first agricultural colony in the province was created in 1856, through a joint venture between a private entrepreneur and the provincial authorities, which had been agreed in 1853. This was soon followed by others near the Indian borderland, where up until then there had been no settlement except for extensive cattle ranches. Land available for these experiments expanded fast, as from 1858 to 1870 the province quadrupled its size at the expense of former Indian territories[34]. The number of colonies grew from three in 1865 to over 400 in 1895 with more than four million hectares, that is, 35 per cent of Santa Fe territory.[35]

Since land in Santa Fe was not as suitable for that purpose as in the northern Buenos Aires province, sheep farming did not develop as fast there. As late as 1889, the province's flock amounted to no more than twenty-two sheep per square Km, as compared to 168 in Buenos Aires.[36] From as early as 1865, the colonies took to growing cash crops to sell in the cities of Santa Fe and Buenos Aires and later in the world market, vastly contributing to Argentina's changing role from an importer to an exporter of wheat since 1880.[37]

The colonies were settled with European immigrants. Each household was granted a farm of no more than thirty-three hectares, and from 1865 onwards, the size of the farm was limited to the farmer's ability to pay mortgage dues.[38] Each farmer had full assurance of land ownership under a written contract. This was in sharp contrast with customary property rights, which in Santa Fe were loosely defined, were not officially recorded and were legally uncertain according to state law, and mostly were without physically marked boundaries. The presence of the state was itself infrequent and very few officials were deployed in the province,[39] whereas the colonies had their own authorities from the beginning, later followed by government-paid officials. While the colonies' land value grew, that of land that remained in extensive cattle ranching was not directly affected. In 1859–1862, one hectare of pastoral land was worth only 0.25 gold pesos in Santa Fe, while in the northern Buenos Aires province its value was 0.87; in 1864–1865, one hectare for extensive cattle ranching was worth 0.98 gold pesos, against 5.7 in Buenos Aires, a price that in Santa Fe was only reached by 1900.[40]

There was political pressure to establish colonies in Buenos Aires as well. Domingo Faustino Sarmiento, president of Argentina between 1868 and 1874, declared his intentions to carry out that policy in the province. However, the agrarian wealth in Buenos Aires then consisted mostly of cattle and sheep, and many policy makers, intellectuals, experts and businessmen argued that the expansion of cereals in the province would be a fatal mistake. Firstly, they believed it would have to face the competition of Santa Fe, which by then had become the 'country's barn', and face a probable fall in prices due to increased supply in a cereal market that they perceived as approaching saturation. Were cattle and sheep be replaced with crops, they argued, the wealth of the province would be depleted and fiscal revenues and exports would suffer badly.[41] Secondly, capital was scarce and the government would have to invest huge amounts of funding in the storage and transport infrastructure that would be needed to take advantage of such crops.

No colonies were created and cereal crops did not expand in the province of Buenos Aires before the late nineteenth century. By the first decade of the twentieth century, the world market offered good prices for cereals, and crops could be combined with improved cattle, allowing for a fast increase in cultivated land along with high-performing cattle raising. By then it was good business to invest capital in the large-scale units that had been consolidated by the former changes in property rights, and as a result, both the average farm size and the percentage of farms under lease were larger in Buenos Aires than in Santa Fe, while the latter had a less unequal distribution of land wealth.[42]

The implementation of modern property rights in Santa Fe was initially bound to the agricultural colonies and therefore linked to intensive crops, while in Buenos Aires it was carried out on extensive cattle ranches and sheep farms that held valuable herds and flocks which were produced for the world market. Contrary to what happened in Santa Fe, when intensive crops were introduced into Pergamino, the scale of the productive units had been fashioned by extensive ranching. As the soil there is very suitable for maize, a massive wave of capital investment for conversion to cash crops gave further support to large-scale units. Throughout this evolution, the practical implementation of new property rights played a role in freezing the former landholding structure, thus impeding wealth inequality among landowners from falling substantially from 1881 to 1914, in spite of agricultural intensification.

Concluding remarks

Economic growth was quite spectacular in the pampas in general, and in Pergamino in particular, during the second half of the nineteenth century. The population rose, driven by an inflow of immigrants. Extensive cattle ranching gave way to sheep farming, and then to maize crops and improved animal farming. Transport infrastructures were put in place. Rural wealth per capita rose from 329 gold pesos in 1854 to 1,112 in 1881, and again to 1,991 in 1914. The number of landowners rose from 2.9 per cent of the rural population in 1867 to 3.7 per cent in 1914. At the same time, inequality in the distribution of land property grew substantially from the 1860s to the 1880s and then remained high, despite some efforts to curb it.

We have argued that this situation was partly a consequence of how modern property rights were implemented by the state and appropriated by the existing agrarian and business elite. Public land was sold under a new legal system of property rights that established full, absolute and exclusive land ownership, guaranteed by the government and secured by official registration procedures, just as technological improvements such as wire fences allowed for a tighter enforcement of property and control over the land. The actual implementation of the new legal framework expropriated former tenures that had rested on locally accepted customary rights, and the newly defined property rights were appropriated by an agrarian elite that controlled a structure of vast landholdings suitable for extensive uses typical of a frontier economy, in which the abundance of land at low cost compensated for the paucity of high-cost labour and capital. In a relatively short time, however, this economy was to be replaced with more intensive uses. Massive capital investment driven by global demand and partly funded by available foreign capital, together with a growing immigrant labour supply, transformed the regional production pattern from creole cattle ranching or sheep farming to more intensive cash crops, and the resulting increased accumulation of land wealth was poured into a property mould that had already congealed at a high peak of inequality.[43]

The contrasting results observed in this respect in the provinces of Santa Fe and Buenos Aires show the weight of path dependence. The political philosophy and the institutional foundations underpinning modern property rights, as well as the administrative tools and the fencing technology supporting them, were the same in both provinces. Therefore, it was the critical differences in the initial conditions and early evolution of the agrarian structure, which may explain the strikingly different distributional outcomes of a formally identical set of institutionalized property rights – namely, the less favourable conditions for sheep ranching in Santa Fe, which encouraged the establishment from an early stage of agricultural colonies geared to higher intensity agriculture that created a middling landowning stratum, and the fact that in Buenos Aires similar policies were blocked by political and business elites.[44]

Once investors realized that extensive areas in the Pergamino district had excellent soil conditions for cash crops, they bought the large landholdings located in those areas and kept them whole, either for their own agricultural ventures or to lease them out to capitalist farmers. As landholdings were converted to large-scale mixed production units combining improved livestock farming with maize crops, landowners could leverage the ongoing rise in land value for capital investment and further accumulation. This in turn enhanced unequal wealth distribution, or at the very least kept it from decreasing substantially in spite of agricultural intensification and a growing number of new landowners.[45] Eventually, this became a factor for social unrest, already noticeable in 1912[46] and which would increase as the agrarian income fell after 1914 due to troubles in the international market for cash crops.

Notes

1   J. Gelman (ed.), *El Mapa de la Desigualdad en la Argentina del Siglo XIX* (Rosario: Prohistoria, 2011).
2   G. Banzato, *La Expansión de la Frontera Bonaerense: Posesión y Propiedad de la Tierra en Chascomús, Ranchos y Monte, 1780–1880* (Bernal: Universidad de Quilmes, 2005); G. Banzato, G. Blanco, M. Blanco, and A. I. Ferreyra (eds), 'Dossier: Acceso y tenencia de la tierra en Argentina: Enfoques locales y regionales, siglos XVIII–XX', *Mundo Agrario: Revista de Estudios Rurales*, 7:14 (2007); M. E. Infesta, 'La enfiteusis en Buenos Aires, 1820–1850', in M. Bonaudo and A. Pucciarelli (eds), *La Problemática Agraria: Nuevas Aproximaciones* (Buenos Aires: CEAL, 1993), pp. 93–120; M. E. Infesta, *La Pampa Criolla: Usufructo y Apropiación Privada de Tierras Públicas en Buenos Aires, 1820–1850* (La Plata: Archivo Histórico de la Provincia de Buenos Aires, 2003); M. Valencia, *Tierras Públicas, Tierras Privadas: Buenos Aires 1852–1876* (La Plata: Editorial de la Universidad de La Plata, 2005).
3   R. Congost, *Tierras, Leyes, Historia: Reflexiones sobre 'La Gran Obra de la Propiedad'* (Barcelona: Crítica, 2007), pp. 15–21.
4   T. Ingold, *Hunters, Pastoralists and Ranchers: Reindeer Economies and Their Transformations* (Cambridge: Cambridge University Press, 1988), pp. 1–10, 201–60.
5   Growth was faster in the second half of the century. Details in R. Cortés Conde, *El Progreso Argentino 1880–1914* (Buenos Aires: Sudamericana, 1979); J. Djenderedjian, *Historia del Capitalismo Agrario Pampeano: Tomo IV: La Agricultura Pampeana en la Primera Mitad del Siglo XIX* (Buenos Aires: Siglo XXI and Universidad de Belgrano, 2008); J. Djenderedjian, S. Bearzotti, and J. L. Martirén, *Historia del Capitalismo Agrario Pampeano: Tomo VI: Expansión Agrícola y Colonización en la Segunda Mitad del Siglo XIX* (Buenos Aires: Teseo, 2010); E. Gallo, *La Pampa Gringa* (Buenos Aires: Sudamericana, 1983); E. Miguez, *Historia Económica de la Argentina: De la Conquista a la Crisis de 1930* (Buenos Aires: Sudamericana, 2008).
6   *Registro Estadístico del Estado de Buenos Aires: Segunda Época* (Buenos Aires: Imprenta del Orden, 1854).
7   O. Barsky and J. Djenderedjian, *Historia del Capitalismo Agrario Pampeano: Tomo I: La Expansión Ganadera Hasta 1895* (Buenos Aires: Siglo XXI, 2003); J. Gelman, 'Unos números sorprendentes: Cambio y continuidad en el mundo agrario bonaerense durante la primera mitad del siglo XIX', *Anuario IEHS*, 11 (1996), pp. 123–46; H. Sábato, *Capitalismo y Ganadería en Buenos Aires: La Fiebre del Lanar, 1850–1890* (Buenos Aires: Sudamericana, 1989); D. Santilli, 'Propiedad y producción en tiempos de Rosas: Quilmes 1837', *Quinto Sol*, 5 (2001), pp. 113–14; C. Sesto, *Historia del Capitalismo Agrario Pampeano: Tomo II: La Vanguardia Ganadera Bonaerense, 1856–1900* (Buenos Aires: Siglo XXI, 2005).
8   *Censo General de la Provincia de Buenos Aires: 9 de Octubre de 1881* (Buenos Aires: El Diario, 1883), p. 462 and ff.; *Tercer Censo Nacional Levantado el 1° de Junio de 1914: Tomo I* (Buenos Aires: L. J. Rosso y Cia., 1916–17); C. Lemée, *Datos para la Estadística Agrícola de la Provincia Correspondientes al Año de 1894* (La Plata: Escuela de Artes y Oficios, 1896), p. 24, wrongly gives a size of 312,640 hectares. A. Dupuy, *El Fin de una Sociedad de Frontera en la Primera Mitad del Siglo XIX: 'Hacendados' y 'Estancieros' en Pergamino* (Mar del Plata: UNMdP/GIHRR, 2004), pp. 43–54. L. E. Giménez Colodrero, *Historia de Pergamino Hasta 1895* (La Plata: Taller de Impresiones Oficiales, 1945), pp. 9–10; G. Sors de Tricerri, 'Pergamino', in R. Levene (ed.), *Historia de la Provincia de Buenos Aires y Formación de Sus Pueblos: Tomo II* (La Plata: Taller de Impresiones Oficiales, 1940–41), p. 529.

9 A. Fernández, *Prontuario de la Provincia de Buenos Aires: Entrega XIV* (20 December 1906), p. 1272.

10 *La Experimentación Agrícola en la República Argentina* (Buenos Aires: Ministerio de Agricultura de la Nación, 1915), p. 93.

11 *Estadística de los Ferrocarriles en Explotación durante el Año 1892* (Buenos Aires: Jacobo Peuser, 1894), p. 46; *Anuario Estadístico de la Provincia de Buenos Aires: 1924: Tomo I* (Buenos Aires: Baiocco, 1926), p. 32 and ff.

12 *Registro Estadístico del Estado de Buenos Aires: Segunda Época* (Buenos Aires: Imprenta del Orden, 1854); *Registro Estadístico de Buenos Aires: 1866* (Buenos Aires: Imprenta del Porvenir, 1867); *Censo General de la Provincia de Buenos Aires, 9 de Octubre de 1881*; *Censo Agrícolo-Pecuario de la Provincia de Buenos Aires, Octubre de 1888* (Buenos Aires: Establecimiento Tipográfico El Censor, 1889); *Tercer Censo Nacional*; *Estadística de los Ferrocarriles*; official statistical data in the series *Registro Estadístico*, 1881–2; *Anuario Geográfico Argentino de 1941* (Buenos Aires: Comité Nacional de Geografía, 1942); N. Avellaneda, *Estudio Sobre las Leyes de Tierras Públicas* (Buenos Aires: Imprenta del Siglo, 1865); F. Latzina, *L'Agriculture et l'Élevage dans la République Argentine* (Paris: Imprimerie Typographique P. Mouillot, 1889); V. M. de Moussy, *Description Géographique et Statistique de la Confédération Argentine* (Paris: Firmin Didot, 1860–4), vol. I, pp. 474–5; H. Miatello, *Investigación Agrícola en la Provincia de Santa Fe* (Buenos Aires: Cía. Sub-Americana [sic.] de Billetes de Banco, 1904); F. D. Seguí, *Memoria Presentada á la Honorable Legislatura de la Provincia por el Ministro de Gobierno . . . 1887–1888* (La Plata: Imprenta Buenos Aires, 1888); F. D. Seguí, *Investigación Parlamentaria sobre Agricultura, Ganadería, Industrias Derivadas y Colonización: Anexo B: Provincia de Buenos Aires* (Buenos Aires: Taller Tipográfico de la Penitenciaría Nacional, 1898); E. Zeballos, *Descripción Amena de la República Argentina: Tomo III: A Través de las Cabañas* (Buenos Aires: Peuser, 1888). Cortés Conde, *Progreso Argentino*; O. Ferreres, *Dos Siglos de Economía Argentina* (Buenos Aires: NorteSur, 2005); C. A. García Belsunce, 'Diezmos y producción agrícola en Buenos Aires virreinal', *Investigaciones y Ensayos*, 38 (1989), p. 349; Santilli, 'Propiedad y producción', pp. 113–42; E. A. Zalduendo, *Libras y Rieles: Las Inversiones Británicas para el Desarrollo de los Ferrocarriles en Argentina, Brasil, Canadá e India Durante el Siglo XIX* (Buenos Aires: El Coloquio, 1975), pp. 384–5. Values for operational equipment were estimated from data in Sábato, *Capitalismo y Ganadería* for 1854 and in *Tercer Censo Nacional* for 1866, and may be underestimated.

13 Considering only fully occupied land in 1854 and 1866.

14 Not considering land used for agriculture.

15 Values estimated only for fully occupied land with owners, from prices in the cited bibliography (1854 and 1866), censuses (1881), market transactions (1888) and tax values (1914). Cultivated land in 1854 was estimated from production of wheat and maize, according to needs for seed and yields offered by de Moussy, *Description,* t. I, pp. 474–5. The censuses and the bibliography used actual transactions and newspaper advertisements and the values seem to reflect market prices. Cereal production was estimated according to García Belsunce, 'Diezmos', p. 349. Crops were valued according to Buenos Aires market prices, less transportation costs in Zalduendo, *Libras y Rieles*, pp. 384–5, and in *Estadística de los Ferrocarriles*. We converted to gold pesos using the tables in J. Álvarez, *Temas de Historia Económica Argentina* (Buenos Aires: El Ateneo, 1929).

16 Includes horses (1854–1914), donkeys, mules and pigs (1881–1914), and poultry (1888–1914).

17 See note 15 on the value of land, capital and crops. We estimated output for crops, cattle and sheep according to expected usual yields or to those actually obtained. We calculated labour from contemporary estimates including sheep farming in Sábato, *Capitalismo y Ganadería*, and cattle ranching in Avellaneda, *Estudio Sobre las Leyes.*

For agriculture, we selected wheat, maize and linen crops and included all related operations. We assumed that half the crops were harvested by tenants and half by landowners, following proportions often found in censuses, which show that nearly half of both farming units and acreage were held by tenants.

18 Mortgage lending was underdeveloped even as late as 1880. H. Quesada, *El Crédito Territorial en la República Argentina* (Buenos Aires: Felix Lajouane, 1888), pp. 113–20.

19 J. R. Scobie, *Revolución en las Pampas* (Buenos Aires: Solar/Hachette, 1968); R. M. Ortiz, *Historia Económica de la Argentina* (Buenos Aires: Plus Ultra, 1974).

20 O. Barsky and J. Gelman, *Historia del Agro Argentino* (Buenos Aires: Grijalbo-Mondadori, 2001); Barsky and Djenderedjian, *Historia del Capitalismo*; R. Hora, *Historia Económica de la Argentina en el Siglo XIX* (Buenos Aires: Siglo XXI and Fundación OSDE, 2010); Cortés Conde, *Progreso Argentino*; Miguez, *Historia Económica*.

21 Barsky and Gelman, *Historia del Agro*; Cortés Conde, *Progreso Argentino*.

22 In 1867, 64 per cent of total land was fully occupied; in 1881, it was 98 per cent. Data from sources cited above in note 12.

23 Infesta, 'Enfiteusis' and *Pampa Criolla*.

24 B. Zeberio, 'Los hombres y las cosas: Cambios y continuidades en los derechos de propiedad (Argentina, siglo XIX)', *Quinto Sol*, 9–10 (2005–2006), pp. 151–83.

25 1839 was not included because of inconsistent data for the area under private ownership. AGN (Archivo General de la Nación), Sala III, 33–5–14, Libros de Contribución Directa, 1855, 33–8–28 a 32, Libros de Contribución Directa, 1867; *Contribución Directa: Rejistro Catastral de la Provincia de Buenos Aires con Exclusión de la Capital: Año de 1863* (Buenos Aires: Publicación oficial, 1863); DGPBA (Archivo de la Dirección de Geodesia de la Provincia de Buenos Aires, La Plata), Plano del Partido de Pergamino y Mensuras no. 62 (1890); *Argentina: Provincia de Buenos Aires: Ministerio de Hacienda* [1914]. The privately owned area was taken from fiscal sources (1855; 1863; 1867; 1914) and the *Cadastre* (1890).

26 The 1855 fiscal records report value, not area. We divided the area by the mean hectare price (0.87 gold pesos) to estimate total privately owned area. This is close enough to the 108,000 ha. counted in the 1854 census as 'occupied by farmers and ranchers'. In 1890, the difference between total district area and privately owned land amounts to urban area and roads, not considered in former years. In 1914, total privately owned area as reported by fiscal records is higher than the total for the whole district. We have not been able to trace the error, no doubt committed in the measurement of some of the holdings.

27 *Registro Oficial de la Provincia de Buenos Aires: 1878* (Buenos Aires: Imprenta del Mercurio, 1878, p. 602.

28 Evolution of the new property rights in Buenos Aires in Infesta, *Pampa Criolla*; Valencia, *Tierras Públicas*, pp. 97 and ff.; new land taxes in D. Santilli, 'El papel de la tributación en la formación del estado: La contribución directa en el siglo XIX en Buenos Aires', *América Latina en la Historia Económica*, 33 (2010), pp. 30–63.

29 Valencia, *Tierras Públicas*, p. 105 and ff.

30 Djenderedjian, Bearzotti and Martirén, *Historia del Capitalismo*, vol. 2, pp. 673 and ff.

31 Population: AGN Sala X 25–6–2, Padrón (1838); *Registro Estadístico del Estado de Buenos Aires* (1854), *Primer Censo Nacional* (1869); *Segundo Censo Nacional* (1895); *Tercer Censo Nacional* (1914). Urban population was negligible in 1838, and remained below 40 per cent until 1895. Land ownership: AGN Sala III 33–4–7 (1839), 33–5–14 (1855); 33–828 to 32 (1867). DGPBA, Plano del Partido de Pergamino y Mensuras no. 62 y 68 (1890), DGPBA, Primera Guía de Contribuyentes de la Provincia de Buenos Aires (1914).

32 J. Gelman and D. Santilli, *De Rivadavia a Rosas: Desigualdad y Crecimiento Económico* (Buenos Aires: Siglo XXI, 2006).

33 Quesada, *Crédito Territorial*, pp. 113–20.

34 Gallo, *Pampa Gringa*, pp. 34–5.
35 *Segundo Censo de la República Argentina*, t. I, pp. 652 and ff.; Djenderedjian, Bearzotti and Martirén, *Historia del Capitalismo*.
36 Latzina, *L'Agriculture et l'Élevage*, p. 354.
37 Djenderedjian, Bearzotti and Martirén, *Historia del Capitalismo*.
38 Djenderedjian, Bearzotti and Martirén, *Historia del Capitalismo*.
39 Each province had its own land record system and land taxes.
40 For Santa Fe, J. Martirén, personal communication; for Buenos Aires, Sábato, *Capitalismo y Ganadería*.
41 *For example,* Olivera to Sarmiento, Buenos Aires, August 11, 1867, in *Anales: Tomo X* (Buenos Aires: Sociedad Rural Argentina, 1875), p. 413 and ff.
42 *Tercer Censo Nacional*, vols. V and VI. Land wealth inequality in Santa Fe versus Buenos Aires: Research cited in Gelman, *Mapa de la Desigualdad* and Martirén, personal communication.
43 I. Iriarte and J. M. Lana make a similar point in chapter seven. (Editors' note.)
44 J. E. Bromley and A. Wolz, in chapter eight present another example of the implementation of a new set of formal property rights being moulded by the pre-existing social and agrarian structure. (Editors' note.)
45 Technological development and increases in capital investment can generate social differentiation and inequality. Among others, M. Piñeiro and I. Llovet (eds), *Transición Tecnológica y Diferenciación Social* (San José: IICA, 1986), pp. 9 and ff., 83 and ff. As early as 1855, many small farmers were selling part of their land to raise the capital to invest in the remaining part, in order to increase their gains. J. Gelman and D. Santilli, 'Movilidad social y desigualdad en el Buenos Aires del siglo XIX: El acceso a la propiedad de la tierra entre el Rosismo y el orden liberal', *Hispanic American Historical Review*, 93:4 (2013), pp. 659–84.
46 Barsky and Gelman, *Historia del Agro*.

5 Taming the platypus

Adaptations of the *colonia* tenancy contract to a changing context in nineteenth-century Madeira

Benedita Câmara and Rui Santos

Introduction

The *colonia* was a customary tenancy contract in Madeira that combined share-cropping with land improvement by conferring on the tenants the ownership of the improvements they had made, such as vines and buildings. It was also a tenancy at will, which in practice became a long-term contract. Each of the afore-mentioned elements is found in several historical instances, most often associated with vineyards, generally in mountainous and often previously uncultivated land where creating them constituted a considerable long-term improvement. From a contract choice perspective, this association has been related to several factors. Firstly, to the landowners' preference for leasing out rather than cultivating vines with hired labour on such terrains. Secondly, to the unlikelihood of small peasants accepting a fixed-rent lease, given the crop's volatility and the conse-quent risk of forfeit, and lastly, to the relatively low share of capital in the inputs, because of the labour-intensiveness of traditional viticulture. The latter meant that a sharecropper's high share of the inputs in long-term improvements had to be compensated for with a stake in their value.[1] In this chapter, we will explore the way these elements came together in the particular context of Madeira, the sets of incentives they defined and how they were appropriated. We will not do so from a contract choice perspective, but rather from one of institutional and practical change.

As with all seigniorial, traditional, and customary institutions, the *colonia* posed a challenge to the nineteenth-century liberal project of perfecting and universalizing property rights, to be brought about by their abstract delineation and individualization out of the fetters of traditional and local particularisms, 'feudality' and 'backwardness' into the realm of 'progress'. Conversely, the mater-ialization of this project posed the problem of striking a balance between the universality of the law and the specificity of custom, under the general principle of contractual freedom, and everyday challenges to the way new institutional forms were appropriated and re-appropriated in concrete social practice.[2]

The splitting of property and its relationship with contract in *colonia* were hard to fit within emerging liberal conceptions and with the 1867 Civil Code's *numerus clausus* of property forms. The customary contract became a sort of juridical platypus, the inner workings of which would have to be regulated on the one hand according to the rules of sharecropping contracts, and on the other according to property law concerning the improvements. The way this played out in Madeira displays elements both of path dependence and adaptation. Changing economic, agricultural, and legal conditions in the course of the nineteenth century were met with practical adjustments in the contract which help account for its resilience. Moreover, practical and juridical solutions to this conundrum remained very much alive in everyday practice, as well as legal reinterpretation, long after the contract's relative weight declined and it was eventually outlawed. An earlier study argued that the Civil Code introduced or accentuated inefficiencies in the contract, which led to a gradual waning of its use from the 1870s onwards.[3] While holding to this view, in this chapter we will look at the process from another angle, by asking ourselves why the waning *was* gradual and left persistent property issues in its wake.

One hundred years after the Civil Code, new *colonia* contracts were forbidden and the ones still in force were partially regulated by law. *Colonia* itself was prohibited by the Portuguese Constitution in 1976, and its extinction was decreed by ensuing national and regional acts, along with much debate concerning its phasing-out.[4] Nevertheless, to this day heated political struggle goes on over the effectiveness and fairness of the extinction process and the reallocation of the resulting bundles of property rights, along with a stream of court rulings concerning transactions of such rights.[5]

The setting

Madeira is an island situated off the northwest coast of Africa, almost 1,000 km southwest of Lisbon. Maderia's geography lent it a strategic role within the expanding Atlantic trade routes, which contributed to a very open economy, ever since its early days in the fifteenth century, and ever more so as trade flows became increasingly globalized.[6]

When the Portuguese first landed there in 1419, Madeira was a deserted island, densely covered with forest. Settlement began shortly afterwards during the 1420s, and with it systematic land clearings.[7] The island's total area is 737 km², over a quarter of which is at altitudes above 1,000 m and one half above 700 m; some 60 per cent of the total surface has slopes of over 25 per cent. As a result, the area suitable for agricultural use would was no more than 20,000 ha. The island's orography had obvious consequences for agricultural occupation, which was literally an uphill struggle from the earliest settlements on the littoral.

In the early stages of settlement, the new colony's 'captains' granted lands in *sesmaria* within their respective jurisdictions, until the king decreed in 1501 that no more land should be granted in that form. The *sesmaria* was a medieval form of granting uncultivated land for settlement and improvement, subject to confirmation after a specified period of time, which the Portuguese adapted to regulate the distribution of entitlements to land in their Atlantic colonies.[8] The Portuguese also brought their institutional templates of agrarian contracts, among which the most relevant for the case at hand were those of *parceria* and emphyteusis. The former was the general legal designation for sharecropping contracts, which were varied in customary detail, were often short-term, and were not typically improvement contracts. The *parceria* was used in Madeira from the early days, and, as we will see, sharecropping formed a major component of the specific contract of *colonia* that concerns us here.

Emphyteutis was traditionally an improvement contract.[9] It split property into two separate *dominia* (henceforth 'domains'). The 'eminent' or 'direct' domain remained with the landlord, mainly consisting of the rights to receive an annual rent, succession and sale fines, and to have the last say concerning the alienation or subdivision of the useful domain. The latter consisted of the remaining property rights that were transferred to the taker. It could be sold, subject to the landlord's agreement, and it was handed down through inheritance.

Wheat was the main crop in the early days, but soon a very lucrative sugar manufacturing and export trade took off in the early 1450s. Sugar became the main driver of Madeira's economy and agriculture from the 1460s to the mid-seventeenth century.[10] Contrary to other sugar producing colonies, in late fifteenth-century Madeira, production was not organized in large plantations, but rather in small and medium landholdings belonging to 'a middling class of landowners with limited assets',[11] under a variety of contractual arrangements, including sharecropping and emphyteusis.

When the island's sugar trade succumbed to growing competition from the rest of the Atlantic complex, wine already had an incipient presence, and in the late sixteenth century exports were reported to India 'and many other parts of the world'.[12] Nevertheless, the actual Madeira wine industry only took off during the eighteenth century, supplying the worldwide British wine trade.[13] In this process, the *colonia* became the major institutional device for the creation of a new vineyard landscape.

The contract

The *colonia* was a customary tenancy that is likely to have evolved from recurrent contractual arrangements. In an open society, where winemakers and land-owners constantly interacted with merchants and seafarers from all over Europe, the influence of imported ideas cannot be ruled out, which, besides a common-ality of practical problems it addressed, might help explain some striking similarities with known contractual forms elsewhere in Europe.[14] The earliest written contracts known that were fully stipulated as *colonias* date from the mid-eighteenth century.[15]

The *colonia* was, firstly, a plantation contract, which provided incentives for the tenants (henceforth *colonos*) to plant and tend the vineyards and to build and keep the necessary infrastructure, in the form of property rights in the stipulated improvements and fines in case of non-compliance. Secondly, it was an eviction contract that could be terminated at will and, while in force, it was hereditary. Lastly, it was a share tenancy by which, as a rule, the main and accessory crops were shared in halves between the *colono* and the landlord, with no obligation of the latter to invest. In the predominant case of grapes, the rent would be half of the resulting must.

The planting of vineyards required considerable investments in vine stocks and labour, with deferred payback due to the growth and maturation period of the vines. When this was carried out on newly cleared land on the slopes, labour was required to build the stone walls supporting the terraced plots. The limited availability of capital in Madeira and the fragmentation of the plots, within a traditional agricultural system in which the main input, besides land, was the peasants' family labour, led landowners to offer the ownership of improvements as the major incentive for the *colonos* to clear new land and plant.[16] This contractual regime proved very effective in the economic context in which it developed, as the *colonos* responded by building and tending the vineyard landscape on which the commercial success of Madeira wines came to rest – a success it shared with several other plantation contracts for vines with the built-in incentive of entitling tenants to indemnification for improvements.[17] The rationale of the *colonia* arrangement was very similar to that of the *vigneronnage* in the Beaujolais, in which sharecropping was also 'linked to the production of better-quality wines, requiring the presence of a specialist wine-maker to supervise operations, and the need for a labour-intensive agriculture to provide the supply of suitable grapes'.[18]

The contract recombined in a new way some elements that were available in the institutional culture toolbox, namely the sharecropping principle of *parceria* and the principle of land improvement, which was a constituting element both for the early land grants in *sesmaria* and for emphyteusis. Improvements were partially compensated for in rent in the case of newly-planted vineyards, in which the landlords usually waived the share-rent for the first four years and reduced it to one third of the crop up to the sixth year. The main feature of *colonia*, however, was the *colonos'* ownership of the improvements they had carried out, provided that this had been authorized by the landlord. Because of this divided property, regional historians have suggested that the *colonia* had evolved from some form of emphyteusis or sub-emphyteusis at its outset.[19] However, in *colonia* there was no splitting of property between two layered domains over the same physical object, but rather the ownership by different persons of two distinct, albeit interdependent sets of objects: the land on the one hand, and the buildings and plants on the other.

The ownership of improvements was not considered as just a right to indemnity for expenditure on leaving, but rather as a right *in rem*. This much was clearly stated by the Funchal Town Hall in representation to the king in 1776: '[the *colonos*] are the owners of the plants, houses and barns',[20] and later a court ruling in 1859 invoked custom, to state that improvements 'are not considered as a right of estimation, but as a real right, [which is] resolvable . . .',[21] the last term meaning that landlords could buy them upon eviction, independently of the *colonos'* will, for an agreed price or one stipulated by a court. A *colono* wishing to leave might offer to sell the improvements directly to the landlord or to a newly incoming tenant, in which case the landlord might wish to enter into an amicable agreement to buy the improvements instead, usually to resell them to a new tenant.

The contract could be terminated at will by either party. Several factors colluded to its becoming, in practice, a long-term arrangement. Firstly, the landlords would have an interest in keeping good tenants whom they knew and trusted, as well as their families. The skills required for vine-growing and the tacit knowledge of the specific terrains in such a demanding environment certainly contributed to human asset specificity, which gave the landlords an interest in long-term cooperation with *colono* families who had proven their worth.[22] Moreover, due to asymmetrical information concerning the quantity and quality of the harvest, a *colonia* carried monitoring and supervision costs to prevent cheating, which the scattering of the plots increased. As in the Catalan *rabassa morta*, a sharecropping contract of indeterminate duration, and in which the sharecroppers owned the vines, gave landlords an economic interest in not overexploiting the tenants in the short run, which lowered the monitoring costs.[23] This was all the more reason for the landlords to invest on continued relationships, to build up 'a kind and confidential feeling . . . between the landlord and tenant', in the words of an English traveller who had made inquiries in Madeira in 1849.[24]

Secondly, the landlord could only evict by paying the *colono* the assessed price for the improvements. The higher the cost that improvements put on eviction, the more they curtailed the landlords' effective power to evict.[25] Supporting walls for terraces often made up a large part of the improvements' financial value, and, since they had to be maintained, added repairs made up for eventual depreciation. Fragmentation played a part in this as well, because improvements would often be divided among heirs. For instance, eviction court cases in the early twentieth century had to deal with one quarter of a house and half a kitchen, or from twelve to sixteen hundredths of assorted improvements.[26] Therefore, to the financial costs of buying the improvements and the transaction costs of assessing their value, further transaction costs accrued due to having to settle deals with multiple owners of shares in plants, walls, and buildings.

Thirdly, as land grew progressively scarce due to population growth, a *colono* would have few exit options. The rural economy provided little opportunity to make a living from wages – in 1847, there was a ratio of only one agricultural wage labourer to 4.6 farmers (many of whom would by then have been *colonos*).[27] Hence, the *colonos'* concern would be to keep as firm a hold as they could on the land, which gave them a powerful incentive to invest in long-standing relationships with their landlords, and to pile up improvements that might insure them against eviction.

In the economic context in which it was created, for both parties the *colonia* was an investment in future growth. Landlords expected to have their bundle of rights increased in land rent, by collecting half of the future produce, with, as a trade-off, a lesser control over the duration of the contract to the extent that the eviction costs would grow in proportion with the improvements made by the *colonos*. The latter expected their bundle to grow through the ownership of the improvements, the increase in the economic worth of the improved land, of which they would retain half the gross output, and the ability, either by consent or weak supervision, to allocate interstitial land to diversify crops.[28] Lastly, the *colonos* would expect the contract to be made more secure by rising eviction costs, as well as by the landlords' own interest in keeping tenants who had proved themselves.[29]

The critical parameters defining the effective distribution of economic (as opposed to simply legal) property rights,[30] and over which tensions, conflict and bargaining were more likely to arise, were the quota of share-rent versus inputs and the compliance with the quota when sharing the crops, and the control over the amount of legitimate improvements, the assessment of their value, and their subdivision through sale or inheritance. More fundamentally, the latter brought up the issue of the relationship between the different ownerships of the two juridically separate but physically interlocked sets of assets. Such tensions, which ran through the history of the contract, were enhanced by changing conjunctures of economic, agricultural and political circumstances in the course of the nineteenth century.

A changing context

As long as the prices for wine were high and the vineyards were forthcoming, the contract seems to have been rewarding enough for both parties. One contract in 1828, in which the *colono* had previously served as a farm hand under his landlord, suggests it could provide a step up the social mobility ladder.[31] Even though this is as yet a poorly researched hypothesis, the *colonia* may have provided a basis for the rise or consolidation of a middling peasant stratum. Latter-day testimonies speak of 'relatively wealthy' *colonos* in the heyday of the Madeira wine trade,[32] some of whom used their future crop shares as collateral for credit, in order to expand or reorganize their holdings by buying improvements from others. In 1848, the Civil Governor of Madeira sent a circular letter to the municipal administrators cautioning them about daily requests by farmers to take over leases of plots and improvements belonging to the Treasury from their current tenants, signalling the existence of competitive demand for improvements.[33] Even after the wine boom subsided, we can find probate inventories like that of a widow in 1863, which reveals considerable wealth in cattle, crops, and improvements in several plots belonging to different landlords.[34] Nevertheless, by the end of the nineteenth century the social and economic status of a *colono* was low, as expressly alleged by the defendants in a law-suit who refused to be called *colonos* once the court found against their pretension of being emphyteuts.[35]

Starting in the second quarter of the nineteenth century, Madeira experienced significant changes in its crop mix, due both to market circumstances and to plant pests and diseases. Vine growing began declining in the 1820s, as a drop in export prices led some producers to look for alternatives. Grapes still remained the main crop up until oidium struck in the early 1850s, and this kept causing losses until the late 1860s. Increases in the production costs and a sluggish external demand for wine dictated a revival of sugar cane production, in parallel with a slow and partial replanting of vines. The decline of the vineyards is patent in the makeup of the rents of an entail with a dispersed estate, which in the second quarter of the nineteenth century still received most of its share-rents in must, whereas during the second half of the century the shares in must were limited to a couple of localized areas, replaced in others with shares in sugar cane and even rents in money, where the crop was onions for export.[36]

From the late 1870s onwards, phylloxera broke out, once more driving up the cost of vine cultivation, concomitantly with a progressive decrease in the export price of Madeira wines. The ensuing changes in the crop mix and agricultural practice followed a trend towards both diversification and intensification, favoured by population growth and the resulting pressure on a virtually unchanged area of agricultural land. From 1864 to 1911, the number of twenty- to sixty-year-old men rose by over 23 per cent, and the area per male head dropped from 0.90 ha to 0.72 ha. Together this, with the fact that the steep slopes of much of the agricultural land prevented the use of animal traction, led to a labour-intensive trend.[37]

That was partly related to changing conditions in the contracts, concerning the enforcement of the landlords' control over accessory and often subsistence crops. In 1822, we can still find a large landowner ordering his steward to forbid the *colonos*' planting of vegetables in-between the vines.[38] The landlord's concern might be that such interstitial cultures would cause over-irrigation, thereby harming the main crop. However, allowing crop diversification in order to spread risk and provide for the tenant household's subsistence was often a requirement of viable sharecropping relationships.[39] This would have been even more the case after wine prices sank and diseases rendered the vines less productive. In a context of population growth, it became impossible to enforce the same degree of crop discipline and the landlords made more allowances for intensifying subsistence crops. Sometimes, this was associated with adjustments to the traditional contractual arrangements, such as in two contracts in 1873 in which different landlords authorized the *colonos* to plant potatoes, cabbage, or beans in-between the vines and waived their half-share in those crops for the first year, but in return did not waive the half-share of the must during the first four years.[40]

By 1911–1914, wine production had recovered to three and a half times the 1868–1869 pre-phylloxera volume, due to replanting with resistant American stocks and substantial inputs of pesticides, whereas the area covered by vineyards had actually decreased. There was a steep recovery of sugar cane, which quadrupled in production between 1862–1863 and 1910–1911, partly as a result of a protectionist policy for sugar from 1895 onwards, after it too had been decimated by pests and diseases during the 1880s. The shift to sugar cane encouraged cattle raising as well, because cane foliage provided forage and cattle supplied much-needed fertilizer for this crop. In roughly the same period, meat production increased by about one-third, while wheat gave way to potatoes as the main staple crop.[41]

Against this background of agricultural change, major political and juridical transformations also took place. After a troubled period beginning in 1820, a new constitutional monarchy was consolidated in Portugal in 1834. In tandem with political Liberalism, the regime change led to the creation of a new institutional framework for property up to the final enactment of a new Civil Code in 1867. Broad steps were taken along that path with the dismantling of the seigniorial regime, the sales of the Crown's and other national assets, and full disentailment in the 1860s. In the mid-nineteenth century, while the reform of the entails was still under way, contemporaries estimated free allodia at no more than one-tenth of the total agricultural land in Madeira. However, property was not overly concentrated, and a lot of the estates were quite small.[42]

Throughout the nineteenth century, there were many land transactions, which may have brought about some degree of change in the social makeup of the *colonia* landlords, and in those attempting to exit the contracts. According to our survey of court cases, up until the 1880s landlords initiating eviction lawsuits remained for the most part the nobility and the *Misericórdia*, a land-wealthy charity; from then onwards, the number of institutional landlords decreased and small landlords, some of whom were themselves farmers or were based in the same locations as the farms, increased proportionally. There was a trend since the 1880s for landlords to buy the improvements and terminate *colonias*, leading to a continued decline of this contract's weight in the island's agriculture, for reasons addressed elsewhere.[43]

Within this broad context of juridical and agricultural change and with falling prices for wine, sugar and wheat during the 1880s, debates took place at the regional and national levels on institutional reforms, as was common to many regions in Europe.[44] Such debates favoured the reform or the downright doing away with of the *colonia* contract, which however did not actually happen until several decades later.[45] Nevertheless, even in the absence of legal reform, all the changes above interplayed with the structural tensions inherent to the *colonia* in ways that affected the reciprocal roles and the power balance between the parties.

Throughout the remaining sections, we will look for evidence of those tensions and readjustments in written sources, such as contracts and court rulings. In a social system in which informal contracting largely predominated it is impossible for us to assess the effectiveness of formal contracts and case law in depicting current practices. In fact, it can be argued that written contracts might be used to escape custom and would therefore stipulate rules contrary to it.[46] Nevertheless, it seems plausible enough that such piecemeal adaptations, as they do reveal, may be read as the tip of an iceberg of ongoing changes and resistances to change.

Rent and supervision

During the expansion of the vineyards, the heavy half-share rent became a matter of contention.[47] In 1774, a group of *colonos* petitioned the king for the landlord's share in the output to be cut down to one-fourth, which was eventually denied.[48] No legal change took place during the whole period and, arguably, the rent burden became relatively lighter during the second half of the nineteenth century, once the landlords started to contribute with more inputs, as explained below. True to liberal principles, the Civil Code placed no boundaries on the rent quota when regulating share tenancies, leaving this entirely to 'what [the parties] agree amongst themselves'.[49]

In reply to the aforementioned petition, the previously-cited representation by the Funchal Town Hall in 1776 established a definite relationship between the high share-rent and the *colonos*' ownership of the improvements, arguing to the effect that the *colonos* had their investment and labour remunerated by earning property in real assets which 'they sell to whomever they wish when they leave the farm, or else the landlord pays for them if they are evicted'.[50]

While the wine industry was thriving, the value of the must and the improvements was high and certainly afforded liquidity. From the 1820s onwards, however, the depreciation of Madeira wines and the drop in exports was reflected in the price the shares of the must could fetch, significantly worsening the economic situation of both landlords and *colonos*. In times of hardship, supervision seems to have become more of an issue to both parties, and thereby a source for endemic conflict. In 1841, the overseer of a large estate complained to the landlord of suffering at the hands of 'malefactors', which is probably related to these issues.[51] It was reported in 1850 that overseers tending the landlords' interests, as well as resident landlords themselves, came under threat of violence against their persons and property, if they were too diligent in supervising the crops and their sharing.[52]

During the second half of the century, vine diseases severely devaluated the plants, not just in terms of production but as collateral for loans as well. This made the *colonos* more dependent on the landlords for short-term advancements, with likely repercussions on their contractual status. Even though by then the Civil Code had made the improvements mortgageable, a renowned reformer and publicist in Madeira reported in 1888 that the *colonos*' improvements were useless for accessing hypotecary bank credit.[53] Moreover, overcoming the oidium and especially the phylloxera outbreaks required capital outlays for replanting, whether with new vines or alternative crops, mostly sugar cane, and for the pesticides, fertilizers and irrigation water increasingly required, just when the *colonos*' ability to invest would have been at its lowest.[54]

Therefore, landlords with an interest in keeping their land productive and tenanted had to invest in capital inputs to a much larger extent than previously, well beyond their traditional obligations. Many landlords took loans at 10 to 12 per cent interest in order to invest.[55] This made them more concerned with supervising both the farming and the output. On the other hand, the *colonos*' capacity for resistance certainly subsided – possibly along with their customary legitimacy within the peasant communities – once they grew more dependent on the landlords' inputs and the effective sharing of costs became a permanent feature of the landlord-tenant relationship.

Controlling improvements

As we saw, it was in the *colonos*' interest to plant and build in order to accumulate capital in the form of improvements – which was indeed the point of the contract. Some deeds in the 1820s show that, as in other improvement contracts such as the most intensely studied ones in eastern Spain, the value of the *colonos'* improvements might also be useful to the landlords as collateral against default and rent arrears.[56] However, since improvements were also a power asset to secure the land, the *colonos'* interest to plant and build extended beyond the economic efficiency, which was in the landlords' interest as well, to become a matter of practical control over the rights in land, and therefore one in which the two groups' interests could become opposed. As with all such contracts, the power balance between the parties to control the improvements was decisive to their effective economic property rights over the land itself. High costs for buying improvements not only hindered the landlords' right to evict the tenants and to dispose of the land, but they also made it more difficult for the former to change the crops.[57]

The first written contracts stipulated that the *colonos* would only be entitled to useful improvements. In 1779, the island's government ruled that the *colonos* had to obtain the landlords' permission, otherwise, the improvements would be deemed superfluous or made in bad faith and the landlords would not be forced to buy them.[58] One month later, in a report to the Portuguese government, the governor (*Capitão-General*) explained this was meant to avoid the *colonos* building 'useless improvements, adorning the lands with unnecessary walls so that the landlords could not evict them without paying for the said improvements'.[59] A court ruling in 1853, which denied the landlord the right to withhold his consent to necessary repairs, shows that the liberal courts would not enforce that obligation to the letter, provided that the improvements were found to have been necessary.[60] Moreover, in a period of demographic growth and expanding urban sprawl, the daily supervision of permissions to build and establishing each disputed improvement's usefulness or (dis)proving the landlord's permission to build certainly would have been daunting tasks, and a never-ending source of conflict.

At a later stage, some landlords tried to control the *colonos'* improvements through contractual specifications, while on the other hand using selective authorization for improvements as a reward for cooperation in agricultural change. For instance, shortly after the enactment of the Civil Code in 1867, the administrator of an entailed estate changed a number of procedures in contracts, mostly with incumbent *colonos*. Specifically where he opted for planting sugar cane, besides co-participating in capital outlays he authorized the *colonos* to build houses and cattle stalls, using this as an extra incentive for the *colonos'* collaboration in changing crops.[61] During the 1880s and 1890s, however, he systematically placed such authorizations under a set of clearly specified restrictions, including measurements and materials to be used and the buying price for the houses being set in advance, regardless of later inflation.[62] A court case in 1875–1876, in which the judge ruled that some house walls be deducted from the *colono's* improvements because they belonged to the landlord, suggests that some landlords might also keep direct control over some of the improvements, either by taking on the costs themselves or by not reselling all those they had acquired from former *colonos*.[63]

Even before the Civil Code, the liberal courts began to reinterpret the customary contract by splitting the issues between the property of the improvements, on the one hand, and the tenancy contract, on the other, according to the more formally defined contractual template of the *parceria*. This played against the landlords' holding of the improvements as collateral for rent: in a court case in 1853, the judge ruled against the landlord by interpreting *colonia* strictly as a sharecropping contract. In sharecropping, he argued, tenants were legally required to farm the land according to the customs of the region, not 'to provide a deposit that serves as a guarantee of compliance . . . and insures the indemnification to the landlord'; to uphold the landlords' pretension would therefore violate the constitutional right that no citizen could be forced to do anything not required by law.[64] This legal understanding, later reinforced by the Civil Code, impaired whatever purview the landlords held on the *colonos'* improvements through debts.

However, the landlords' larger share in the inputs could provide a basis for adaptations in the contract that recovered the use of the improvements as collateral. In one previously-mentioned contract in 1867, in which the landlord provided funds as an advance for a sugar cane plantation, he required the *colono*, if he was unable to fulfil his obligations, 'to choose either to pay a fine in cash or to deliver his own improvements without opposition'. Similar arrangements were made in another contract by a different landlord in 1871.[65] In these instances, the landlords used their capital outlays, which the customary contract did not require them to provide, as leverage to adapt the formula of the *colonia* contract to their new role as investors.

Valuing improvements

Valuing the improvements obviously was another crucial issue. When, upon a tenant's leaving or eviction, the parties could not reach an agreement over the valuation, they resorted to the courts. The judges decided according to their prudent discretion, based on assessments by experts chosen by the parties and the court. The improvements were customarily assessed according to the state in which they were found.[66] Buildings were valued in terms of the estimated building costs, often involving craftsmen as assessment experts.[67] Vines were also valued for their intrinsic value, by pricing the number of stems according to quality, age and size. In 1822, the Madeira Board of the Portuguese Treasury valued *colonia* improvements in vines in those terms, instead of their estimated added value to the revenue of the land, as they should according to the Treasury's instructions. The Board alleged that otherwise vine plantations would cease, the supporting walls would no longer be kept and the whole island would be reduced to wastelands and rubble.[68]

The 1867 Civil Code, if applied to the letter, would have made this more complex. The rules for land lease tenancies, which applied to sharecropping as well, distinguished between, on the one hand, improvements consented to by the landlord in writing, or which were necessary and made by the tenant after legally citing the landlord for omission, and, on the other hand, improvements which the tenant had made without meeting those conditions, but which were proven to be necessary or useful. Upon contract termination, the tenant had the right to the intrinsic value of the improvements only in the former situations – which were rare, given the informality prevailing in *colonia* relationships, even though they became increasingly used during the second half of the nineteenth century. In the latter situations, the improvements were to be compensated according to the estimate of their added value to the annual income of the landholding.[69]

A draft law to regulate the *colonia* in the same year, pointed out that the second criterion would tip the existing balance in favour of the landlords.[70] However, where buildings and vines were concerned, the customary valuation criteria were never called into question in practical valuations. In one court case in the mid-1870s, the *colono* proposed a valuation of his improvements in view of an amicable resolution, which the landlord rejected. After the *colono* in turn rejected the second valuation carried out before the judge, the latter turned down his request for a third valuation. Accepting it, he argued, would go against 'the use and customs of the *colonia*', which were 'customary, adopted and followed in the courts'.[71]

The courts' use of custom in their rulings over the new problems posed by the changes in crops appears rather to have favoured the *colonos*. The same 1867 draft law, cited previously, defined a different valuation criterion for sugar cane plants, based on the cost of planting and not counting the intrinsic value of the ratoons. It was argued that, contrary to vines, a valuation based on counting the plants was 'absurdly prejudicial to the landlord', as the first cane production would by itself fully repay that expenditure.[72] In line with this argument, a landlord's lawyer in an eviction case in 1875, in which the planted ratoons accounted for a significant proportion of total valuation, alleged that because it needed periodical replanting, sugar cane 'served as a pretext ... to attribute fantastic values to improvements'.[73] Nevertheless, court rulings on eviction lawsuits such as this one show that judges kept valuing improvements in sugar cane according to the custom.

Interlocked assets and fragmented properties

Once a *colono*'s improvements – especially the plants – were transmitted to a third party, either through sale, forfeit or inheritance, the new owner succeeded in the right to use the productive assets. Since the land and the productive improvements were interlocked assets, a new owner of the whole or a part of those improvements acquired the former tenant's rights in the corresponding land, that is to say, to use it as the new *colono*. The landowners' right to choose tenants therefore depended either on them buying the improvements pre-emptively, acting as middlemen between leaving *colonos* and new ones of their choice; on using their power not to authorize sales as a way of imposing conditions regarding the buyers; or, lastly, on evicting the new owners by buying the improvements when they could not help but accept the transfers, as was the case with inheritances.

Given the ease with which the *colonos* could enter into informal agreements to transact improvements and use them as loan collaterals, surveillance was required, but all forms of controlling the entry of new *colonos* carried financial or transaction costs. Even so, before the Civil Code landlords could take action against undesired tenants, as a large landowner did in 1864, filing a lawsuit to expel a *colono* who had entered onto the land without making it known to him, as 'he was obliged to do'.[74] *Colonos* would circumvent the need for the landlords' consent by stipulating in sales contracts that the seller was liable for the buyer's losses, should the landlord refuse to acknowledge the sale.[75] Even though this certainly allowed for improvements to be sold outside the landlords' *ex ante* control, it came at a risk to the sellers, which still afforded the landlords some degree of *ex post* control.

An additional consequence of the interlocking of property rights in improvements and in land was the increasing morcellation of the landholdings. During the second half of the nineteenth century, in a context of population growth, increasing demand for land, and agricultural intensification, there was a trend for dividing up the property in improvements. When the new owner of a fraction of the planted improvements entered as a new *colono* in the corresponding land, effective landholding morcellation ensued. In the absence of legal rules stipulating otherwise for the inheritance of improvements, the landlords had no way of avoiding this unless they bought the improvements from the heirs. This is probably the reason for an eviction in 1875, in which the *colono* was a widow whose household included several children of marrying age.[76]

We have already explained how the fragmentation of the ownership of improvements checked the landlords' contractual power by raising the transaction costs of evictions, and as a consequence their economic rights regarding the land itself. Morcellation posed an additional threat to the economic viability of the *colonos*' households, and thereby to rent security, besides a further hindrance to crop changes. Not surprisingly, by the mid-nineteenth century checking the subdivision of improvements had become a major concern to those who favoured the landlords' interests and agricultural change. The most important attempt to achieve that was the draft law proposed in 1854 by a Portuguese MP and former Civil Governor of Madeira, which would have enacted the same impartibility rules that applied to the emphyteutic useful domain for the inheritance of *colonia* improvements.[77] However, even though the draft was voted favourably, the law was never actually passed.

The interlocking of properties in the *colonia* proved hard to conceptualize within the new liberal frame of mind. In 1855, an apparently perplexed Portuguese Home Secretary agreed with the proposal by the same MP to conduct an informal survey concerning the island's 'sort of agrarian legislation' in which 'the ideas of the property of the land and the property of the cultivator are singularly understood'.[78] In spite of all attempts to regulate it, however, the 1867 Civil Code ended up not acknowledging the *colonia* at all, as either a form of imperfect property or a specific type of contract.

Strictly speaking, according to the Code's abstract definitions the *colonia* would come under the general category of sharecropping contracts, to which applied most of the rules concerning land leases, including those regulating the indemnification for improvements.[79] The latter was defined as the tenants' right to be reimbursed upon contract termination of the expenditure they had made in improvements and repairs that had been formally asked or agreed upon by the landlords, or those that were proven to be necessary, provided the landlords had not done them after being formally notified. Expenditure on necessary or useful repairs not coming under the previous situations would not be reimbursed, but rather paid according to the estimated increase in land income resulting from them.[80] The improvements were conceived of as a sort of a loan to the landlords, and therefore they only constituted a property right for the tenants in the future indemnification value, not in the things themselves.

This, however, would not be applied to the *colonia*. At the regional level even the landlords, let alone the *colonos*, acknowledged the legitimacy both of the constituted property rights in the improvements under customary norms and of the customary contract itself, which moreover the liberal courts had validated over the previous decades. The state had further reinforced this by having improvements registered as property for tax purposes, by admitting them to collateralize debts to the Treasury, and by the Treasury leasing out those that it had come to own. Therefore, the formerly organic whole of the *colonia* became a composite beast, partly coming under contract law concerning the sharecropping and partly under property law concerning the improvements, and moreover overlaying within the latter the two distinct properties in land and in improvements. This is why in 1971 a property law scholar considered that the *colonia* was the most complex real right in the Portuguese juridical order.[81] In practice, legislative power left it to jurisprudence and future legislation to extricate all those components, which were inextricably enmeshed in the customary contract and in everyday practice, into 'perfect properties' and 'pure contract'. As we have seen, some court rulings had already been implementing this to deal with specific cases. However, dissecting these different components under the property conception of the Civil Code caused important changes in their balance.

The Civil Code defined perfect and imperfect property and enumerated the latter's forms, none of which applied to *colonia* improvements. Therefore, these were owned as perfect property, which 'consist[ed] in the enjoyment of all the rights included in the right of property', namely, those of 'fruition, transformation, exclusion and defence, restitution and indemnification, and alienation'. The only limitation to property in the improvements came from it being resolvable, which was defined as 'the property that, according to its constituting title, is subject to being revoked independently of the proprietor's will' and therefore was not 'absolute', albeit being 'perfect'.[82]

Barring the landowners' use of their right to evict by buying the improvements from the *colonos*', the latter could legally do with their property as they wanted, provided that they kept using the land and the improvements according to the terms of their contract. Under the newly institutionalized concept of property and the liberal design to unfetter free trade,[83] the landlords' customary rights to authorize sales and leases of improvements – which, difficult as they were to exert before, could still be used as deterrents and brought to justice as a last resort – were no longer tenable in court.[84] Moreover, the improvements became mortgageable property. As we have seen, under the social and economic circumstances in which the *colonia* operated, this largely removed what power the landlords previously had to choose tenants, and a freer market in improvements resulted in further morcellation of the landholdings.[85]

Since all this made the landlords' economic property rights increasingly slimmer, the *colonia* became less and less attractive to landowners, who furthermore were betting on alternative crops to vines. This certainly helps explain the contract gradually fading out of the agrarian contractual mix. However, because those changes increased the landlords' exit costs, they also can explain why, rather than because of some irrational atavism, the *colonia* seems to have outlived its effectiveness for so long. At the turn of the twentieth century, after evictions had been facilitated for emigrating *colonos*, we can still find the improvements being paid for by new entrants in the contracts, after the landlord had filed the eviction process.[86] This can be understood as one way for landlords to pass on the cost of terminating the existing contracts, thereby contributing to the survival of the *colonia*.

Finally, under the right of accession stipulated by the Civil Code, the assets accrued to a landowner's property by a tenant's work and belonging to the latter could be incorporated to the landed property by either the landowner buying them, if their value was inferior to that of the land, or the tenant buying the land if the value of the added assets was higher.[87] Even though at the moment we have no empirical corroboration for this, it seems a likely hypothesis that in cases of extreme morcellation of the landholdings the latter form of accession may have been both a landlord's way out of a puny contract and a tenant's way to become a small landowner. If such was the case, this could in turn partly explain the microfundia landholding structure that persists in Madeira to this day.[88]

Conclusions

The *colonia* has a long history of being looked at as an insular oddity, a contractual species which evolved out of feudal institutions and survived there because it served the exploitive landowners' interests. Contrary to this view, it seems clear to us that while, like all such customary arrangements, it did have its local singularities; in its essence the *colonia* was but one in a family of contracts that have developed in many different places across Europe, linked with the spread of vines and a market-oriented wine industry. If at some point the *colonia* came to be considered an unnatural mix of disparate contractual and property forms – our metaphorical platypus – that was because politicians, jurists and historians looked at it through the lenses of the liberal concepts of perfect property and contract, and forcing it into the legal rules enacted according to those concepts eventually did turn it into a platypus.

In Madeira, as elsewhere, this contract, while certainly affording large and small, full and emphyteutic landowners a half-share rent in valued commercial produce at low cost, proved a very effective incentive for peasants to invest labour, capital and skills to create a productive landscape, and it also seems to have provided opportunities for property accumulation and social mobility within the peasantry.

However, the contract's effectiveness during the eighteenth and the early nineteenth centuries hinged on two things. Firstly, on the high demand for Madeira wines in the global market. When this subsided and vine diseases hit in the course of the nineteenth century, the *colonia* entered a long period of crisis. Secondly, on the alignment of goals and incentives and the balance of power between landlords and tenants. The *colonos'* ownership of the improvements was of key importance to that power balance. The changes introduced in the property rules following the establishment of the liberal regime, culminating with the enactment of the Civil Code in 1867, altered this and from the landlords' perspective, they made the *colonia* increasingly inefficient in the face of changing economic opportunities.

The breakdown of those factors may explain the platypus's gradual extinction from the late eighteenth century onwards. Precisely how this extinction process came about, with what intensity over time, and to whose benefit still begs systematic research. The puzzle that motivated us here was rather that of understanding why and how the contract lasted for so long after it had become inefficient for the landlords.

We believe that the major cause underlying the contract's resilience was the high exit costs that the *colonos'* property in improvements imposed on landlords wishing to terminate the contracts to allocate the land otherwise. The customary contract structure had created those costs to begin with, but they were greatly enhanced by the *colono*'s accumulation and subdivision strategies, by the action of the courts in upholding customary valuation procedures while at the same time enforcing new legal rules of contract and property, and by the liberal rules themselves which 'perfected' the *colono*'s property away from the landlords' control. The element of path dependence in this process, which made the customary contract more resilient to change, seems to have been caused not by the landowning elite appropriating the institutional changes, but largely by those changes having disempowered the customary property rights of the landlords.

This does not mean that the *colonia* remained static. While the *colonos*, often supported by the courts, held on to whatever customary and legal rules which empowered them, the landlords – at least those with more resources – to the extent that they were stuck with the *colonia*, imposed stricter limits on improvements and used selective authorizations, along with their higher participation in inputs, to reward the *colonos'* collaboration in changing crops. The platypus may well have been doomed from the moment of its inception by the liberal property laws. However, while the beast survived, it had to be tamed.

Acknowledgements

While this chapter resulted from collaborative writing, all credits for the empirical research belong to Benedita Câmara. We thank Samuel Garrido for letting us have the final manuscript of his cited article 'Sharecropping was sometimes efficient', which has just been accepted for publication in *Economic History Review*.

Notes

1 S. Garrido, 'Sharecropping was sometimes efficient: Sharecropping with compensation for improvements in European viticulture', *Economic History Review* (forthcoming).
2 R. Congost, *Tierras, Leyes, Historia: Estudios Sobre la 'Gran Obra de la Propiedad'* (Barcelona: Crítica, 2007); F. Fortunet, 'Uniformité du droit et usages locaux: L'économie juridique des contrats agraires en France au XIXe siècle', in G. Béaur, M. Arnoux and A. Varet-Vitu (eds), *Exploiter la Terre: Les Contrats Agraires de l'Antiquité à nos Jours: Actes du Coloque de Caen (10–13 Septembre 1997)* (Rennes: Association d'Histoire des Sociétés Rurales, 2003), pp. 167–220.
3 B. Câmara, 'The Portuguese Civil Code and the colonia tenancy contract in Madeira (1867–1967)', *Continuity and Change*, 21:2 (2006), pp. 213–33.
4 Decreto-Lei no. 47937 (15 September 1967); Decreto de Aprovação da Constituição de 10 de Abril (10 April 1976), Art. 101 par. 2; Lei no. 77/77 (29 September 1977), Art. 55.
5 For example, the papers read in a meeting in 2007 organized by the Communist MPs in the Regional Parliament of Madeira, in J. Lizardo (ed.), *Caseiros e Senhorios nos Finais do Século XX na Madeira: O Processo de Extinção da Colonia* (Porto: Afrontamento, 2009), among many other such initiatives, press articles and pamphlets; Supremo Tribunal de Justiça, Case no. 592/03.2TCFUN.S1, at www.dgsi.pt/jstj.nsf/954f0ce6ad9dd8b980256b5f003fa814/2dc8ea8cf229d2fd80257810005eca2b?OpenDocument [last accessed 10 March 2016].
6 J. M. Azevedo e Silva, *A Madeira e a Construção do Mundo Atlântico (Séculos XV–XVII)* (Funchal: Secretaria Geral de Turismo e Cultura, Centro de Estudos de História do Atlântico, 1995), pp. 25–35; V. M. Godinho, 'Portugal and the making of the Atlantic world: Sugar fleets and gold fleets, the seventeenth to the eighteenth centuries', *Review: Fernand Braudel Center*, 28:4 (2005), pp. 313–37.
7 Azevedo e Silva, *Madeira*, pp. 59–61, 70–7.
8 V. Rau, *Sesmarias Medievais Portuguesas* (Lisbon: Presença, 1982). J. V. Serrão and E. Rodrigues also refer to *sesmarias* in chapter one. (Editors' note.)
9 Concerning the improvement principle underlying emphyteusis, see A. M. Cordeiro, 'Da enfiteuse: Extinção e sobrevivência', in J. Miranda (ed.), *Estudos em Homenagem ao Prof. Doutor Martim de Albuquerque*, vol. 1 (Lisbon: Faculdade de Direito da Universidade de Lisboa, 2010), pp. 101–29, on pp. 108–10.
10 Azevedo e Silva, *Madeira*, pp. 237–9, 245–75; V. M. Godinho, *Os Descobrimentos e a Economia Mundial* (Lisbon: Presença, 1987), vol. 3, pp. 221–3, 232–7, 248; vol. 4, pp. 73–83.
11 V. Rau and J. de Macedo, *O Açúcar na Madeira nos Fins do Século XV: Problemas de Produção e Comércio* (Funchal: Junta Geral do Distrito Autónomo do Funchal, 1962).
12 G. Frutuoso, *As Saudades da Terra pelo Doutor Gaspar Fructuoso* [book II]: *Historia das Ilhas do Porto-Sancto, Madeira, Desertas e Selvagens: Manuscripto do Seculo XVI Annotado por Alvaro Rodrigues de Azevedo* [. . .] (Funchal: Typ. Funchalense, 1873), p. 113.
13 A. B. Cardoso, 'Os vinhos macios e a História', *Douro: Estudos & Documentos*, 8:16 (2003), pp. 39–53, on pp. 46–7.
14 For a review, see Garrido, 'Sharecropping'.
15 Azevedo e Silva, *A Madeira*, pp. 198–9; Sousa, *História Rural da Madeira*, pp. 345 and 354. *Colonia* contracts dated 1756 and 1757 in Arquivo Nacional/Torre do Tombo: Convento de Santa Clara, Funchal, PT/TT/CSCF/008/0013, fls 164v and 176; PT/TT/CSCF/010/0008.
16 J. V. Serrão, 'Land management responses to market changes: Portugal, seventeenth – nineteenth centuries', in V. Pinilla (ed.), *Markets and Agricultural Change in Europe from the Thirteenth to the Twentieth Century* (Turnhout: Brepols, 2009), pp. 47–73, on pp. 54–5.

17 J. Carmona and J. Simpson, 'The "rabassa morta" in Catalan viticulture: The rise and decline of a long-term sharecropping contract, 1670s–1920s', *Journal of Economic History*, 59:2 (1999), pp. 290–315, on pp. 294–6; R. Congost, J. Planas, E. Saguer and E. Vicedo, '¿Quién transformó la agricultura catalana?: Los campesinos como actores del cambio agrario en Cataluña, Siglos XVIII–XX', in R. Robledo (ed.), *Sombras del Progreso: Las Huellas de la Historia Agraria* (Barcelona: Crítica, 2010), pp. 171–97, on pp. 176–80; Garrido, 'Sharecropping', Table 2; L. Lorenzetti, 'Property relations, socio-economic change and the state: The Valtellina in the nineteenth century', in G. Béaur, P. R. Schofield, J.-M. Chevet and M. T. Pérez Picazo (eds), *Property Rights, Land Markets and Economic Growth in the European Countryside (Thirteenth–Twentieth Centuries)* (Turnhout: Brepols, 2013), pp. 179–94, on pp. 181–2.
18 J. Carmona and J. Simpson, 'Explaining contract choice: Vertical coordination, sharecropping, and wine in Europe, 1850–1950', *Economic History Review*, 65:3 (2012), pp. 887–909, on p. 901.
19 Azevedo, note XIV to Frutuoso, *Saudades da Terra*, p. 472.
20 Arquivo Histórico Ultramarino, Lisbon, Madeira e Porto Santo (hereinafter AHU), (box 2: doc. 449), Representação da Câmara do Funchal, 24 May 1776.
21 J. P. Sanches e Castro, *Sentenças de um Juiz de Direito* (Lisbon: Typographia do Panorama), pp. 130–1.
22 Carmona and Simpson, 'Explaining contract choice', pp. 892, 896, 899.
23 Carmona and Simpson, 'Rabassa morta', pp. 292–3.
24 G. Peacock, 'The agriculture and the tenure of land', in *A Treatise on the Climate and Meteorology of Madeira; by the Late J. A. Mason [. . .]: To which Are Attached A Review of the State of Agriculture and of the Tenure of Land; by George Peacock [. . .]* (London: John Churchill, and Liverpool: Deighton and Laughton, 1850), pp. 227–84, on p. 261.
25 S. Garrido and S. Calatayud, 'The price of improvements: Agrarian contracts and agrarian development in nineteenth-century eastern Spain', *Economic History Review*, 64:2 (2011), pp. 598–620, on p. 610.
26 Arquivo Regional da Madeira (hereinafter ARM), Judiciais (box 890: doc. 5), 1900–1901; ARM (2599:8), 1924–1929.
27 The figures as reported by the governor were 20,253 farmers, 4,404 labourers and 1,153 landowners. 'Classificação da população por géneros de indústria, profissões, Mesteres & c.' [1847], in S. D. de Menezes (ed.), *Uma Época Administrativa da Madeira e Porto Santo, a Contar do Dia 7 de Outubro de 1846*, vol. 2 (Funchal: Typographia Nacional, 1860).
28 B. Câmara, *A Economia da Madeira (1850–1914)* (Lisbon: Imprensa de Ciências Sociais, 2002), p. 113 and footnote 205.
29 For the analytical framework this summary draws on, see R. Santos and J. V. Serrão, 'Property rights, social appropriations and economic outcomes: Agrarian contracts in southern Portugal in the late-eighteenth century', in Béaur *et al.*, *Property Rights*, pp. 475–94, on p. 471.
30 Y. Barzel, *Economic Analysis of Property Rights* (Cambridge: Cambridge University Press, 1997), p. 4.
31 ARM, Notários, 1649, fl. 28.
32 A. C. Heredia, *Observações Sobre a Situação Económica da Ilha da Madeira e a Reforma das Alfândegas* (Lisbon: Typ. Mattos Moreira, 1888), p. 4.
33 Menezes, *Uma Epoca Administrativa*, vol. 1 (Funchal: Typographia Nacional, 1849), pp. 276–8.
34 ARM (TCSCR-10-2: mç.18), Inventário Orfanológico, 5 March 1863.
35 ARM, Judiciais (238:1), 1897–1903.
36 ARM, Família Ornelas e Vasconcelos (hereinafter FOV), several boxes.
37 Câmara, *Economia da Madeira*, pp. 89–91, 103–20.

38 ARM, Notários, 1591, fl. 34.
39 Carmona and Simpson, 'Explaining contract choice', p. 890.
40 ARM, Notários, 822, fl. 20 and 849, fl. 26.
41 Câmara, *Economia da Madeira*, pp. 303–4.
42 According to the governor José Silvestre Ribeiro in 1850. Menezes, *Uma Epoca Administrativa*, vol. 2.
43 Câmara, 'Portuguese Civil Code'.
44 J. F. M. Swinnen, 'Political reforms, rural crises, and land tenure in Western Europe', *Food Policy*, 27:4 (2002), pp. 371–94, on p. 382.
45 B. Câmara, 'The colonia contract: Ambiguity between sharecropping, fixed-rent and emphyteusis', in R. Congost, G. Béaur and P. Luna (eds), *Almost Landowners: Emphyteusis and Other Long-term Practices in Europe (16th–20th centuries)* (Turnhout: Brepols, forthcoming); A. C. Heredia, *Observações sobre a Situação Económica da Ilha da Madeira e sobre a Reforma das Alfândegas* (Lisboa: Typographia Mattos Moreira, 1888); *Inquérito Sobre a Situação Económica da Ilha da Madeira e Medidas Convenientes para a Melhorar Ordenado por Decreto de 31 de Dezembro de 1887* (Lisbon: Imprensa Nacional, 1888), pp. 23, 129–32; H. F. F. Valle, *A Revolta da Madeira e a Comissão de Inquérito: Breves Considerações e Apontamentos* (Funchal: Typografia Funchalense, 1888); M. J. Vieira, *Discurso Pronunciado na Camara dos Senhores Deputados na Sessão de 7 de Julho de 1888* (Funchal: Typographia do Direito), p. 19.
46 Garrido, 'Sharecropping'.
47 In comparable contracts, the share-rent was usually lower than this, at between one sixth and one third of the crop. Garrido, 'Sharecropping'; Carmona and Simpson, 'Rabassa morta', p. 297.
48 AHU, (3:418). The *colonos'* representation, dated 1773, was actually sent on 1 March 1774.
49 *Codigo Civil Portuguez Approvado por Carta de Lei de 1 de Julho de 1867* (Lisbon: Imprensa Nacional, 1867), Art. no. 1299.
50 AHU (2:449), Representação; Câmara, 'Portuguese Civil Code', p. 222.
51 ARM, FOV (17:2), Letter to the landlord, 22 December 1841.
52 Peacock, *Review*, pp. 260–1.
53 Heredia, *Observações*, pp. 16–18.
54 ARM, FOV (18:10).
55 Heredia, *Observações*, p. 7.
56 ARM, Notários, 1649, fls 82 and 89; S. Garrido, 'Improve and sit: The surrendering of land at rents below marginal product in nineteenth-century Valencia, Spain', in C. Hanes and S. Wolcott (eds), *Research in Economic History*, vol. 29 (Bingley: Emerald, 2013), pp. 97–144, on p. 110; Garrido and Calatayud, 'Price of improvements', pp. 609–10.
57 Câmara, 'Portuguese Civil Code', p. 229; Garrido and Calatayud, 'Price of improvements', 615.
58 AHU (Avulsos: 4), Governor's Letter, 22 October 1779.
59 Officio do Capitão-General João Gonçalves da Câmara Coutinho ao Governo do Reino, 18 November 1779, cited in Azevedo e Silva, *Madeira*, p. 200.
60 Castro, *Sentenças*, pp. 72–3.
61 ARM, FOV (18:10).
62 ARM, FOV (13: mç. 45–7, 52, 54, 57–9, 61–3), 1880–1900.
63 ARM, Judiciais (833:19).
64 Castro, *Sentenças*, p.76.
65 ARM, FOV (18:10), 1867; ARM, Notários, 3620, fl. 6v, 1871.
66 Castro, *Sentenças*, pp. 130–1.
67 Castro, *Sentenças*, pp. 40–4; for example, ARM, Judiciais (674: 21), 1857.

68 AHU (XIX:6476), Representação da Junta da Fazenda Nacional da Madeira ao Congresso, 30 March 1822.
69 *Codigo Civil Portuguez*, Arts no. 1303, 1611, and 1614–15.
70 J. R. Trindade e Vasconcellos and J. A. d'Almada, *Projecto de Lei Regulamentar do Contrato de Colonia ou Parceria Agricola na Ilha da Madeira* (Funchal: Typographia da Gazeta da Madeira, 1867), p. 35.
71 ARM, Judiciais (374–A:10).
72 Trindade e Vasconcellos and d'Almada, *Projecto de Lei*, p. 36.
73 ARM, Judiciais (374–A:10).
74 ARM, Judiciais (674:16), 1864–65.
75 Câmara, 'Portuguese Civil Code', p. 227.
76 ARM, Judiciais (374–A:10).
77 Draft law proposed by José Silvestre Ribeiro MP, *Diário da Câmara dos Senhores Deputados* (17 March 1854); Câmara, 'Ambiguity'.
78 Rodrigo Fonseca Magalhães, Ministro do Reino, *Diário da Câmara dos Senhores Deputados* (25 February 1855).
79 *Codigo Civil Portuguez*, Arts no. 1299–332, 1606–22, and 1627–32.
80 *Codigo Civil Portuguez*, Arts no. 1611 and 1614–15.
81 J. A. Ascensão, *Direitos Reais* (Lisbon: Minerva, 1971), p. 513.
82 *Codigo Civil Portuguez*, Arts no. 2168, 2171, and 2187–9, quotes from Arts no. 2187 and 2171.
83 A. M. Hespanha, 'Instituições e quadro legal', in P. Lains and A. F. Silva (eds), *História Económica de Portugal*, vol. 2 (Lisbon: Imprensa de Ciências Sociais, 2005), pp. 421–46, on pp. 421–5.
84 Câmara, 'Portuguese Civil Code', pp. 225–8.
85 Concerning the relationship between perfect land markets and morcellation, see B. M. S. Campbell, 'Land markets and morcellation of holdings in pre-Plague England and pre-Famine Ireland', in Béaur *et al.*, *Property Rights*, pp. 197–218.
86 ARM, Judiciais (906:17), 1903–4.
87 *Codigo Civil Portuguez*, Art. no. 2306.
88 According to the *Statistical Yearbook of Região Autónoma da Madeira 2013* (Funchal: Direcção Geral de Estatística da Madeira, 2014), p. 233, the average agricultural surface per landholding is 0.4 hectares, by far the lowest in Portugal, with the highest agricultural productivity per land surface and the lowest per labour unit. Available at http://estatistica.gov-madeira.pt/index.php/download-now/multitematicas-pt/mutitematicas-anuario-pt/multitematicas-anuario-publicacoes-pt/finish/196-anuario-publicacoes/3080-anuario-estatistico-da-ram-2013 [last accessed 10 March 2016].

6 Demythologizing and de-idealizing the commons

Ostrom's eight design principles and the irrigation institutions in eastern Spain

Samuel Garrido

Introduction

In *Governing the Commons*, one of the most thought-provoking books ever written on common property, economic institutions or cooperation, Elinor Ostrom drew on a broad sample of local cases for empirical information to base her theory about the conditions required for successful collective action.[1] Among those cases were four irrigation communities in eastern Spain (Valencia, Alicante, Murcia and Orihuela), and from then on Spanish *huertas* began to be mentioned quite frequently in the international literature on the commons and the management of natural resources.[2]

However, as we shall see below, much of the Spanish historical scholarship on irrigation systems has cast doubt on the accuracy of the accounts she relied on, portraying them as a sort of idealized myth. The purpose of this chapter is to reassess the analytical usefulness of the theory in the light of actual social practice, as revealed by historical evidence.

In Ostrom's terms, the areas of irrigated farmland where a collective right exists to use water fall under the concept of 'common pool resource'. This applies to commonly used resource systems, either natural or man-made, which are large enough to make it difficult (though not impossible) for those with the right to use them in common to monitor how they are used.

Ostrom took great care in distinguishing between the commonly used resource *system* and the resource *units* which flow from the system and cannot be used in common. When a given amount of water from a common pool is used to irrigate an individual user's field it ceases to be available to other users, just as a fish caught by an individual fisherman in a common fishery is no longer available to other fishermen. The process by which someone uses resource units for their own particular benefit is called 'appropriation' and that person is an 'appropriator'. On the other hand, any contribution towards replenishing the resource system and preventing its deterioration is a 'provision', and someone who makes such a contribution is a 'provider' of a common good. Thus, any single individual can act as an appropriator, a provider, or both.

Appropriation and provision underlie two sorts of collective action problems that may lead to a so-called tragedy of the commons.[3] Appropriation problems arise from the absence of strict rules to avoid overuse and effective mechanisms to ensure compliance, because in that case each individual appropriator has an incentive to overexploit the common pool, with the collective result of depleting it. If each user of scarce irrigation water from a common source believes other users will irrigate without restraint, all will tend to irrigate above the source's replenishing capacity, since by restraining use unilaterally each one would forgo present appropriation, while still suffering from future droughts caused by others. Provision problems arise from the fact that providing common goods (such as, for instance, cleaning irrigation canals) involves costs to providers, yet the resulting goods are made available to all regardless of each one's individual contribution. Each individual who cannot be excluded as an appropriator will, therefore, shirk from acting as a provider and be motivated instead to free-ride the public goods provided at the cost of others, resulting in an undersupply of collective action and the resulting public goods.[4]

In order to curb appropriation and provision problems, and to preserve the common resources, it becomes necessary to design and implement norms, monitor behaviour and enforce compliance. All these pose a collective action problem as well, since they too involve time and effort-consuming activities to produce common goods. Hence, the belief by early collective action theorists that the users of a shared resource would hardly be likely to provide and enforce common norms by themselves.

These sets of problems are obviously intertwined and if they were generally true, then 'tragedies of the commons' could only be avoided either by privatizing the commons or by the state managing them. Contrary to these assumptions, Ostrom's theoretical argument unfolds in the first two chapters of *Governing the Commons* to demonstrate that supervision costs will tend to be lower when the common system users, rather than an external authority, carry out monitoring and enforcement for themselves, provided that the rules were collectively designed by the users to begin with and can be adjusted by collective deliberation. The book goes on to compare a considerable number of empirical cases of institutions set up by communities of users to regulate common pool resources. Some, like the Spanish irrigation communities, were successful and have survived for a long time, affording individuals enduring access to common resources sustained by collective action, despite operating in contexts in which the temptation to adopt non-cooperative behaviour is always present. Others were not as successful. She compared those cases systematically in order to sort out the conditions underlying their success or failure, and to thereby enrich her theory.

Ostrom's team collected the empirical evidence from:

> case studies written by historians, anthropologists, engineers, political scientists, economists, and other social scientists and started the challenging task of coding them systematically in the common-pool resources (CPR) database

housed at the Workshop in Political Theory and Policy Analysis at Indiana University'.[5]

Data on the Spanish irrigation communities were provided by case studies by Thomas Glick and mostly by Arthur Maass and Raymond L. Anderson.[6] These are high-quality works that, nevertheless, put forward some controversial interpretations. As a result, Ostrom took it for granted that the Spanish cases offered a set of circumstances that most Spanish specialists on this topic claim were not in fact present, such as internal democracy and the collective capacity of the irrigators to change and adapt their norms.[7] However, during the last few years the scholarship on Spanish irrigation systems has become more responsive to Ostrom's outlook and nuanced some of the previous reservations, as evidenced by many of the papers given to a recent congress.[8]

Ostrom famously identified eight 'design principles' – meaning empirically reported good practices systematized *ex post*, rather than blueprints existing *ex ante* – that tended to underlie successful institutions.[9] In order to contribute to the ongoing reassessment of her take on Spanish irrigation institutions, the eight sections that follow in turn contrast each of these 'design principles' with historical evidence on actual social practice in eastern Spanish *huertas*. The concluding section sums up the findings: the complexity of these historical institutions and the actual social practices surrounding them do belie some of the empirical generalizations that supported Ostrom's design principles, and some idealized interpretations built on them. Nonetheless, the theory retains its heuristic potential as a challenging tool for historical analysis.

First principle: Clearly defined boundaries

Individuals or households who have rights to withdraw resource units from the CPR [Common Pool Resource] must be clearly defined, as must the boundaries of the CPR itself.[10]

If the resource units in a common pool are in wide demand and in unrestrained, free-for-all access, the common pool will tend to be overexploited. Therefore, defining the boundaries of the common pool and clearly specifying who can appropriate its resources is a necessary, albeit not sufficient, condition to achieve its sustainable management. In the irrigation communities in eastern Spain, the common pool of water is defined by the amount of water available at any given moment from the sources under each community's control, mostly consisting of rivers and also sometimes of springs and wells.

The boundary of appropriators, on the other hand, was almost always defined indirectly. The most usual arrangement was that all who owned land within the irrigated *huerta*, and they alone, partook of the right to appropriate water from the common pool. The amount of water allocated to each particular plot was free, and it could only be used to irrigate that same plot; it could neither be traded nor given away. Since private property rights in land were the gauge for the private appropriation of water, the set of legitimate appropriators was delimited by the territorial boundaries of irrigable land. In a few communities though, such as in Alicante and Elche, the right to appropriate water was allocated directly to individuals or households. Some landowners on the *huerta* might hold no rights in water, and conversely some owners of rights in water might own no land in the *huerta*, which eventually gave rise to local markets trading private rights in common water.[11]

If a community widened its irrigated *huerta*, this would expand the private demand for water, while not affecting the boundaries of the common pool itself and, therefore, the total available supply. The wider the irrigated area in the *huerta*, the less water there was per unit of surface area, and the more frequent and intense the conflicts between irrigators became during times of drought. In order to prevent the system from collapsing, some buffering device was needed to control total demand during shortages. This is probably why most communities were very conservative concerning the size of their *huertas*.[12] However, this did not mean that those boundaries remained unchanged in the long run.

On the one hand, in those communities where the rights in water were separate from those in land and a market in water had developed, those appropriators who were not actual users became market brokers between the common supply pool and the effective demand of users who had to buy the water they needed. Under these conditions, for a part of the appropriators the relative scarcity of water would be an incentive rather than a deterrent to enlarge the irrigated area, and the way this turned out would depend on the relative power such brokers had in the community to affect the boundary rules.[13] I will come back to this point.

On the other hand, even in the majority of communities where the appropriation of water was tied to land it was only apparently that the irrigated areas remained unaltered for centuries. Take the *huertas* irrigated by the river Mijares in the district of La Plana, administered by five irrigation communities – one of which being the community of Castellón, studied by Glick – and those irrigated by the river Turia in Huerta de Valencia – studied by Glick and by Maass and Anderson. When the communities of La Plana reached an agreement on the distribution of the flow of the river Mijares in 1346, each settled a maximum area for their *huertas*. This was officially recorded as the actual irrigated area for centuries to come. However, the areas actually irrigated by each community in 1346 were well below that limit, which was eventually only attained by the mid-nineteenth century.[14] Something similar happened in Huerta de Valencia, which was administered by eight communities.[15] Prior to the nineteenth century, in most communities in eastern Spain there was land within the theoretical limits of the *huertas* that, in practice, did not confer rights in water.[16]

Bearing in mind that the monetary returns from one hectare of irrigated land were four or fivefold those from one hectare employed for dry-farming, and that once the major canal was in place, expanding irrigation was normally a relatively simple and cheap undertaking, it is safe to assume that some form of institutional restriction kept the area actually irrigated from growing faster, although unfortunately, we do not know how that worked. But in spite of restrictions, quite often the irrigated areas kept growing, almost always as the result of the ongoing piecemeal encroaching of secondary canals in periods of more relaxed surveillance, which created 'practical appropriators', which were eventually legalized after going to the courts to have their acquired rights recognized.[17] But as the next section will show, it is not obvious that there would be a strong positive correlation between the size of the irrigated *huertas* and their productivity, at least before river flows became regulated by dams and reservoirs.

Second principle: Congruence between appropriation and provision rules and local conditions

> Appropriation rules restricting time, place, technology, and/or quantity of resource units are related to local conditions and to provision rules requiring labour, materials, and/or money.[18]

It seems safe to state that, when drawing up their ordinances, Spanish irrigation communities attempted to adapt the rules governing their use of water to the specific local circumstances in which they operated. Even so, the resource was managed in some communities better than in others. I will pay special attention to the three cases considered by Ostrom, namely Valencia, Murcia-Orihuela and Alicante.

Maass and Anderson concluded that the efficiency of the institutional management of water was correlated with the toughness of the environmental conditions. According to them, the relative abundance in Huerta de Valencia created no incentive to save on water; when it was their turn to irrigate, farmers could use as much as they wanted, provided they did not waste it. In Murcia-Orihuela, with greater scarcity than Valencia, the communities responded with the *tanda* procedure that assigned a number of minutes of water flow to each plot, in proportion to its surface area. Lastly, extreme scarcity in Alicante had led to one of those situations in which the right to appropriate water was separate from land ownership and was traded in a market, which according to Maass and Anderson was the most efficient institutional method to deal with scarcity.

Historical evidence rather turns upside down this kind of challenge–response explanation. It was not the eleven cubic metres per second, carried by the river Turia in summer, that made water relatively abundant in Huerta de Valencia, allowing more flexible and seemingly less efficient rules, but rather the strict rule decided and implemented by the community that the maximum irrigable surface area should remain small in relation to the river flow rate, at about 10,500 hectares, taking into account the availability of water in the frequent periods of moderate scarcity. Similar limits were in place in all the large irrigation communities in the provinces of Valencia and Castellón. Around 1900, the average 8.7 m³ per second, which the river Mijares carried in summer in La Plana, were used to irrigate some 10,000 hectares. Although such precautions did not prevent the occasional violent dispute among irrigators,[19] overall they did mitigate the degree of conflict. During severe droughts, the *tanda* procedure was enforced in Huerta de Valencia as well, but in regular times the community institutions allowed farmers to use the water with a great deal of flexibility, which was very important in an agriculture based on the rotation of many different crops with a wide range of needs in terms of water.

In contrast, Murcia–Orihuela had rather extended *huertas* in relation to the amount of water available. With a flow rate of between eight and nine cubic metres per second, in the late nineteenth century the river Segura irrigated around 11,000 hectares in Murcia and 19,000 hectares in Orihuela. It was this disproportion that created relative scarcity, which 'condemned' a substantial part of the irrigated land in Orihuela to crops that did not require large amounts of water.[20] Paradoxically, the scarcity was the result of an adaptive response to the physical surroundings. Part of the land in Murcia–Orihuela rests upon an impermeable layer of clay that hindered irrigation water filtering down into the soil. Because of that, a network of drainage ditches was needed in order to prevent salinization and waterlogging. The surplus water collected by this drainage system was then used to irrigate a relatively large surface area – 20 per cent of the *huerta* of Murcia and 30 per cent of that of Orihuela.[21]

It is likely that the peripheral areas irrigated in this way were included in the *huerta* as a by-product of the sustainability of its core. But this would then be an exception which still begs historical explanation. Communities elsewhere, as for instance in Huerta de Valencia, usually did not allow peripheral fields irrigated with surplus water to become institutionalized as part of their irrigated *huertas*, making it quite clear that they had no right to water in periods of drought. Moreover, in order to prevent disputes during droughts, they only allowed surplus water to be used on peripheral land that had access to alternative irrigation sources such as wells and springs.

Lastly, the major cause of water scarcity in the *huerta* of Alicante was its disproportionate size relative to the common water pool:[22] the 0.26 m^3 per second carried on average by the extremely irregular river Montnegre (theoretically 0.5 m^3 per second after the Tibi dam was built in 1594) provided water for 3,600 hectares. This was not the only irrigation community with a water market in which the water to land ratio was very low. With a flow rate of one m^3 per second, the Guadalentín irrigated 11,000 hectares in Lorca in the early twentieth century, and the Vinalopó irrigated 12,000 hectares in Elche with no more than 0.36 m^3 per second. Initially, the right to appropriate water in these communities had been tied to land ownership as well. It may well be that their irrigated *huertas* were too large to begin with, but everything points to it only being *after* the rights in water were assigned individually and a market was set up that the *huertas* began to grow out of all proportion. It was the appropriators, usually economically and politically powerful people, who pressed for the expansion of the irrigable area to increase effective demand and hence the price of the water that they brokered, while at the same time actively opposing the creation of alternative supplies such as wells. This gave rise to an extensive and undersupplied irrigated area that was mainly used for crops such as cereals, vines, olives and carob trees, cultivated with low intensity. Far from being the most efficient institutional response to water scarcity, the development of a market in water at least partially caused this.[23]

In short, institutions did not simply arise as efficient responses to scarcity, and it appears that not all irrigation communities adapted the usage of their water to the surroundings with equally good results. Nevertheless, there are no reports of poor adaptation having led to the disappearance of a community.

As regards the congruence between the rules of appropriation and provision, Ostrom believed the major issue to be that of the proportional contribution by each participant towards the upkeep of the system, relative to the resource units that they appropriate, or 'fiscal equivalence'.[24] Without such equivalence, those who contribute in excess will feel exploited and tend to display a low level of compliance with the rules, which in turn can lead to a cascade of violations. Given this, those who use the most water should contribute to maintenance costs correspondingly, and Ostrom made it a particular point to state that this occurred in all instances of the Spanish *huertas*.[25]

But this was not really the case in Valencia. It is true that common expenses each year were shared among the owners of land in the *huertas* in proportion to the surface they owned and consequently to the amount of water they were *entitled* to. But those who appropriated the most water were not necessarily those who contributed the most, because the amount per hectare charged for a plot that had not been irrigated at all was the same as for one that had been irrigated twenty times or more. In some communities like those in Borriana and Murcia, the land was divided into categories, according to the frequency with which different areas might be irrigated, and the contribution amount per surface unit was rated differently between categories. However, a given plot in the lowest category might actually have consumed more water in a given year than another rated the highest. In practice, the landowners paid a flat rate per surface unit that entitled them to irrigate as often as they needed, up to the ceiling amount in each land category.

Even though it breached the principle of fiscal equivalence, this method seems to have been widely accepted and I found no evidence that it was ever disputed. Perhaps it was the case that as farmers could choose from among a great variety of crops with very different needs in terms of irrigation, they placed more value on keeping open both their entitlement to water and their freedom of crop options, than they did on strict fiscal equivalence even if their particular choice in a given year might require less water than they were entitled to.

Third principle: Collective choice arrangements

> Most individuals affected by the operational rules can participate in modifying the operational rules.[26]

According to Ostrom, it will be easier for the rules to be consistent with the local conditions if they are drawn up by the users of the common resource themselves, since they know each other and their milieu best.

Maass and Anderson reported that the communities in Huerta de Valencia held general board meetings where, among other things, they discussed the pros and cons of modifying the Ordinances.[27] In reality, such assemblies did meet regularly in the Middle Ages, but that was sometimes no longer the case from the seventeenth century on. Moreover, the case of Huerta de Valencia was an exception. Elsewhere the water was not usually administered by the irrigators themselves, but rather by the authorities of the towns around which the *huertas* were located. It seems medieval Ordinances were mostly designed and modified over the years by the municipal authorities rather than by the communities of irrigators.

Moreover, even in Huerta de Valencia not all those who had a right of say in the general assemblies were really irrigators, and very few of the actual irrigators could attend the assemblies. As in all the *huertas*, land ownership was distributed very unequally, especially before the twentieth century. Most landowners lived in the city of Valencia and about 90 per cent of the total surface area was farmed by tenants. The latter enjoyed a great deal of stability, and leases were usually passed on from father to son,[28] but tenants were not allowed to attend the general assemblies. For instance, 326 out of the 536 individuals who could attend the Rovella community assemblies around 1890 were not farmers, and there were as many as 851 farmers who could not attend.[29] Since the Ordinances established that the executive committees responsible for governing the communities should be made up exclusively of landowners, historians who sustain that the Valencian 'democracies of irrigators' never existed are largely right.

Nevertheless, the lack of democratic decision-making does not rule out the fact that the irrigators might participate indirectly in designing the rules, to the extent that their participation was in the landowners' interest. The great stability enjoyed by the tenants in Huerta de Valencia, as in the *huertas* of Gandía and Murcia, was related to the fact that the landowners had gradually stopped investing in improvements and had left it to their tenants to decide upon the different aspects of farming operations. In the course of the twentieth century, the farmers ended up buying most of the plots at low prices.[30] It is not realistic to suppose that the absentee landlords would have managed irrigation matters on a daily basis. The overall management was incumbent on the syndic, a paid office that was open only to landowners who were also themselves irrigators, and such a complex system could not work without the vast majority of irrigators somehow participating in its practical arrangements.

Although they were not set out in the Ordinances, criteria to allocate the water during droughts existed and they were gradually modified over the years. In times of severe droughts, it was not unusual for many irrigators to believe that unfair modifications had been introduced in the method of distribution, which they were not willing to accept. Communities would then resort to the army or the local police force to keep watch day and night to prevent the stealing of water. However, it was not feasible to use such costly surveillance on a permanent basis. Overall, the system must have rested on compliance.

A commitment to comply with norms is usually one of a conditional nature. For individuals to commit to respecting norms, a perception is required that (a) the collective aim that is the goal of such norms is indeed being achieved, and that (b) the other participants are respecting the norms as well.[31] If a significant number of irrigators in a community were willing to commit offences because they believed they were being treated unfairly, the commitment of the other members of the community to the norms would also suffer, threatening the survival of the institution itself. Therefore, those who had a say and the right to vote in the assemblies had an interest in allowing those who did not to participate in the agreement, albeit informally.

These considerations do not apply to the irrigation communities in which water rights were not tied to land and where there was a water market. In Alicante, as in other such communities, the actual irrigators repeatedly struggled against the water appropriators to abolish the water market, which they would only achieve in the course of the twentieth century (in Alicante, this happened shortly after Maass and Anderson's book was published). Previously, there had been a structural conflict between those who owned water and those that cultivated the land, and the separation between land and water tended to cause 'the stagnation of agricultural progress'.[32] But, yet again, none of those communities ended up collapsing.

Fourth principle: Monitoring

> Monitors, who actively audit CPR conditions and appropriators' behaviour, are accountable to the appropriators or are the appropriators.[33]

The use of third party guards is costly and relatively ineffective, because their knowledge of the milieu is not as good as that of the potential offenders. In long-enduring common institutions, according to Ostrom, both monitoring to prevent offences and meting out sanctions to offenders are carried out either by the users themselves or by personnel directly accountable to them. As explained previously, collective action theorists have assumed that users would shirk monitoring and enforcing because those are activities that involve high individual costs to produce public goods. Ostrom in turn pointed out that users will not shirk this if surveillance can be done at low cost or with high individual benefits.

In fact, both of these conditions were met in the traditional irrigation communities in eastern Spain. Monitoring incurs two kinds of costs related to the problems outlined previously: those resulting from the maintenance and improvement of the system (provision problems) and those needed to ensure that nobody wastes or steals resource units (appropriation problems). Provision problems are more costly to monitor, for it is harder to measure the contribution made by each individual and to exclude free riders from the benefits than to identify outright misappropriation.

In the Spanish irrigation communities, the payment of an annual fee proportional to the units of land owned provided a simple way to solve these problems. It was quite easy to know whether somebody had paid or not, and those who had failed to pay could easily be denied access to water until they settled. With the money thus collected, the communities employed paid workers to clean out the major canal and perform other maintenance tasks. The irrigators themselves were personally responsible for cleaning the sections of the secondary irrigation canals that ran alongside their plots, which besides being in their own direct interest, was easy to monitor.

The users of some of the irrigation systems studied by Ostrom might prefer to do some days' work for the community rather than paying in cash, in order to ensure that their contribution was used to improve the system instead of lining some civil servant's pocket.[34] But in the *huertas*, the preference for payments in cash was already widespread in medieval times. Contributions in labour would have forced the Spanish communities to incur huge organization and supervision costs, because they were often made up of many irrigators, most of whom owned or farmed tiny plots and, therefore, would each contribute very little work time. The Orihuela Ordinances warned against the irrigators cleaning the major canal themselves, which 'results in serious problems and should therefore be avoided as much as possible'. If in spite of this warning the major canals were to be cleaned by the irrigators, the Ordinances stipulated that each should clean a stretch of canal proportional to the surface they farmed and they would not be allowed to irrigate until a community official certified that they had cleaned it properly.[35] This was the solution to a problem that Ostrom claimed might arise when the contribution was made in the form of days' labour, namely that the families would send children or elderly people to do the work. In Orihuela, it was the outcome of the work that would be supervised, which was easier to assess than the intensity of the work.

Monitoring for appropriation problems will be cheap if the participants do not have to invest additional resources to be able to carry it out, and the personal benefits from monitoring will be high when it prevents infractions that would cause significant personal harm to those who perform it. Therefore, the rules that put potential offenders under direct surveillance by potential victims are easier to enforce than those where compliance depends mainly on reports made by people only indirectly harmed by the infractions.[36]

What usually occurred in Spanish irrigation communities was that each round began with the plot whose water inlet was the closest to the head of the secondary irrigation canal being used, followed by the second closest and so on. Farmers had to wait by their plots some time before their turn came, because they would not know exactly when the water would reach them and if they missed a turn they would forfeit their right in that round. Since each had an interest in monitoring the use of the water by their immediate neighbours, especially during critical junctures like droughts when some kind of rationing system was in place, monitoring was an inherent part of the irrigation process done at close to no additional cost, and each irrigator had a significant incentive to perform it and report infractions.

However, irrigating out of turn and diverting water in an untimely manner from the major to a secondary canal was less likely to be seen by the offender's neighbours, and if they did witness the infraction they were less likely to report it because doing so would only produce diffuse benefits.[37] That was why the fines

Table 6.1 Complaints lodged by the irrigators themselves (*I*) and by officials (*O*) in the
Vila-real community

Subject of the complaint	1899–1903		1919–1923	
	I	*O*	*I*	*O*
Stealing water	2	36	3	34
Flooding a neighbour's field	32	0	18	0
Wasting water	1	43	0	128
Irrigating out of turn	2	59	0	125
Irrigating land not belonging to the *huerta*	0	24	0	0
Failing to clean the irrigation canals[a]	—	—	0	283
Others	4	10	0	8
Total	41	172	21	578

Source: Archive of the Irrigation Community of Vila-real, books of fines.

Note [a]In 1899–1903, reports for this motive were placed under 'others'.

were usually heavier in the case of offences that did not directly affect the offender's neighbours, and in order to encourage reporting it was common before the nineteenth century for the Ordinances to award the complainant part of the fine. Besides such incentives to direct reporting, the communities kept a team of paid guards to monitor those offences, who often had to pay a deposit when they came into office to cover any harm they might cause through negligence or corruption, and who could in turn be reported by the irrigators.

Table 6.1 concerning the *huerta* of Vila-real in the early twentieth century suggests that it was actually the paid guards who lodged most reports.[38] The Vila-real community underwent continuous growth in members throughout the period. Around 1900, it had about 4,100 members, whose holdings were fragmented into more than 10,000 dispersed plots, and water flowed past each of them about twenty times a year. As such, the annual average of forty-three official complaints lodged between 1899 and 1903 and even the 120 between 1919 and 1923 are very low numbers.

Thanks to the comments noted in the record books, we know that all complaints lodged by the irrigators themselves concerned offences that caused them some direct personal harm. There were on average eight of these per year over the period 1899–1903 and four during 1919–1923. One of the keys to the success of the system lies in these small numbers: when intensive collective monitoring by community members uncovers few violations and those who carry it out can be certain that few offences are actually taking place, they will tend not to commit offences themselves, both because they will be certain that that they are not being taken advantage of and because they realize that the chances of being discovered are very high. In such a situation, the rules come to be met with 'quasi-voluntary compliance'.[39]

As often happens in successful community irrigation institutions,[40] the physical design of the system allowed community members to observe the behaviour of each member in a simple and inexpensive way. Since the plots were not fenced off, the effects of untimely irrigation would remain in plain sight for several days. Moreover, from the mid-nineteenth century on the communities adopted a technical improvement that lowered supervision costs even more, as the sluice gates and screw pumps regulating the water distribution from the major to secondary canals started being made of iron and protected with padlocks.

While few offences were normally committed, that would not be the case in times of severe drought. Then the frequency of infractions would rise, and in some places this is known to have remained high for a long period. The two neighbouring *huertas* of Vila-real and Borriana offer good examples of such conflicting situations. Conflict in Vila-real basically arose from new and more water-demanding crops replacing traditional ones in many holdings throughout the nineteenth century. The following factors ended up playing an essential role in re-establishing an agreement: the generalized diffusion of orange groves, which needed a moderate amount of water, changes in the rules governing water allocation during droughts, and the fact that as of 1869, the irrigators themselves (instead of the Town Council) took charge of managing irrigation through a formal Community backed by the 1866 *Ley de Aguas* (Waters Act). In Borriana, besides similar causes that were dealt with in identical ways, disputes with irrigators from the neighbouring town of Nules also spilled over into the community. These disputes came to an end following the building of a new canal in 1897, when Nules stopped using Borriana's major canal to carry the water from the river Mijares into its own *huerta*.

Since the troubled times, when the intensity of disputes was highest, left deeper impressions in archival records, they have also attracted most attention from specialists in the history of irrigation, which might give the impression that conflict was the rule in the social life of these communities. The significant point to be made, however, is that these were really exceptional situations, and that those that broke out indeed tended to be managed by the communities' own devices.

Fifth principle: Graduated sanctions

> Appropriators who violate operational rules are likely to be assessed graduated sanctions (depending on the seriousness and context of the offence) by other appropriators, by officials accountable to these appropriators, or by both.[41]

If someone who usually abides by the rules is sanctioned harshly for a sporadic offence, they are likely to feel resentful and less committed to respecting the norms in the future. This is Ostrom's starting point in considering the question of sanctions. Her argument can be summed up as follows. Since there will be many occasions for the users of a common pool resource to behave opportunistically, at some point even those who usually comply with the rules are likely to fall into temptation and misbehave. If it is the users themselves or officials directly accountable to them who carry out monitoring and enforcement, they will have detailed information on the past behaviour of other participants. If someone occasionally breaks a rule, a small sanction will be enough to remind them of the importance of not repeating this, since occasional offenders know that the whole community is aware of what has happened and that if they recur, besides harsher sanctions they will suffer reputational losses. Recurrent offenders will be sanctioned more harshly in order to prevent them from becoming habitual offenders and malfeasance from becoming generalized.

Indeed, the fines actually meted out to offenders in mediaeval Castellón were usually lower than those established in the Ordinances, and the same offence could be sanctioned differently depending on who had committed it and under which conditions;[42] it is very likely that something similar took place in Huerta de Valencia. The Ordinances of the communities of Quart (1709) and Mislata (1751) assigned the same penalty for nearly all offences, and those of Tormos (1843) laid down fines so high that, in general, it would have been difficult to enforce their payment. In all cases, it can be supposed that the fines stipulated in the Ordinances would work as maximum amounts, up to which the community body responsible for applying the sanctions would enjoy wide discretionary leeway.

By the mid-nineteenth century, as the Ordinances were reformed they often started to stipulate a maximum and a minimum fine for each sanction, to which those of the Júcar irrigation canal (1844) added that 'the first recurring offence shall be punished with double the fine'. The use of such 'floor' and 'ceiling' fines became generalized when the communities' Ordinances were modified to comply with the *Leyes de Aguas* of 1866 and 1879. Very wide ranges were usually adopted, as was the case in Vila-real (1869), Castellón (1878) and Borriana (1906). For instance, the Ordinances of Vila-real set the 'floor' fine for all offences at 2.5 pesetas and the 'ceiling' at 25 pesetas for most of them, rising to as high 75 pesetas for very serious offences.

In the 1870s, when the level of disputes among irrigators became exceptionally high in Vila-real, as explained in the previous section, it became relatively common to enforce the maximum fines allowed by the Ordinances. For instance, each of the 145 persons found guilty of a collective theft of water on 14 and 15 August 1870 was fined 75 pesetas, which by then was more than a typical wage worker's monthly earnings.

While they are needed for ongoing cooperation, sanctions can also work against this because they may encourage reprisals. It was undoubtedly to offset this peril that the use of minimum penalties became increasingly more frequent after internal conflicts subsided around 1880. Even though this ceased to be the case since the early twentieth century, the deflated total amounts of fines in Figure 6.1 suggest that the absolute increases in fines actually resulted from the communities using the higher end of the penalty range to compensate for inflation, as current prices were 90 per cent higher in 1935 as compared to 1900 and 464 per cent higher in 1958 as compared to 1941.

A generalized culture of observance may emerge if besides fear of sanctions and reputational loss participants widely believe that by complying they are contributing to collective aims for their own benefit.[43] This indeed seems to have been the case in the *huertas*. That would account for the fact that between 1905

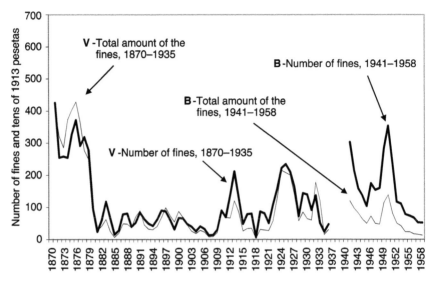

Figure 6.1 Number and amount (in constant pesetas) of the fines imposed by the Vila-real (*V*) and Borriana (*B*) irrigation communities. Three-year moving averages.

Source: Archives of the Irrigation Communities of Vila-real and Borriana, books of fines.

and 1942, those who owned land in Huerta de Vila-real but lived elsewhere accounted for 29 per cent of all the irrigators, yet their share in all sanctions was no more than 21 per cent. Similar figures occurred in Huerta de Borriana between 1941 and 1958: 25 and 20 per cent, respectively. If the operative factor was only the fear of losing reputation, one would expect foreign irrigators to commit more offences than the locals, who were virtually in daily contact with each other.

According to Ostrom, some community institutions tolerate violations of the norms up to a certain extent during especially hard times, while in others anyone's failure to abide by the rules can have such harmful effects on the remaining participants as to make it essential to ensure full compliance as close as possible.[44] Clearly the *huertas* fell into the latter category. The Ordinances frequently stipu-lated that top sanctions should be applied during droughts. The greater the amount of water carried by the river Mijares, the fewer fines were imposed in both Vila-real and in Borriana.[45] This might be partly because participants would be less tempted to use water illegally when it was abundant, and partly because during periods of ample supply monitoring would be more relaxed, permis-siveness would increase and offences would be more likely to be overlooked. Such were also the periods that favoured the expansion of irrigated areas through encroachment, as mentioned above in the first section.

Sixth principle: Conflict resolution mechanisms

Appropriators and their officials have rapid access to low-cost local arenas to resolve conflicts among appropriators or between appropriators and officials.[46]

In Huerta de Valencia, mediating to settle disputes and impose sanctions have long been the responsibility of the *Tribunal de las Aguas*, made up of the syndics, the chief executives of the seven communities. This tribunal holds weekly public sessions to hear the complaints brought against irrigators and officials, and after hearing both the complainant's and the defendant's cases, it proffers an immediate oral ruling which cannot be appealed.

The presence of similar entities in the other communities seems to be relatively recent. It seems that where water was administered by the municipal authorities, it was either they or their officials who acted as judges, not the irrigators themselves or their employees. Tribunals made up of irrigators only began spreading in the 1840s, as they were first adopted by many of the communities that redrafted their Ordinances at that time.[47] Afterwards, the 1866 *Ley de Aguas* and its 1879 amendment stated that Irrigation Communities should consist of three bodies: a general assembly (the *Comunidad*), an executive committee (the *Sindicato*, elected by the general assembly) and an irrigation tribunal (the *Jurado de Riegos*, also elected by the general assembly and which carried out similar duties to the Valencian *Tribunal de las Aguas*).

Two intervening circumstances made the work of mediators and judges easier. Firstly, during severe droughts the margin for interpreting the norms became narrower, as contingency procedures to allocate water would then replace those that were in place during times of regular supply. Such alternative procedures empowered the communities' management and employees to distribute the water the way they thought best to satisfy both general and individual interests. At such times, everyone suffered increased exposure to arbitrariness, but this was offset by the imposition of heavy fines on elected officials and employees who, once reported by an irrigator, were found guilty of unfair conduct.

Secondly, the more users within an irrigation system have their plots distributed between the beginning and the end of the major canals, the more they are likely to agree to the criteria used to share water when it becomes scarce.[48] In the *huertas*, the estates were usually broken up into many non-adjacent plots, often set apart by considerable distances.[49] This dispersion of plots was a way to optimize the use of the household workforce, by ensuring that plots were irrigated at different times and thus the optimum times for working them would not coincide.[50] Therefore, many landowners had their plots spread over areas irrigated by different secondary canals with entry points distributed along the length of the major canal, which as a by-effect would act as a mitigating factor for internal disputes.

Seventh principle: Minimal recognition of rights to organize

> The rights of appropriators to devise their own institutions are not challenged by external government authorities.[51]

According to Ostrom, the recognition of the right of users of a common pool resource to organize themselves implies at least three things. Firstly, it should be they who, *at least partially*, draw up the norms. Secondly, all users should know that when someone does not agree to those norms, they cannot easily have them overturned by an external authority. Thirdly, the community of users should be able to rely on external support to help defend their common property rights against third parties.

With regard to the first aspect, most Spanish scholars' belief can be summed up in the words of Enric Guinot, who claims that it is a 'myth' that the *huertas* were 'an agricultural space managed essentially by the farmers themselves'.[52] It seems beyond doubt, however, that in Huerta de Valencia the landowners did have a fair degree of autonomy when it came to devising the rules of the game, and as already argued above, it would have gone against their own interests to do so without taking into account the daily activities of the tenants who actually farmed their holdings and eventually came to own most of them. It is true that before the legislative changes, which took place from the mid-nineteenth century to the 1879 amendment to the *Ley de Aguas*, the model of irrigation management used in Huerta de Valencia was an exception.[53] Up until then, most *huertas* were governed by the municipal authorities. Even then, in view of the social makeup of the municipal bodies and the landowning interests of their members, a similar reflection to the one I have used for Huerta de Valencia would apply; but the adhesion of Ostrom's principle to historical reality is nevertheless flawed in this respect.

With regard to the second aspect, external authorities (the courts of law, the Crown and its representatives under the *Ancien Régime* and afterwards the Ministry of Public Works) did have a great capacity to repeal and modify the norms, as a number of examples show relating to the *huertas* by the rivers Mijares and Palancia.[54] Affairs between the irrigation communities and 'the exterior' (including the neighbouring communities) were nearly always settled by the intervention of these authorities, and the irrigation communities often had to undertake internal changes as an indirect result. To be fair, what Ostrom argues is not that the intervention of external authorities necessarily leads to poor results, but rather that it will produce poor results if it imposes practices that are considered inappropriate by most users of the resource.[55]

Lastly, external coercion certainly played a fundamental role in regulating the relationships of the irrigation communities with outsiders. It was essential for instance to make sure that those who lived upriver resigned themselves to watching the precious water flow past their land towards the coastal *huertas* and not have the right to use it. And as a last resort, external coercion also ensured that the justice delivered by the irrigation tribunals was binding.

Eighth principle: Nested enterprises

> Appropriation, provision, monitoring, enforcement, conflict resolution, and governance activities are organized in multiple layers of nested enterprises.[56]

According to Ostrom, '[b]y nesting layers of organization within one another irrigators can take advantage of many different scales of organization'.[57] This undoubtedly happened in the *huertas*. The large *huertas* were located on or close to the coast, which was the area that enjoyed the most favourable climatic conditions for water to be put to use to create wealth. After the Christian conquest in the thirteenth century, the kings of Aragon and Castile (sometimes ratifying arrangements that had been in place since the Muslim period) granted coastal irrigation communities a preferential right to use the water from the rivers. This contributed to the appearance, as from the Middle Ages, of a first level of organ-ization: the communities joined forces to stand up for their privileges before those who lived along the middle and upper reaches of the rivers and would take more water than they were legally entitled to.[58] The second organizational level consisted of the communities themselves. Each of them usually had a single weir and one major canal, although there might be more, as was the case in Murcia and Orihuela. The major distributaries branching off from the major canal made up the third level, and so on.

In some cases, organization by levels was formally stipulated. For example, each of the twenty-one towns that used the Júcar canal had its own particular set of regulations. And the Ordinances of Murcia recognized the existence of three layers of assemblies: that of the whole *huerta*, that of its two major subsections (*heredamientos*), and that of the numerous territorial subdivisions within the latter. In most communities, however, such layers were established implicitly. The ordinances simply indicated that each secondary canal (and each of the successive distributaries branching off from them) would have the right to use a certain portion of the water from the major canal, or to be filled for a certain number of hours after being in the dry for a certain period of time. For most everyday purposes (including, besides irrigation itself, monitoring and maintenance tasks, as referred to above), users organized around those spaces.

The fact that decisions can be taken at different levels makes it easier to adapt to specific surrounding conditions, while at the same time the system as a whole can be monitored in a far more economical and effective way.[59] Ever since the Middle Ages, each community had had the right to divert a certain amount of water from its river. As a result, communities monitored each other – a task normally undertaken by paid officials known as *azuderos* – so that none would use more water than they were entitled to.

Once the water was in its major canal, each community could do with it as it pleased. As said above, the larger the area to be irrigated, the less water there would be per hectare. But this average was of little practical significance. Normally, the oldest areas of the *huertas* were allocated more water per surface unit, whereas the canals that irrigated the later extensions were entitled to pro-gressively smaller amounts. As a consequence, those who had their holdings on the edges of the *huertas* usually irrigated their land by means of the system's capillaries. They were the ones with a more direct interest in fighting illegal expansions, and they were perfectly aware of where the area with the right to be irrigated ended. The expansion of the system's boundaries through 'practical appropriation', as referred to in the first section, would therefore be unlikely to occur without either their collective participation or tacit consent; in this sense, important decisions for the system might be taken at this informal organizational level as well.

Conclusions

Granted that the commons are not condemned to an unavoidable 'tragedy', one should not over-idealize them either, at the cost of turning them into myths. Since the sustainable management of the commons requires, among other things, that not everybody can have access to them, dynamic community institutions are quite compatible with the exclusion of many and with the maintenance of high levels of social inequality in the society as a whole.

The society in which the Spanish irrigation communities were embedded was highly unequal, especially before the twentieth century. This was carried over into the distribution of land ownership in the *huertas* – the private property rights that for the most part defined the appropriation rule for the common water. Where that was not the case, the owners of private rights in common water were among the most powerful families, both economically and politically. Some commoners were clearly less common than others: economic resources and power relations were uneven both within the irrigation communities and between them and the external powers that managed their institutions. Even where the formal institutions were directly managed by the actual users of the commons, they were far from democratic, let alone equalitarian. Social power imbalances certainly translated into the decisions being made with respect to the common pool institutions.

Yet there is no doubt that the centuries-long irrigation communities in eastern Spain are historically successful entities. That was precisely why Elinor Ostrom looked into them for empirical material on which to ground her theoretical construct. The fact that her information contains a number of inaccurate idealizations about the actual social practices that conformed and used institutions poses a paradox. The theory predicts that institutions with characteristics similar to some of the irrigation communities – which were not guided by a strict principle of fiscal equivalence, did not operate democratically, and were either managed by external authorities or dependent on their rulings – would have had little chance of surviving. However, this chapter shows that in the light of Ostrom's powerful theoretical tools, it is still possible to draw on concrete historical situations not just to criticize such idealizations, but also to go beyond the mythology and attempt to make some explanations that may help understand what actually made it possible for them to survive.

Acknowledgements

This chapter is a revised version of S. Garrido, 'Las instituciones de riego en la España del Este: Una reflexión a la luz de la obra de Elinor Ostrom', *Historia Agraria* 53 (2011), pp. 13–42, which resulted of the research project ECO2009-10739, funded by the Spanish Ministry of Science and Innovation.

Notes

1 E. Ostrom, *Governing the Commons: The Evolution of Institutions for Collective Action* (New York: Cambridge University Press, 1990).
2 When in lower case, the Spanish term *huerta* refers to the territory administered by a particular community. 'Huerta' in upper case is a part of a district's name. Such districts sometimes are made up of several specific *huertas*, as in Huerta de Valencia and Huerta de Gandia.
3 G. Hardin, 'The tragedy of the commons', *Science,* 162 (1968), pp. 1243–8.
4 M. Olson, *The Logic of Collective Action: Public Goods and the Theory of Groups* (Cambridge MA: Harvard University Press, 1970).
5 E. Ostrom, 'Design principles of robust property rights institutions: What have we learned?', in G. K. Ingram and Y. H. Hong (eds), *Property Rights and Land Policies* (Cambridge MA: Lincoln Institute of Land Policy, 2009), pp. 25–51, on p. 27.
6 T. Glick, *Irrigation and Society in Medieval Valencia* (Cambridge MA: Harvard University Press, 1970); A. Maass and R. L. Anderson, . . . *And the Desert Shall Rejoice: Conflict, Growth and Justice in Arid Environments* (Cambridge MA: MIT Press, 1978).
7 E. Guinot, 'Comunidad rural: Municipios y gestión del agua en las huertas medievales valencianas', in A. Rodríguez (ed.), *El Lugar del Campesino* (Valencia: Universitat de València, 2007), pp. 309–30; M. T. Pérez Picazo, 'El agua y las comunidades de regantes', in A. López and M. Ortiz (eds), *Entre Surcos y Arados* (Cuenca: Universidad de Castilla–La Mancha 2001), pp. 77–97; T. Peris, 'La conflictividad hidráulica en el País Valenciano entre los siglos XII y XVIII', *Areas:* 17 (1997), pp. 44–60; J. Romero and J. Mateu, 'Introducción', in J. Jaubert de Passà, *Canales de Riego de Cataluña y el Reino de Valencia*, vol. 1 (Madrid: Ministerio de Agricultura, 1991), pp. 7–101.
8 C. Sanchis-Ibor, G. Palau-Salvador, I. Mangue Alférez and L. P. Martinez-Sanmartín (eds), *Irrigation, Society, Landscape: Tribute to T. F. Glick* (Valencia: Editorial Universitat Politècnica de València, 2014), at http://dx.doi.org/10.4995/ISL2014. 2014.225 [last accessed 10 March 2016].
9 In a later book, she recommended these principles for designing irrigation projects in developing countries: E. Ostrom, *Crafting Institutions for Self-Governing Irrigation Systems* (San Francisco: International Centre for Self-Governance, 1992). She later referred to them in several works, including her Nobel Prize acceptance speech: E. Ostrom, 'Beyond markets and states', *American Economic Review*, 100:3 (2010), pp. 641–72.
10 Ostrom, *Governing the Commons*, p. 91.
11 S. Garrido, 'Governing scarcity: Water markets, equity and efficiency in pre-1950s eastern Spain', *International Journal of the Commons*, 2:5 (2011), pp. 513–34, at http://doi.org/10.18352/ijc.274 [last accessed 10 March 2016].
12 S. Garrido, 'Ampliación del regadío, regulación institucional y sostenibilidad en las Huertas Tradicionales de la España mediterránea', *Investigaciones de Historia Económica*, 8:2 (2012), pp. 94–103.
13 Garrido, 'Governing scarcity', pp. 523–4.
14 S. Garrido, *Cànem Gentil: L'Evolució de les Estructures Agràries a la Plana de Castelló* (Castellón: Ayuntamiento, 2004), pp. 20–1.
15 E. Burriel, *La Huerta de Valencia: Zona Sur* (Valencia: Instituto Alfonso el Magnánimo, 1970), p. 135; Maass and Anderson, *And the Desert Shall Rejoice*, p. 20.
16 S. Calatayud, 'El regadío ante la expansión agraria valenciana (1800–1916)', *Agricultura y Sociedad*, 67 (1993), pp. 47–92, on p. 61.
17 Garrido, 'Ampliación del regadío', pp. 98–9. I use 'practical appropriators' after the notion of 'practical owners', in R. Congost, *Tierras, Leyes, Historia: Reflexiones sobre 'La Gran Obra de la Propiedad'* (Barcelona: Crítica, 2007), pp. 15–21.

18 Ostrom, *Governing the Commons*, p. 92. Cox, Arnold, and Villamayor proposed dividing Principle 2 into 2A, 'Appropriation rules restricting time, place, technology, and/or quantity of resource units are related to local conditions' and 2B 'The benefits obtained by users from a CPR, as determined by appropriation rules, are proportional to the amount of inputs required in the form of labour, material, or money, as determined by provision rules'. M. Cox, G. Arnold and S. Villamayor, 'A review of design principles for community-based natural resource management', *Ecology and Society* 15:4 (2010), n.pag, at www.ecologyandsociety.org/vol15/iss4/art38/ [last accessed 10 March 2016].

19 S. Calatayud, J. Millán and M. C. Romeo, 'Une administration apolitique? Bravo Murillo face à la société civile libérale dans les campagnes valenciennes', in P. Fournier, J.-Ph. Louis, L. P. Martin and N. Planas (eds), *Institutions & Représentations du Politique: Espagne, France, Italie, XVIIème–XXème Siècles* (Clermont-Ferrand: Presses Universitaires Blaise-Pascal, 2006), pp. 121–55.

20 J. Millán, *El Poder de la Tierra: La Sociedad Agraria en el Bajo Segura en la Época del Liberalismo* (Alicante: Gil-Albert, 1999).

21 A. Llauradó, *Tratado de Aguas y Riegos* (Madrid: Moreno, 1884), pp. 223 and 252.

22 Garrido, 'Governing scarcity' for further details on the sources for the information in this paragraph.

23 Garrido, 'Ampliación del regadío', pp. 100–2.

24 M. Olson, 'The principle of "fiscal equivalence"', *American Economic Review*, 59:2 (1969), pp. 479–87.

25 Ostrom, *Governing the Commons*, p. 92, and *Crafting Institutions*, pp. 70 and 77–8.

26 Ostrom, *Governing the Commons*, p. 93.

27 Maass and Anderson, *And the Desert Shall Rejoice*, p. 22. I have analysed the topic of this section in greater detail in S. Garrido, 'Water management, Spanish irrigation communities and colonial engineers', *Journal of Agrarian Change*, 14:3 (2014), pp. 400–18.

28 S. Garrido, 'Improve and sit: The surrendering of land at rents below marginal product in nineteenth-century Valencia, Spain', *Research in Economic History*, 29 (2013), pp. 97–144.

29 Burriel, *Huerta de Valencia*, p. 312.

30 Garrido, 'Improve and sit'; S. Garrido and S. Calatayud, 'La compra silenciosa: arrendamientos, estabilidad y mejoras en la agricultura valenciana de regadío (1850–1930)', *Investigaciones de Historia Económica*, 8:3 (2007), pp. 77–108; S. Garrido and S. Calatayud, 'The price of improvements: Agrarian contracts and agrarian development in nineteenth-century eastern Spain', *Economic History Review*, 2:64 (2011), pp. 598–620.

31 M. Levi, *Of Rule and Revenue* (Berkeley: University of California Press, 1988); Ostrom, *Governing the Commons*, p. 95.

32 P. Díaz Cassou, *Ordenanzas y Costumbres de la Huerta de Murcia* (Madrid: Fortanet, 1889), p. 121.

33 Ostrom, *Governing the Commons*, p. 94.

34 Ostrom, *Governing the Commons*, pp. 86 and 228; *Crafting Institutions*, p. 55.

35 Jaubert, *Canales de Riego*, vol. 2, p. 115.

36 Ostrom, *Governing the Commons*, pp. 204–5.

37 T. Peris, 'Gobierno y administración de la Acequia Real del Xúquer', in *Historia y Constitución de las Comunidades de Regantes de las Riberas del Júcar (Valencia)* (Madrid: Ministerio de Agricultura, 1992), pp. 159–264; I. Román, *El Regadío de Vila-Real durante los Siglos XIII–XV* (Vila-real: Ayuntamiento, 2000).

38 Glick, *Irrigation and Society*, p. 56 stated the same about mediaeval Castellón.

39 An expression coined for the taxpayers' behaviour in countries with low tax evasion. Levi, *Of Rule and Revenue*.

40 Ostrom, *Crafting Institutions*, p. 55.

41 Ostrom, *Governing the Commons*, p. 94.
42 Glick, *Irrigation and Society*, pp. 54–64.
43 Ostrom, *Crafting Institutions*, p. 57.
44 Ostrom, *Governing the Commons*, p. 99.
45 Garrido, 'Instituciones de Riego', p. 32.
46 Ostrom, *Governing the Commons*, p. 100.
47 M. Ferri, 'Reorganización de los regadíos valencianos en el siglo XIX', *Areas: Revista Internacional de Ciencias Sociales*, 17 (1997), pp. 77–89.
48 Ostrom, *Crafting Institutions*, p. 74.
49 Garrido, 'Instituciones de riego', p. 35.
50 Garrido and Calatayud, 'Price of improvements', p. 604.
51 Ostrom, *Governing the Commons*, p. 101.
52 Guinot, 'Comunidad rural', p. 309.
53 S. Calatayud, 'Cambios institucionales en el regadío valenciano, 1830–1866', *Ayer*, 69 (2008), pp. 221–52; Ferri, 'Reorganización de los regadíos valencianos'.
54 M. Ferri, *Terratinents, Camperols i Soldats* (Valencia: Universitat de València, 2002); V. García Edo, *Derechos Históricos de los Pueblos de la Plana a las Aguas del Río Mijares* (Castellón: Diputación, 1994).
55 Ostrom, *Crafting Institutions*, p. 52.
56 Ostrom, *Governing the Commons*, p. 101.
57 Ostrom, *Crafting Institutions*, p. 76.
58 Calatayud, 'El regadío ante la expansión agraria', pp. 72–3.
59 Ostrom, *Governing the Commons*, p. 102; *Crafting Institutions*, p. 56.

7 Hopes of recovery

Struggles over the right to common lands in the Spanish countryside, 1931–1936

Iñaki Iriarte-Goñi and José-Miguel Lana

Introduction

The build-up of capitalism in Spain went hand-in-hand with an in-depth redefinition of property rights in land, which mainly followed the stream of the rest of the Western world; namely the establishment of the dominance of private individual property rights.[1] Nevertheless, since this was a complex social process, every country and even every region followed their own specific paths within that general movement.

One issue within this process in Spain, which has aroused much research interest, concerns the changes affecting common lands. A large part of the historical literature on Spanish common lands has focused on the privatization process, which took off in the early modern period, accelerated at the end of the eighteenth century and was institutionalized in specific laws during the second half of the nineteenth century along with the dismantling of the seigniorial regime and the land disentailment acts, which freed the landed assets of *ancien régime* corporate bodies into the market. As a result, millions of hectares lost their communal nature and no longer carried out their associated social and economic functions.[2] Recent historiography has complemented this view by highlighting that far from being linear, such changes were quite complex depending on the social, economic and cultural features of regional or local societies, which has also resulted in the survival of many commons in certain areas of the country. Moreover, in some historical situations that process could be stopped and even reversed.[3]

This chapter focuses on the period in modern Spanish history when opportunities were most available for the recovery of common lands, within the framework of the agrarian reform launched by the government of the Second Spanish Republic (1931–1936). As contemporary policymakers understood it, such a recovery was an important part of the agrarian reform. They asked local councils and workers' associations to submit dossiers containing information about commons that had been misappropriated, as a means for their possible restoration. We have located and thoroughly explored those dossiers, which are kept in the archives of the former Institute for Agrarian Reform and Development (IRYDA), and we have conducted an initial analysis on their contents.

The actual recovery of the commons never took place. To begin with, administrative and political problems delayed the process and then the outbreak of the Spanish Civil War cut short any further development. The information in the dossiers is nonetheless of great interest. Some of the literature on the republican agrarian reform has pointed out the significance of these recovery proceedings for a thorough understanding of the aims and design of the land reform project.[4] However, besides that, the dossiers also contain highly detailed historical information about local privatization processes and their consequences, as seen through the memories and arguments of the social sectors that had felt harmed by the loss of their commons. Despite the short period concerned, six years, the dossiers shed new light on the long-term changes in property rights, which makes it possible to better understand their social nature.

The rest of this chapter consists of four sections. The first provides the historical background to the Second Republic's project and assesses the role that the recovery of commons might have played in the reform. The second describes in some detail the dossiers and the different phases during which they were submitted to the government, and explores the main factors that might explain the submissions. The third section focuses on a few specific areas and explores in more depth the qualitative information in the dossiers. The sample was chosen both from *latifundium* regions, a system of concentrated land ownership that prevailed in the southern Spanish provinces of Andalusia and Extremadura, and from areas in the northern regions of Castile and León where family smallholdings predominated. The closing section discusses the main preliminary conclusions and indicates topics for further research.

The agrarian reform in the Second Spanish Republic: Background and the role of the commons

The Second Spanish Republic's land reform must be contextualized within the political programmes that were designed in the inter-war period to reallocate property rights in land in many European countries.[5] Nineteenth-century Spain had seen the modernization of state administration, a deregulation of agricultural markets, and the wholesale transfer of land from the Church and local councils to the urban bourgeoisie, the wealthier peasants and the aristocracy. Social and political tensions flared up in the first decades of the twentieth century. After the First World War, labour struggles increased sharply in both city and countryside, especially in the southern provinces of Andalusia and Extremadura, where the structure of land ownership was more imbalanced and a higher percentage of labourers and peasants were starved for land.

Meanwhile, the two-party political system and the informal arrangement jocularly referred to as the '*turno*' (shift), by which Liberals and Conservatives took turns at government by manipulating the electoral system supported by the politics of '*caciquismo*' – the rule of local bosses – broke down because of divisions within the ruling parties and because of the rise of new mass parties (socialists, republicans, and Basque and Catalan nationalists). However, parliamentary attempts between 1917 and 1923 to introduce structural reforms repeatedly failed, placing the country in a dilemma as how to solve the impasse within the political system: either more democracy or more authority. The military coup headed by General Primo de Rivera in 1923 imposed the latter, enabling some reforms to be introduced from above, albeit insufficient to resolve the structural problems. The regime's political crisis following the dictator's resignation in 1930 brought down the monarchy, leading to the proclamation of the Second Spanish Republic. The new government came into office on a broad reformist agenda based on the promises made by its constituent political parties, which for the first time in Spain were placed to the centre and left of the ideological spectrum.

The redistribution of landed property was a key lever in this political agenda for social and economic change.[6] The underlying approach had surfaced many years earlier, in the writings of some of Spain's leading economic thinkers, such as Costa, Flores de Lemus and Carrión.[7] In fact, the problem of the *latifundia* that dominated the southern half of the country had long been identified as an economic and social stumbling block, due to the low agricultural yields of the large estates and to their inability to generate sufficient employment. In Carrión's words, where ownership was 'shared out' the potential of the land was fully used, while where it was 'monopolized' by a handful of landowners there was no incentive to intensify production. Thus the private interests of large landowners favoured more extensive farming, which was detrimental to the interests of the local community.[8] Redistributing land ownership might therefore have a double advantage of improving output and creating jobs to rescue landless peasants from unemployment and poverty. This summarizes the argument made, in more or less developed forms, by many subsequent studies that have considered land redistribution policies a major lever for rural development and the eradication of poverty.[9]

Therefore, the novelty in 1931 was not in the ideas about *latifundia* but in a government's firm commitment to design and enact land redistribution. Moreover, the reformist legislation was not restricted to breaking up the *latifundia* to provide for peasant settlements. It had broader objectives: firstly, to revise some of the measures taken by nineteenth-century liberal governments, in order to achieve the total abolition of the remaining quasi-feudal seigniorial rights and a review of farming contracts. Secondly, several measures related to land-use intensification and to rural labour markets were designed to uphold a model of labour-intensive agriculture based on smallholdings, as the best way to avoid recurring unemployment crises.[10]

The recovery of the commons made full sense in this context. The prevalent notion concerning common lands in republican reformist policies was that in the course of time, and especially due to the nineteenth-century privatization process, common property had been misappropriated on a huge scale by the wealthy. In that light, the problem of concentration of ownership was interwoven with that of misappropriated commons, the devolution of which would have a major bearing on the intended redistributive policy.

Again, the use of common lands to favour smallholdings was not invented by republican lawmakers. Ever since the eighteenth century, the distribution of communal wastelands had been used to promote peasant settlements. But the nineteenth-century liberal legislation tended to annul the commons' social function through a double process of privatization and municipalization. The law broadly considered surviving common land as municipal property, empowering local councils instead of peasant communities to decide upon its use.[11] Up until the 1920s, several million hectares of land ceased to be in commons, both as a result of property being conveyed by force of the disentailment acts and of different forms of individual appropriation.[12] In spite of that, the remaining commons continued to play a crucial role in the socio-economic fabric of some areas, even reinforcing their function in terms of social fairness.[13] In many places, the distribution of the commons among the peasantry was used to curb the effects of agrarian crises, as in the late nineteenth century. In the first decades of the twentieth century, the commons also played a part in colonization projects for new peasant settlements.[14] Underlying these earlier redistributive processes, there were the claims of a diverse range of social movements that were being organized in the countryside, along with an interest by some elites in using the commons as a social buffer to defuse conflict.

In short, during the nineteenth and the early decades of the twentieth century, two kinds of processes had run in parallel: while the private appropriation of a significant part of the commons helped to reinforce the huge concentration of land ownership, on the other hand they were also used to facilitate farming by smallholders, through land distribution either for growing crops or for complementary agricultural uses. Within this context, the Second Republic legislation on common lands was a two-pronged attempt to reverse the first process and reinforce the second. The political aim was to help recover the commons, the misappropriation of which had contributed to the concentration of ownership, encouraging their use as complementary assets to consolidate smallholders' farming concerns.

An overview of the dossiers

The dossiers on common lands submitted by local councils and workers' associations can be grouped into three specific time windows, which coincided with three distinct phases the issue of the commons went through during the republican period.[15] The first window opened up almost immediately after the proclamation of the Republic in June 1931, when the Agrarian Technical Committee at the Ministry of Labour called on local councils to provide information on the common lands within their municipal boundaries and on their eventual dispossession. This initial request was not part of a specifically arranged scheme. Apparently its purpose was purely informative, but it clearly shows that from the very start, the intention was there to use the common lands in the economic and social transformations being planned. This first step led to a wave of dossiers, in which many local councils submitted information on their common lands and the ones they had lost.

The second window opened in September 1932, with the passing of a frame-work law on agrarian reform. Its guideline 20 allowed local councils to '[s]ubmit a petition to the IRA for the recovery of those properties and rights of which they find they have been dispossessed, according to proven data or simply by test-ifying to their former existence'.[16] This made it quite clear that the recovery of misappropriated commons was to play a part in the land redistribution policy.

Guideline 20 required subsequent legislative specification as to how the recoveries would take effect. Accordingly, a decree in January 1933 explained how to make the requests, including a description of the situation and characteristics of the former common properties to be recovered and the evidence required to establish that they had been misappropriated and by whom. Local councils could make these requests, but if they did not any private person or legal entity might file a claim as well. The 1933 decree has been aptly called a 'phantom decree', as it was published without the President's signature and was subsequently repealed even before it came into force.[17] Nevertheless, the information reached many villages, which in the spring and summer of 1933 compiled their recovery dossiers roughly according to what the decree stipulated. These months in 1933 account for the highest number of applications kept in the IRYDA archive.

Finally, the third window opened up with the electoral victory of the Popular Front in the spring of 1936. The new overtly left-wing government showed a special interest in enacting guideline 20 of the 1932 law by having it debated in the Parliament. The new legislative project not only extended the definition of misappropriation, but also backdated the misappropriations that might be recovered as commons to 1808.[18] The military coup in 18 July 1936 and the ensuing civil war put an end to any chance of a new law being passed.[19] From then on, in the context of war, the number of land seizures soared but the legal recovery of common lands based on dossiers does not seem to have played a significant role in this phase, as land seizures were carried out by the much more expedient mechanisms of revolutionary collectivization.[20]

Our initial approach to the vast volume of documents pertaining to the recovery of common lands draws on the contents of sixty-seven boxes in the section *Reforma Agraria Parte 1* of the IRYDA archive, which according to the catalogue contain all documents directly related to the applications, which might be consider-ed as a sort of *cahiers de doléances*.[21] We drew up a first provisional summary based on these documents and on an undated list by the Legal Sub-Directorate of the IRA.[22] Out of the 866 claims included in the IRA list, we have managed to find the dossiers for 490 villages, which, in addition to a further 312 dossiers we have found whose villages were not included on that list, make up a total of 802 dossiers. We have been unable to find the remaining 371 claims listed in IRA's 'general catalogue', which may however still come to light in future searches.[23]

By combining the list and the non-listed dossiers, we were able to identify 1,139 villages that provide a first snapshot of the overall importance of these recovery applications across the Spanish regions. In Table 7.1, we used the 1930 population figures to assess whether population size was a factor in the move toward the recovery of common lands. One should bear in mind that the numbers

Table 7.1 Number of villages in the municipalities that applied to the IRA for the recovery of common lands between 1931 and 1936 and their population in 1930, according to regions

Region	Number of villages					Population in 1930	
	1	*2*	*3*	*Total*	*%*	*Total*	*% of region*
Andalusia	57	110	18	185	15.8	1,050,663	28.0
Aragón	14	39	54	107	9.1	175,670	21.2
Asturias	9	11	4	24	2.0	196,506	27.4
Balearic Isles	2	0	0	2	0.2	8,560	3.1
Basque Country	7	1	2	10	0.9	26,007	4.3
Canary Islands	1	7	4	12	1.0	52,790	12.7
Cantabria	5	2	2	9	0.8	20,397	7.3
Castilla y León	91	111	121	323	27.5	349,829	16.0
Catalonia	14	10	2	26	2.2	41,533	2.5
Extremadura	92	37	27	156	13.3	492,205	45.5
Galicia	9	6	5	20	1.7	164,828	8.0
La Mancha	50	76	38	164	14.0	353,391	20.8
La Rioja	5	5	1	11	0.9	12,379	7.3
Madrid	6	18	1	25	2.1	29,102	6.8
Murcia	3	6	0	9	0.8	62,132	12.8
Navarre	3	29	26	58	4.9	115,346	38.0
Valencia	3	22	7	32	2.7	196,420	13.4
Total	371	490	312	1173	100	3,347,758	18.1

Sources: *Catálogo General de Reclamaciones*; IRYDA Ref.Agr.1, box 23(1); Population Census for 1930, INEbase Historia www.ine.es/inebaseweb/hist.do.

Legend

1 – Villages in the *Catálogo General* whose dossiers have not been found.
2 – Villages in the *Catálogo General* whose dossiers have been found.
3 – Villages not in the *Catálogo General* for which dossiers have been found.
Population does not include provincial capitals, both in the numerator and in the denominator.

in the table reflect the haste with which these villages sought to resolve a long-standing issue by appealing to a legal process in which they apparently placed high hopes. Since the recovery law was never actually passed, these statistics are but the tip of an iceberg. The figures are nonetheless significant.

The bulk of applications came from some of the larger and most populated regions. What is now the autonomous region of Castilla y León alone accounted for 27 per cent of the claims, followed by Andalusia (16 per cent), La Mancha (14 per cent) and Extremadura (13 per cent). Taken together, these regions accounted for 70 per cent of the claims, while they covered 60 per cent of Spain's area and accounted for 43 per cent of its population in 1930.

The population involved in these claims amounted to 18 per cent of the overall total in 1930 (excluding provincial capitals), with huge regional variation (Figure 7.1). There were three focal areas in the recovery claims: the middle Ebro valley, with Navarre and Zaragoza; the south-western quadrant, with Extremadura

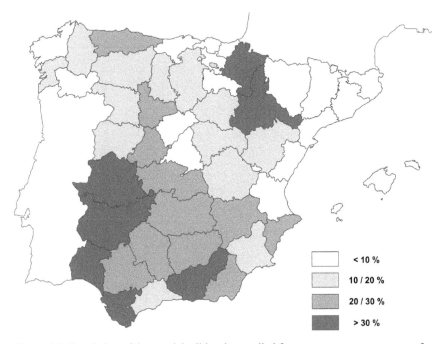

Figure 7.1 Population of the municipalities that applied for recovery as a percentage of the province's population (excluding provincial capitals).

Source: Table 7.1

and the Andalusian provinces of Cadiz and Huelva, and the Penibaetic region in southern Andalusia, centred on the province of Granada. The rest of the Spanish countryside has figures of between 10 and 30 per cent of the population involved in recovery applications, with a greater weight in the southern half than in the northern *meseta* and in the central mountain range. The priority given to the southern *latifundia* regions for the application of the agrarian reform law may explain their higher share of claims for the recovery of common lands, given how much the two issues were connected.

In a first approach to explaining this regional pattern, we have tested two simple hypotheses about the factors that might have stimulated the submission of claims. The first and most obvious one involves the presumable link between recovery applications and the previous privatization processes. The second deals with the so-called 'land hunger', related to population growth facing fixed land resources.

Concerning the former, Robledo has already argued along these lines by comparing the maps of the regional distributions of recovery claims and of the consequences of the nineteenth-century disentailment process.[24]

We have taken a simple statistical approach to the same question. Figure 7.2 relates the rate of privatization in forty-five Spanish provinces (measured as a

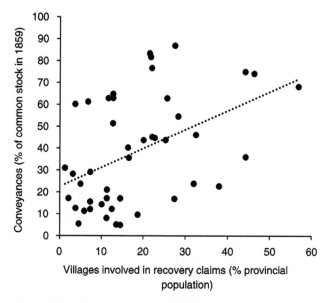

Figure 7.2 Relationship between the privatization of common lands (1859–1926) and recovery applications in 1931–1936 in Spanish provinces.

Sources: Table 7.1; GEHR, 'Más allá de la "propiedad perfecta"', appendix 4, p. 142.

percentage of common lands existing in 1859 that were privatized between 1859 and 1926) to the rate of recovery claims (expressed as the percentage of the population in the claimant municipalities over the respective provincial totals). As expected, there is a positive relationship.[25] The regression line shows that people in the provinces recording the most privatizations did tend to be more active in recovery claims. Nevertheless, the relationship between these two variables is far from perfect. The correlation coefficient of 0.42, making for an explained variance of 18 per cent, shows quite clearly that other circumstances were at play besides the volume of land privatized during the seventy-five preceding years.

Some of the provinces with the highest rate of claims did indeed rank high in privatization (Cadiz, Cáceres, and Badajoz), but then there were the exceptions of Huelva and Navarre, both with high claim rates but relatively low privatization rates. We do know that the volume of land conveyed in Navarre had been very high between 1808 and 1859,[26] therefore the correlation between the variables might have been higher if we could include the sales made before the 1855 privatization act for all the provinces. But conversely, there were provinces in which over 70 per cent of the uncultivated common lands were privatized (Ciudad Real, Córdoba, Toledo, and Seville) and in which the recovery claims nevertheless had much smaller impact than in the preceding cases.

Concerning the second hypothesis, in Table 7.2 we proxied 'land hunger' with population growth between 1860 and 1930, even though we are aware that an

Table 7.2 Population growth rates (1860–1930) in the villages that applied for recoveries and in the regions, with and without provincial capitals

Growth rates	In claimant villages		In regions		In regions without capitals	
Regions	1860 1930	1900 1930	1860 1930	1900 1930	1860 1930	1900 1930
Castilla León	**0.28**	**0.28**	0.24	0.24	0.16	0.13
Andalusia	0.52	0.77	0.62	0.83	0.57	0.74
La Mancha	**0.67**	**0.97**	0.58	0.89	0.55	0.86
Extremadura	**0.73**	**0.87**	0.71	0.86	0.69	0.84
Aragón	**0.18**	**0.38**	0.21	0.39	0.05	0.16
Navarre	**0.26**	**0.34**	0.20	0.38	0.13	0.28
Valencia	**0.60**	**0.71**	0.56	0.57	0.38	0.40
Catalonia	0.15	0.35	0.72	1.13	0.24	0.68
Asturias	0.11	0.11	0.54	0.75	0.47	0.69
Madrid	0.45	0.65	1.46	1.87	1.15	1.95
Galicia	**0.42**	**0.62**	0.30	0.38	0.25	0.33
Canary Islands	**0.92**	**1.46**	1.20	1.41	0.87	0.84
La Rioja	−0.22	−0.31	0.21	0.24	0.05	−0.01
Basque Country	**0.90**	0.95	1.03	1.26	0.67	0.97
Cantabria	**0.84**	**0.96**	0.71	0.89	0.54	0.75
Murcia	0.71	**0.65**	0.74	0.36	0.71	0.14
Balearic Isles	0.25	0.24	0.43	0.51	0.35	0.36
Total	**0.48**	**0.66**	0.58	0.76	0.41	0.56

Sources: Population censuses for 1860, 1900 and 1930, INEbase Historia: www.ine.es/inebaseweb/hist.do

Legend
Regions are ordered by decreasing number of claims. Figures in bold indicate where claimant villages exceeded regional rates (provincial capitals excluded).

accurate measurement of the pressure added by population growth and market forces on land would require considering further environmental and economic variables. It is evident from the table that at the national scale, population growth in the claimant villages or municipalities had outpaced that of the country as a whole (provincial capitals excluded from both counts), not only between 1860 and 1930 but also in the shorter term, between 1900 and 1930. This is consistent with the hypothesis that to some extent the claims responded to a greater pressure on available resources.

At a regional level, in most of the regions ranking higher in terms of the number of recovery applications (Castilla y León, La Mancha, Navarre and Aragón), population growth in the claimant villages was markedly higher than the regional rate, and moreover in the former three it was higher even counting the provincial capitals. Thus, the villages in Castilla y León that filed claims had grown during the first third of the twentieth century at a yearly rate of 0.31 per cent, outpacing the 0.24 per cent recorded for this region overall (0.13 per cent when the capitals are excluded). The situation was repeated in Castilla La Mancha (1.01 per cent, 0.89 per cent and 0.86 per cent, respectively) and in Navarre (0.73 per cent, 0.38 per cent and 0.28 per cent), and to a lesser extent in Aragón (0.38 per cent, 0.39 per cent and 0.16 per cent). Yet in two of the regions with the highest number of claims (Extremadura and Andalusia), the growth rates in the claimant villages were almost exactly on a par with the regional average, indicating that population growth played no significant role there. Furthermore, precisely the opposite is true in other regions, with lower population growth rates in municipalities submitting recovery applications. It is true that these are regions with a lower number of claims than those mentioned beforehand, therefore constituting a more residual phenomenon. Conversely, in several regions that had a lesser number of claimant villages and a lower rate of claims to the provincial population, the claimant villages had experienced faster population growth.

Be that as may, we cannot establish a clear-cut relationship between population growth and recovery claims, either. As we shall see below, many of the Castilian villages submitting their applications to the IRA reinforced their arguments by conjuring up a looming spectre of mass emigration; yet that scaremongering was never used in the applications submitted from Andalusia and Extremadura, which used plain poverty and hunger instead as the rhetorical device to try and sway the administration, which they nevertheless attributed to demographic pressure, besides the unequal distribution of land and capital.

It is clear that none of the two most immediate macro-level hypotheses satisfactorily explain the geography of recovery claims. In order to gain a deeper level of understanding, it may therefore prove interesting to change scale and identify the reasons, or at least the identities, the conjured up factors and the argumentative rationale of those who lobbied for the recovery of the commons.

'Undoing the unfair enrichment of certain powerful people': The applications for recovery in Andalusia, Extremadura and Old Castile

In the areas we have investigated in more detail, the proceedings for the recovery of commons were mostly instigated by local councils, although in several villages the councils' claims were accompanied by requests from workers' societies, many of which were of socialist persuasion. We have found mutually reinforcing applications submitted by workers' associations and local councils. Other local administrative bodies, such as the governing boards of lower entities and the district councils that replaced the former 'communities of town and countryside', also played a major part in recovery applications. Such were for instance the cases of the *Comunidad de Ciudad y Tierra* of Segovia, which included 129 villages, and the *Asocio de Mombeltrán* in Ávila.[27]

Some local councils, however, seemed to be somewhat remiss in this respect, and then it befell workers' associations to take the initiative, not without denouncing not just the councillors' inaction but indeed their resistance to provide the required documents from their archives (Fuente del Olmo de Fuentidueña,

Segovia and Valbuena de Pisuerga, Palencia).[28] This is little wonder, since in some cases the local councils had hitherto played a major part in the privatizations. In 1908, the Supreme Court ruled against a large-claim lawsuit filed by four villagers of Villar del Buey (Zamora), who alleged that the Land Registry had recorded misappropriated council lands. The ruling alleged that under current municipal law, only the local council was entitled to file such a claim, which in this case it obviously had not.[29] Moreover, some local workers' societies reported misappropriations of commons by members of the local council itself (Santa Eufemia, Córdoba), as well as abuse of power by the mayor, in collusion with other local administration officials (Aceituna, Cáceres).[30]

One dossier after the other complain of the usurpation of the commons that had once existed within the municipal boundaries, providing a wide array of explanations for their origins, as well as varied kinds of evidence to their past existence and misappropriation. Some local councils could refer back to ancient documents, such as the thirteenth-century *Libros de Baldíos* (Books of Commons) (Coripe, Seville).[31] Rather more usually, they resorted to nineteenth-century documents of different natures and origins, particularly the abundant paperwork created during the disentailment process. However, following the nineteenth-century spawning of abrupt political upheaval, municipal archives could hardly be trusted to be particularly well preserved. A council secretary might complain of the arranged disappearance of documents that were important for the defence of common rights (Tornavacas, Cáceres).[32] In Trigueros (Huelva), the dossier also told of the vicissitudes of a file for exemption of land sales, which 'was made to vanish whenever convenient, until the force of *fait accompli* left the local council with no choice but to accept the situation'.[33]

Therefore, as there were not always reliable documents to prove the former existence of commons, numerous statements were given under oath by locals of more or less advanced age, who claimed to remember the existence of common land within the municipality and even provided the approximate location of their boundaries. It may well seem that such witness statements were somewhat shaky evidence to prove the existence of the commons before the law. Yet the dossier from the municipality of Cazalla (Seville) is a reminder that throughout the nineteenth century, part of the privatizations had proceeded precisely on the basis of ownership information provided by two 'landowning' witnesses appearing before the local justice of peace, which was deemed sufficient to record the property in the Land Registry, or of witness statements being accepted by some courts as sufficient proof for granting private property rights.[34]

The allegations of misappropriation presented in the dossiers also covered a wide range of causes, as each village's case involved a specific process with its own time span. It is nonetheless possible to systematize some general features of the most typical situations. Some of the claims seem to have been motivated by sundry lawsuits between villages and the nobility, possibly due to unresolved matters involving the dissolution of the seigniorial regime. Villamartín (Cádiz) reported that the Marquis of Las Amarillas refused to acknowledge common use rights, in spite of a court ruling in favour of the village. This had caused long-term litigation, which apparently was revived whenever a major political change took place.[35] In Dos Torres (Córdoba), a lawsuit had been filed concerning a dispute between the village and the Marquis of La Guardia over the use of allegedly common lands. The first instance court had ruled for the village, but in 1909 a Supreme Court ruling reversed this in favour of the Marquis.[36]

Such tensions between villagers and noblemen concerning common lands also appeared in Arcos de la Frontera (Cádiz), Lucena (Córdoba) and Corbesín (Soria).[37] In the districts of Sayago and Pan (Zamora), they concerned the ownership of pastureland estates (*dehesas*). The villages had bought the *dehesas* from the Crown back in 1741, but between 1891 and 1905 the Land Registry registered their property to a handful of private individuals, many of whom of titled nobility.[38] The alleged misappropriation seems to have been based on a generous interpretation of ancient feudal rights by the deciding official bodies, whether the Land Registry itself or the courts.

Most of the claims involved the commons that had been privatized during the nineteenth century, especially under the Civil Disentailment Act of 1 May 1855, which targeted among others the property of local corporate bodies. As the local council of Ayllón (Segovia) argued in 1933, 'faced with the disentailing rule of those laws, the council could not invoke any right as it was dispossessed of that land that belonged to it legitimately and by legal deeds of ownership'.[39] Some villages that had had their commons sold following disentailment reported that even though the purchasers had never paid for the land, it had not been reinstated to the local council (Vicar and Alcudía de Monteagudo, both in Almería).[40] Others also stated that they had neither received payment of the price nor any rent since the sale, and asked to be afforded at least public debt certificates amounting to 80 per cent of the value of the transactions (Navalmanzano, Segovia and Valbuena de Pisuerga, Palencia).[41]

Some villages pursued a different line of argumentation, claiming that the post-disentailment sales should be considered null and void in their case because their land had in fact been declared a villagers' commons and therefore inalienable (Casas del Castañar, Cáceres; Rinconada, Seville, and Trigueros, Almería).[42] This coincides with the findings of several studies on disentailment, which emphasize that as the land to be sold in the civil disentailment was being identified, the difference in legal ownership status between the property of local corporate bodies such as municipalities (*bienes de propios*), and the villages' own communal properties (*bienes de comunes de los pueblos*) was of scant effectiveness, allowing the latter to be sold in spite of being legally protected.[43]

In yet other cases, the privatization of the commons had been independent of disentailment, such as the sale to private individuals of the right of use over pastures, while the ploughing rights had remained in the hands of the local villagers (Plasenzuela, Calzadilla, Cañaveral and Casas de don Gómez, all in Cáceres).[44] The historical literature reports that over time the purchasers of the pastures had sought, often successfully, to extend their rights to other usages, sometimes even to the point of achieving full ownership.[45] Even where the villagers had retained their right to plough, they sometimes alleged that the yield fell short of the community's needs to request that the former purchasers be expropriated of the right to use the pastures and have it returned to the villages. Along these lines, the Republican legislation proposed to redefine property boundaries, but without specifying how this should be achieved. In its application dossier, the local council of Cañaveral (Cáceres) proposed to proceed quite simply by seizure in favour of the local councils.[46]

Complaints were particularly bitter about the so-called *fetosines*, lands that in some villages of the province of Segovia were reserved for the use of 'the most senior or elderly' villagers. The 110 hectares of *fetosines* in Domingo-García had been sold in 1868 to 'wealthy people for a tenth of their value'.[47] The application made by four labourers in Marazuela complained that following their conveyance pursuant to the disentailment act:

> the local people have been left unprotected and since then there has been almost no help for the aged and no land to be farmed by the dwellers, while a fortune hunter has been made rich by buying the plots made up by those *fetosines* for a ludicrous price.[48]

The same bitterness pervades the dossiers denouncing those who had once undertaken to act on behalf of the local community to preserve the uncultivated common lands, and had finally opted to snatch them for themselves. In Villanueva del Rebollar (Palencia), the socialist trade union complained in January 1932 that 'the husband of this local feudal lady bought it under pretence of sharing it out among all the villagers, by having his shepherd place the highest bid, but then he kept it all for himself'.[49] In May 1936, their fellow socialists in Fuente del Olmo de Fuentidueña (Segovia) accused the buyer of 600 hectares of uncultivated common land of 'tricking the local villagers by telling them he would attend the auctions on behalf of the entire village and then keeping the land for himself'.[50]

Another cause of complaint present in several municipalities was the encroachment of plots by purchasers who over time extended their property to much larger areas, taking advantage of the lack of a land survey that clearly demarcated the plots. The local council of Valdehúncar (Cáceres), for instance, stated that a pasture estate sold in 1860 with an area of 534 hectares, had without apparent explanation extended to 944 hectares by the 1930s.[51] In Olleros de Tera (Zamora), an area called El Teso which the Marquis of Los Salados had bought in 1860 with a surface of 330 hectares, was recorded in the 1885 land survey with 756 hectares.[52] Something similar was reported about the meadow of Pelazas in Villar del Buey (Zamora), which had increased from 1,270 hectares in 1852 and 1879 to 4,182 hectares at the beginning of the twentieth century.[53] More dramatic still was the case of Cazalla (Seville), where the village itself had bought disentailed land in 1893. Interspersed among those lands were a number of other plots that had been sold beforehand to private individuals. Allegedly, one of these plots that was registered with thirty-nine hectares on purchase (1876) had ended up with a massive 1,540 hectares in 1910, with the acquiescence of the Spanish government who by ruling in favour of the owners set a precedent before the courts, which finally acknowledged them full legal ownership.[54]

Not all privatizations had originated in sales. Claims of alleged misappropriation were commonplace even where no sales had taken place and the commons had remained in the hands of local councils. In some cases, it involved court rulings, as a result of the communities' default on mortgage annuities on the use of the land, or due to an interpretation of property law that favoured the rich and powerful. For instance, during the Peninsular War the local council of Coomonte (Zamora) had mortgaged a thirty-hectare meadow and had honoured the annuities up until 1924, when 'they steadfastly refused to pay the rent, as they believed they had already paid too much for the sums borrowed in 1812'. The claim filed by the creditor culminated in 1932 with a ruling for the reinstatement of the meadow, whereby the local council stated in February 1933 that 'they feel fearful and melancholic upon seeing that they have been dispossessed of the meadow belonging to the entire community', being left without 'even a tiny patch of meadowland for separating the grain and threshing the corn'.[55] Much the same was reported by Fuentes de Ropel (Zamora), where the refusal to go on paying mortgage annuities to the Seminary of Valderas on twenty hectares of meadows led to a lawsuit and ultimately a ruling in favour of the creditor. In this case, the village avoided the court order by authorizing the sale of the meadows in 1898 with the permission of the government, and two years later negotiating with the buyer for the transfer of the land to a large group of villagers.[56]

In Huercal (Almería), the local council made the most of the land survey operation in 1930 to compare it with a 1889 tax assessment, pointing out that several tracts of common land had vanished during the intervening years, while no sales transactions had been recorded.[57] Claims were also filed against encroachments by adjacent landowners into the commons, as in San Esteban de Molar (Zamora) and Valdespina (Palencia); the fencing in of common lands by privates, such the parish priest of Pedrazales (Zamora), and the arbitrary ploughing of lands that the local council had sequestered or attempted to, in Matute, Alcózar and Añavieja (Soria) and in Valle de Cerrato (Palencia).[58]

In yet other instances, a minority of villagers eventually monopolized the commons that initially were shared among all for farming on an equitable basis (Vejer de la Frontera – Cadiz, and Santa Eufemía – Córdoba).[59] This is similar to what had happened to the communal exploitation of the marble quarries in Macael (Almería), which initially pertained to the whole village but ended up in the hands of three families who at some unknown date had taken the operation under lease and in 1899 had the local council grant them operating rights in perpetuity. In 1927, some of the dispossessed villagers managed to achieve legal recognition of ownership in a trial that, in the words of the local council, ruled 'in favour of bandits and scoundrels'.[60]

In short, just as there had been plenty of opportunities and many sorts of ways to privatize the commons, there were always sectors of the rural population who saw them as misappropriations and their recovery as a form of social justice. Above all, their sense of grievance was compounded by a dismal economic and social situation, which they saw recovery as a means of overcoming. One common denominator running through most of the applications is the lack of economic means due to the privatization of the pastures for grazing livestock or the land for growing crops, combined with having been forced to give up leases in other villages or the damaging spread of unemployment.

References to mass emigration, either past or future, abound in the dossiers of Castilian villages to justify their claims for recovery, as in the case of Ayllón (Segovia), Manzanar del Barco, Olleros de Tera, Riofrío de Aliste (Zamora) and Centenera de Andaluz (Soria).[61] Frequent references were made to unemployment, poverty and hunger. The workers' society in Fuente del Olmo de Fuentidueña (Segovia) stated in December 1932 that it was submitting such data as it had managed to gather:

> for the peace of mind of the workers who are now waiting impatiently to recover these lands, who cannot wait to farm these lands and start working again, as they cannot find a job either in the province or outside it, even though they have looked in part of the province of Madrid.[62]

Moreover, this was a crucial issue for the trade unions themselves, 'otherwise the societies become demoralised, as they do not see any of the promises being kept, and instead of increasing numbers are tailing off, which is of great concern to us in leadership', trade union leaders admitted in Villanueva del Rebollar (Palencia) in January 1932.[63] They sometimes hinted at threats of violence, as when the socialist trade union in Santervás de la Vega (Palencia) stated that 'due to the job crisis, they lacked the wherewithal or means to remedy unemployment and satisfy their family's hunger, even though they had no wish to resort to violence but rather to act within the law',[64] and the local committee in Villapún (Palencia) noted that the recovery of the land would avoid 'insidious ideas taking root which might compromise our beloved homeland'.[65]

It should come as no surprise, therefore, that as reported in April 1936 from Ayllón (Segovia) the delay in the passing of the recovery act was met with 'the utmost impatience on the part of the local villagers'. The urgency of the recovery was also related to the landowners' reaction to this threat. The same petition from Ayllón also noted that the incumbent owners of the claimed land:

> foreseeing the effects of the agrarian reform, sold it to three villagers in Ayllón, and these took possession of the land most violently, proceeding to plough it without respecting tracks, paths or rights of way, causing considerable inconvenience to the owners of around fifteen cattle sheds and livestock pens and to the community at large.[66]

Still in the province of Segovia, Navalmanzano reported the felling of a pine-wood used for the extraction of resin 'because it is being cut down and used as timber, undoubtedly out of fear that it may one day be recovered by the municipality'.[67]

As was to be expected in an essentially redistributive project, the vision of the Republic's agrarian reform, as well as the expectations of the peasants who eagerly awaited it, was often linked to the partition of the land into smallholdings to be used solely for agricultural purposes, to the detriment of other uses like livestock or forestry. Paraleda de la Mata (Cáceres), for instance, proposed that one of the two *dehesas* to be recovered should be auctioned for ploughing and grazing, and the other divided into smallholdings to be farmed by the villagers.[68] Specific requests for land sharing and ploughing rights are found as well in Valdespina, Santervás de la Vega, Villarrabejo and Valle de Cerrato (all in Palencia), Vega de Villalobos (Zamora) and Santa María de Riaza (Segovia).

It has nonetheless been indicated that the agrarian reform might have taken other paths besides the distribution of ploughing rights and the division of plots for sowing.[69] In some cases, especially when the applicants were workers' societies, rather than dividing the land into plots the aim was to use the recovery for collective farming projects, as in Villamuriel de Cerrato and Villanueva del Rebollar (Palencia), Alcubilla de Nogales (Zamora), Fuente Olmo de Fuentidueña (Segovia) and Corbesín (Soria).[70] On the other hand, we found applications that appeared to exclude plot division in favour of uses primarily for livestock or forestry, as in Castillejo de San Pedro (Soria), where the local council stated that the 672 hectares that it sought to recover 'are of the poorest soils, very difficult to plough, but they can be put to good use for grazing and firewood, so that this minor entity might earn some benefit'.[71] Centenera de Andaluz (Soria) stated that 'when the commons was sold it had been fully forested; there were trees used for making charcoal that produced ten to twelve metric quintals'. Tree felling had seriously harmed the environment, because 'to some extent this has caused the loss of the countryside's ability to attract rainfall' and the erosion of the gravelly soil by torrential rains, threatening 'the rich topsoil in the lowest lying plots'. Accordingly, they proposed using it only for grazing and household firewood.[72] Indeed, the priority for the peasant labourers' society in Fuentenebro (Burgos) in May 1936 in recovering the common land that had been sold back in 1839 was reforestation 'which for the time being will solve the serious problem of unemployment in this village'.[73]

Summing up, underneath these variations the overall aim at the time was to correct the legacy of the liberal changes started in the nineteenth century in order to redress the wrongs they had done to village life. In the words used in November 1932 by four day-labourers in Marazuela (Segovia), 'one of the things the current laws want is precisely to undo the unfair enrichment of certain people that has often been achieved through their influence on the powers that be'.[74] Put more simply, as the society of land labourers of Villanueva del Rebollar (Palencia) had stated a few months earlier: 'We want land and the independence to work it'.[75]

Discussion and conclusions

Having looked at the arguments made in the recovery claims concerning a number of key issues, we can now discuss what we have learned to make a few general points. The first is that the Republican agrarian reform can be understood as one specific episode in a long-term process of redefining property rights in land. The dossiers we investigated suggest that as late as the 1930s, the liberal changes in property rights that began in the nineteenth century, far from a done and dusted affair, remained an ongoing process of conflict. One should therefore avoid simplistic interpretations such as seeing the 'liberal agrarian reform' as an aseptic definition of modern property rights, which painlessly managed to introduce economic efficiency in agriculture. Matters were in fact much more complex, because such redefinition involved not only the efficiency of modern property rights in improving market performance, but also the greater or lesser equity being generated in the process.[76]

It seems clear in this regard that some sectors in rural society felt illegitimately expropriated by the changes that had taken place in the preceding decades. Seen from a historical perspective, and taking into account that besides efficiency, the allocation of property rights has consequences in the distribution of income and work opportunities, it seems a fair conclusion that the gains in efficiency were not enough to compensate those who had felt prejudiced by the changes, and that this lay at the heart of the endless frictions and disputes that had gone on since.

On the other hand, the feelings of mistrust and bitterness that pervade many of the dossiers may be partially explained by the often muddied way the redefinition of rights was carried out in nineteenth-century Spain, which was a far cry from the clear-cut delineation of rights associated with the ideal-type of 'modern property'. As pointed out elsewhere, the laws that allowed the privatization of commons were lax enough, in both definitions and procedures, to be applied in each case according to the local balance of forces among the interested parties.[77] Indeed, the recovery claims show that privatizations often proceeded on the edge of the law and even in outright illegal ways. Common lands and grazing grounds that belonged collectively to the villagers, not to the *ancien régime* corporate bodies, and were thereby inalienable, were redefined as municipal property so that they could be privatized. Some purchases were never paid for, without the land ever being reinstated. Landowners encroached into much larger land surfaces than those they had legally purchased. Lands legally acknowledged as commons were privately ploughed without permission, and ended up being legalized as private ownership. The catalogue of denounced misappropriations is so long and varied that such cases cannot simply be considered exceptions to the rule, but rather as an informal *de facto* rule that ran parallel to legal privatizations, apparently affecting vast tracts of land. This murky side of the process that we could identify in our cases converges with Robledo's argument about the problems caused by the lack of a land survey to verify the entries in the Land Registry, and by Congost about 'the deeds that were never requested'.[78]

Such situations had caused those affected to protest, often turning to the courts for justice. In the courts, the lawsuits for allegedly unlawful privatizations ran alongside others related to the legal redefinition of property rights. Many involved long, drawn-out proceedings, probably because the courts had neither the means nor the inclination to act quickly, and certainly because the more powerful parties could appeal unfavourable rulings almost indefinitely. What does seem clear is that during the first third of the twentieth century, a fairly significant part of the privatization process was still undergoing court litigation. This may have contributed both to keeping alive the memory of the commons among the dispossessed groups and idealizing them, along with reinforcing feelings of social injustice.

Therefore, rather than having created a new problem, the Republican project for the recovery of the commons placed the spotlight on a latent one.[79] From 1931 onwards, the Republican authorities made the first attempt at drawing up a surprisingly extensive catalogue of improper proceedings. Since this was in itself a process involving conflict, the new political regime created a watershed in the balance of forces involved. The stances adopted by the workers' societies in favour of the Republic and the policies rolled out by the government (especially during the so-called Progressive Biennium, from 1931 to 1933) were especially enthusiastic, and a clear expression of the hopes for political change that had been raised among a part of the rural population. The Republic was clearly seen by those sectors as an opportunity for the establishment of what they considered 'social justice', as opposed to – to glean a few typical and telling expressions from the dossiers – the 'hated tyranny of the local bosses', the 'monarchical absolutism' and the 'power of the feudal lords'. The fact that they argued that the liberal regime had not entirely done away with unfair *ancien régime* power structures may itself be understood as a way of de-legitimizing the changes it had introduced in property rights.

Beyond these feelings, the specific factors explaining differences in the geography of the recovery claims remain to be understood. The degree of privatization achieved since the mid-nineteenth century and the pressure of population growth may each have played a part in those differences, but they are clearly not enough to explain them. More research is needed to unearth more complex sets of causes. Some may be related to ecological characteristics: people may have been more encouraged to apply for recovery in those areas were the misappropriated commons provided more farming potential. Others may involve local political contexts, namely the composition of the local councils in the new democratic scenario ushered in by the Republic and the presence and relative strength of workers' associations. Yet other factors are more difficult to trace, such as the varying strength of past communal institutions and the survival of a more or less lively and idealized social memory of the commons in the local collective conscience – more exactly, in the collective conscience of the dispossessed local groups – that might have provided the incentive to take action and lobby for their recovery.[80]

What does seem clear is that the issue of the commons was destined to play a significant role in the Republic's agrarian reform process. The recoveries could have been a means to provide land in response to the claims made by local councils, without the need to pay compensation for compulsory seizures. For landless peasants and for those who owned smallholdings, the recovery of commons might have opened up an alley for fairly speedy access to work opportunities, land, and other resources.

However, although they had the lack of resources as a common denominator, the problems the recovery was supposed to alleviate were expressed in different ways, according to the different agrarian and social structures. In the *latifundium* areas, the claims seem to have been more related to the need for farming land in order to fight unemployment, poverty and hunger. In the smallholding areas, the claims alluded to the use of the commons providing an alternative to emigration, and the recoveries were more often associated with grazing and forestry uses, besides farming land. And even though in most cases the claims converged in an attempt to consolidate agricultural development based on smallholdings, a few of them aimed instead at collective farming.

Acknowledgements

This chapter resulted of the projects in non-oriented basic research HUM2006-01277, HAR2009-09700 and HAR2012-30732, funded by Spain's Directorate General for Scientific and Technological Research (DGICYT). The authors thank the assistance of Metxi Bogino Larrambebere in archival tasks and Alvaro Adot Lerga in data processing.

Notes

1 D. C. North and P. Thomas, *The Rise of the Western World: A New Economic History* (Cambridge: Cambridge University Press, 1976); P. Grossi, *Historia del Derecho de Propiedad* (Barcelona: Ariel, 1986).

2 Grupo de Estudios de Historia Rural (GEHR), 'Más allá de la "propiedad perfecta": El proceso de privatización de los montes públicos Españoles (1859–1926)'. *Historia Agraria*, 8, 1994, pp. 99–152. A. Ortega Santos, *La Tragedia de los Cerramientos* (Valencia: Centro Francisco Tomas y Valiente, 2002).

3 D. Gallego, I. Iriarte and Lana, J. M. 'Las Españas rurales y el Estado, 1800–1931', in R. Robledo (ed.), *Sombras del Progreso: Las Huellas de la Historia Agraria: Ramón Garrabou* (Barcelona: Crítica, 2010), pp. 85–116.

4 Among others, S. Riesco Roche, *La Reforma Agraria y los Orígenes de la Guerra Civil: Cuestión Yuntera y Radicalización Patronal en la Provincia de Cáceres (1931–1940)* (Madrid: Biblioteca Nueva, 2006); R. Robledo, 'Política y reforma agraria: De la restauración a la II República (1868/74–1939)', in A. García Sanz and J. Sanz Fernández (eds), *Reformas y Políticas Agrarias en la Historia de España* (Madrid: Ministerio de Agricultura Pescas y Alimentación, 1996), pp. 247–349; R. Robledo, 'Los economistas ante la reforma agraria de la Segunda República', in E. Fuentes Quintana and F. Comín (eds), *Economía y Economistas Españoles en la Guerra Civil*, vol. 2 (Madrid: Real Academia de Ciencias Morales y Políticas, Galaxia Gutenberg and círculo de lectores, 2008), pp. 243–76; R. Robledo, 'Los males del latifundismo: La hora de la reforma agraria', in A. Viñas (ed.), *En el Combate por la Historia: La República, la Guerra Civil, el Franquismo* (Barcelona: Pasado y Presente, 2012), pp. 101–21; J. A. Serrano Álvarez, '"Reviviendo el sueño de varias generaciones": Comunales y reforma agraria en León en la II República (1931–1936)', *Historia Agraria*, 62 (2014), pp. 147–75.

5 P. Brassley, 'Land reform and reallocation in interwar Europe', in R. Congost and R. Santos (eds), *Contexts of Property in Europe: The Social Embeddedness of Property Rights in Land in Historical Perspective* (Turnhout: Brepols, 2010), pp. 145–64; H. Jörgensen, 'The inter-war land reforms in Estonia, Finland and Bulgaria: A comparative study', *Scandinavian Economic History Review*, 54:1 (2006), pp. 64–97.

6 E. Malefakis, *Reforma Agraria y Revolución Campesina en la España del Siglo XX* (Barcelona: Ariel, 1971).

7 R. Robledo, *Economistas y Reformadores Españoles: La Cuestión Agraria, 1760–1935* (Madrid: Ministerio de Agricultura, Pescas y Alimentación, 1993).

8 P. Carrión, *Estudios Sobre la Agricultura Española* (Madrid: Ediciones de la Revista de Trabajo, 1974 [1934]), pp. 239–42.

9 A. de Janvry, 'The role of land reform in economic development: Policies and politics', *American Journal of Agricultural Economics*, 63:2 (1981), pp. 384–92; K. Deininger, *Land Policies for Growth and Poverty Reduction* (Washington: World Bank and Oxford University Press, 2003); K. Deininger and H. Binswanger, 'The evolution of the World Bank's land policy: Principles, experiences, and future challenges', *World Bank Research Observer*, 14:2 (1999), pp. 247–76; K. Griffin, A. R. Khan and A. Ickowitz, 'Poverty and the distribution of land', *Journal of Agrarian Change*, 2:3 (2002), pp. 279–330; P. Rosset, 'Mirando hacia el futuro: La reforma agraria y la soberanía alimentaria', *Areas: Revista Internacional de Ciencias Sociales*, 26 (2007), pp. 167–82. A critique of this approach in G. Dyer, 'Redistributive land reform: No April rose. The poverty of Berry and Cline and GKI on the inverse relationship', *Journal of Agrarian Change*, 4:1 (2004), pp. 45–72.

10 Robledo, 'Política y reforma agraria'.

11 X. Balboa López, 'La historia de los montes públicos españoles (1812–1936): Un balance y algunas propuestas', *Historia Agraria*, 18 (1999), pp. 95–128; I. Iriarte-Goñi, 'Common lands in Spain, 1800–1995: Persistence, change and adaptation', *Rural History*, 13:1 (2002), pp. 19–37; J. I. Jiménez Blanco, 'El monte: Una atalaya de la Historia', *Historia Agraria*, 26 (2002), pp. 141–92.

12 A. López Estudillo, 'Los montes públicos y las diversas vías de su privatización en el siglo XIX', *Agricultura y Sociedad*, 65 (1992), pp. 65–100.

13 J. M. Lana Berasain, 'From equilibrium to equity: The survival of the commons in the Ebro basin: Navarra, from the 15th to the 20th centuries', *International Journal of the Commons*, 2:2 (2008), pp. 162–91, at http://doi.org/10.18352/ijc.49 [last accessed 10 March 2016).

14 A. Paniagua Mazorra, *Repercusiones Sociodemográficas de la Política de Colonización Durante el Siglo XIX y Primer Tercio del XX* (Madrid: Ministerio de Agricultura, Pescas y Alimentación, 1992); Riesco, *Reforma Agraria*; Robledo, 'Política y reforma agraria'.

15 Riesco, *Reforma Agraria*.

16 The Institute of Agrarian Reform (IRA) was created in September 1932 to implement the land reform project. It ceased to exist after the Civil War. 'Ley relativa a la reforma agraria', *Gaceta de Madrid*, 265 (21 September 1932), pp. 2095–102.

17 Robledo, 'Política y reforma agraria', p. 295.

18 Robledo, 'Política y reforma agraria'.

19 The parliamentary debate on the bill presented by Ruiz Funes, which began on 28 June 1936, is described by M. Tuñón de Lara, *Tres Claves de la Segunda República* (Madrid: Alianza, 1985), pp. 187–92.

20 J. Casanova, *Anarquismo y Revolución en la Sociedad Rural Aragonesa, 1936–1938* (Madrid: Siglo XXI, 1985).

21 J. L. Martín (ed.), *Archivos de la Reforma Agraria Conservados por el IRYDA* (Madrid: UNED, 1996). The analogy with the *cahiers de doleàncs* in S. Riesco, 'Viriato en las Cortes de la República: Los comunales en la escena política de la España contemporánea hasta la Guerra Civil', in J. A. Martínez Martín, E. González Calleja, S. Souto Kustrin and J. A. Blanco Rodríguez (eds), *El Valor de la Historia: Homenaje al Profesor Julio Aróstegui* (Madrid: Editorial Complutense, 2009), p. 256. The boxes we investigated in depth for this article are numbered as follows: 17, 20, 21, 22, 23, 26, 28, 30, 32, 33, 34, 35, 48, 62, 86, 87 and 88, all labelled *Reforma Agraria: Parte Primera*, hereinafter referred to as A.IRYDA, Ref.Agr.1 (box no.:process no.).

22   A.IRYDA, Ref.Agr.1 (23:1), *Catálogo General de Reclamaciones sobre Bienes Comunales* (n.d.).
23   We could not identify five villages mentioned in the catalogue, two of them in Ciudad Real (Hinojosas, Retuerta de los Montes), two in Cáceres (Pajaromillo and Freganal de la Sierra), and one in Badajoz (Ejea de los Caballeros). We have assumed that these names are wrong and repeat villages already included in the list. We have assumed six other cases to be wrong attributions to a province: those of Barreiros, Boñar, Villares de la Reina, Sotovellanos, Los Pozuelos, and Callosa de Segura. On the cover of the catalogue, an anonymous hand wrote the figure of 872 claims, but after several recounts we found no more than the 866 indicated.
24   R. Robledo, 'Introducción y estudio', in Martín, *Archivos*, pp. 7–36; GEHR, 'Más allá de la "propiedad perfecta".
25   The correlation is statistically significant at the 99 per cent level.
26   J. M. Lana Berasain, 'Commons for sale: Economic and institutional change in nineteenth-century northern Spain', *Documentos de Trabajo de la AEHE*, 604 (Madrid: Asociación Española de Historia Agraria, 2006), at www.aehe.es/wp-content/uploads/2015/04/dt-aehe-06041.pdf [last acessed 10 March 2016].
27   A.IRYDA, Ref.Agr.1 (17:67,69), (28: 58,59).
28   A.IRYDA, Ref.Agr.1 (17:44,59).
29   A.IRYDA, Ref.Agr.1 (20:3). The wave of unrest from 1904 to 1906 aroused the interest of Spanish socialist circles in the agrarian question. S. Cruz Artacho, M. González de Molina and A. Herrera González de Molina, 'Los bienes comunales y el Socialismo español', in J. A. Piqueras Arenas (ed.), *Bienes Comunales: Propiedad, Arraigo y Apropiación* (Madrid: Ministerio de Agricultura, Pescas y Alimentación, 2002), pp. 251–97, on pp. 266–7; M. González de Molina and A. Ortega Santos, 'Bienes comunales y conflictos por los recursos en las sociedades rurales, siglos XIX y XX', *Historia Social*, 38 (2000), pp. 95–116.
30   A.IRYDA, Ref.Agr.1 (62:21), (17:14), (21:29,30).
31   A.IRYDA, Ref.Agr.1 (21:4), (22:7).
32   A.IRYDA, Ref.Agr.1 (21:8).
33   A.IRYDA, Ref.Agr.1 (62:5).
34   A.IRYDA, Ref.Agr.1 (22:5,6).
35   A.IRYDA, Ref.Agr.1 (21:51,52).
36   A.IRYDA, Ref.Agr.1 (7:10).
37   A.IRYDA, Ref.Agr.1 (21:12,13), (17:13), (22:14).
38   A.IRYDA, Ref.Agr.1 (20:3,19).
39   A.IRYDA, Ref.Agr.1 (17:55).
40   A.IRYDA, Ref.Agr.1 (33:86,8).
41   A.IRYDA, Ref.Agr.1 (17:55,44).
42   A.IRYDA, Ref.Agr.1 (21:40), (22:10), (28:14), (62:15).
43   *E.g.*, I. Iriarte Goñi, *Bienes Comunales y Capitalismo Agrario en Navarra, 1855–1935* (Madrid: Ministerio de Agricultura, Pescas y Alimentación, 1996); A. Sabio, *Tierra, Comunal y Capitalismo Agrario en Aragón: Uso de los Recursos Naturales y Campesinado en Cinco Villas, 1830–1935* (Huesca: Instituto de Estudios Alto-Aragoneses, 2002).
44   A.IRYDA, Ref.Agr.1 (21:25,36,38,39,41).
45   J. M. Gastón, *¡Vivan los Comunes!: Movimiento Comunero y Sucesos Corraliceros en Navarra (1896–1930)* (Tafalla: Txalaparta, 2010); J. M. Lana Berasain, 'Los aprovechamientos agrícolas comunales en el sur de Navarra entre los siglos XIX y XX', *Agricultura y Sociedad*, 65 (1992), pp. 115–36; F. Sánchez Marroyo, *Dehesas y Terratenientes en Extremadura: La Propiedad de la Tierra en la Provincia de Cáceres en los Siglos XIX y XX* (Mérida: Asamblea de Extremadura, 1993).
46   A.IRYDA, Ref.Agr.1 (21:38,39).
47   A.IRYDA, Ref.Agr.1 (17:58).

48 A.IRYDA, Ref.Agr.1 (17:62).
49 A.IRYDA, Ref.Agr.1 (17:50).
50 A.IRYDA, Ref.Agr.1 (17:61).
51 A.IRYDA, Ref.Agr.1 (21:10).
52 A.IRYDA, Ref.Agr.1 (20:11).
53 A.IRYDA, Ref.Agr.1 (20:3).
54 A.IRYDA, Ref.Agr.1 (22:5,6).
55 A.IRYDA, Ref.Agr.1 (20:5).
56 A.IRYDA, Ref.Agr.1 (20:9).
57 A.IRYDA, Ref.Agr.1 (33:40).
58 A.IRYDA, Ref.Agr.1 (20:15,12), (17:45,46), (22:12,13,19).
59 A.IRYDA, Ref.Agr.1 (21:49,50), (17:14), (62:21).
60 A.IRYDA, Ref.Agr.1 (28:49,50), (33:52).
61 A.IRYDA, Ref.Agr.1 (17:53), (20:10, 11,13), (22:16).
62 A.IRYDA, Ref.Agr.1 (17:59).
63 A.IRYDA, Ref.Agr.1 (17:50).
64 A.IRYDA, Ref.Agr.1 (17:42).
65 A.IRYDA, Ref.Agr.1 (17:51).
66 A.IRYDA, Ref.Agr.1 (17:53).
67 A.IRYDA, Ref.Agr.1 (17:63).
68 A.IRYDA, Ref.Agr.1 (21:24).
69 Robledo, 'Economistas'; Artacho *et al.*, 'Bienes comunales', p. 292.
70 A.IRYDA, Ref.Agr.1 (17:49,50,61), (20:1), (22:14). The socialist defence of collective farming was studied by S. Cruz Artacho, F. Acosta Ramírez, F. Cobo Romero, M. González de Molina Navarro and A. Herrera González de Molina, 'El Socialismo español y la cuestión agraria (1879–1923): Luces y sombras en el debate teórico y en la práctica sindical y política', *Ayer*, 54 (2004), pp. 129–63.
71 A.IRYDA, Ref.Agr.1 (22:15).
72 A.IRYDA, Ref.Agr.1 (22:16).
73 A.IRYDA, Ref.Agr.1 (17:3).
74 A.IRYDA, Ref.Agr.1 (17:62).
75 A.IRYDA, Ref.Agr.1 (17:50).
76 J. Djenderedjian and D. Santilli make a similar point in chapter four. (Editors' note.)
77 Gallego, Iriarte and Lana, 'Españas rurales'.
78 R. Congost, *Tierras, Leyes, Historia: Estudios sobre la 'Gran Obra de la Propiedad'* (Barcelona: Crítica, 2007), p. 275; R. Robledo, 'El fin de la cuestión agraria en España (1931–1939)', in Robledo, *Sombras del Progreso*, pp. 117–50.
79 G. Ranzato, 'El peso de la violencia en los orígenes de la Guerra Civil de 1936–1939', *Espacio, Tiempo y Forma: Serie V: Historia Contemporánea*, 20 (2008), pp. 159–82.
80 J. Bromley and D. Wolz provide another example of clashing memories and their use in social disputes over property rights in chapter eight (Editors'note.)

8 Hurdles to reunification

Cultural memories and control over property in post-socialist rural East Germany

Joyce E. Bromley and Axel Wolz

Introduction

At the time of German reunification in October 1990, any one village in the former GDR might have a mélange of five distinct and often conflicting memories, those of (1) returning large landowners who had been expropriated immediately after World War II (*Alteigentümer*, 'old proprietors'); (2) returning farmers of medium and large-sized farms (*Großbauern*, 'large farmers') who had fled during collectivization; (3) returning farmers of smaller parcels who had also fled during collectivization (*Kleinbauern*, 'small farmers'); (4) German-speaking refugees from further east as well as industrial workers and landless farm labourers, who had been newly established after the war on land expropriated from the large landowners (*Neubauern*, 'new farmers'); they had been the early beneficiaries of the expropriated estates and eventually became members of collective farms; (5) long-term settled farmers, who had remained and became members of farming collectives or worked on state farms.

The historian interested in cultural memories is presented with the obligation and the opportunity to capture the remembered accounts of people's lives – reflecting both what the research subjects claim they now are and what they say they once were. When those recalled memories have occurred across profoundly conflicting political circumstances, the historian's task is both enriched and complicated. In this chapter we will confront this challenge by embedding within German history the recalled memories of eighty returnee *Alteigentümer* and *Großbauern* families from the former Soviet-occupied region of East Germany who returned to their ancestral homes upon reunification. More specifically, we will look at how memories were used to legitimize and in some cases to overcome the resistance that some returnees' attempts to acquire property met from the practical incumbents and enforcers of the property relations, as they were established after the collapse of the communist regime.[1]

Reconstituting Germans

Stalin's ghost still stalks the land.

(*Moscow News*, 14 July 1988)

For Stalin, peasants were scum.

(Nikita Khrushchev).[2]

Our first task is to set the historical context within which these recalled memories were forged – the coerced 'reconstitution' of East Germany immediately follow-ing the Second World War to eliminate German agricultural traditions. This was achieved through the wholesale dispossession of farmers, forced evictions of families from large farms, selective economic pressure to ensure failure of those medium-sized farms that had escaped eviction, finally leading to complete collectivization.

Our story begins when Soviet troops entered present-day eastern Germany in April 1945. The central issue to be addressed here concerns Stalin's impact on an extensive part of Germany and its culture. His goal was to reconstitute agrarian practices in the Soviet Occupation Zone (SOZ), so as to re-constitute Germans by supplanting their memory and practice of family-based agriculture and replacing it with the Soviet model. The Soviet rulers, aided by German communists, began to transform eastern Germany on these principles.

Even before the war had ended in May 1945, Germany was being over-whelmed by refugees, primarily ethnic Germans from territories that had been incorporated into Poland and the Soviet Union. By 1946, about 3.6 million refugees had arrived in eastern Germany, most of whom had to be accommodated in rural areas.[3] The urgent refugee problem fitted well within Stalin's emerging agenda. The first decisive act of Soviet military rule was the expropriation of farms and homes of those who owned more than 100 hectares. The mass eviction of over 11,000 farm families vacated land on which hundreds of thousands of refugees could be settled.

The abiding problem, for Soviet leaders as for the ensuing GDR government, had always been how to acquire the farmers' grain without having to pay for it. However, the full significance of these early dispossessions and of the extensive agrarian reconstruction project in eastern Germany over the following fifteen years must be understood on philosophical grounds, as well as logistical necessity. Marx's notorious likening of the French peasantry to a sack of potatoes had been passed down to mainstream Soviet politics. The point was the need felt to purge Germans of their 'false consciousness': the cultural memory of a historic relation-ship between families and the land on which they and their forebears had worked, whether as owners or tenants, which seemed to instill a sense of personal owner-ship. Such a possessive relationship with land, a fundamental means of production, and thereby with its produce, represented a serious obstacle to socialist develop-ment. The only way to break the peasants of this 'false' idea of ownership of the produce and their legitimacy to name the price at which they were willing to sell it was to deprive them of land ownership. Peasants had to be reconstituted from entrepreneurs into wage labourers, 'new socialist men' who would work hard and produce foodstuffs for the common benefit embodied in the 'workers' state'.[4]

Thus, while in appearance Stalin wished to eliminate the large landowning class and to settle displaced persons on these lands, his ulterior target was the ownership nexus between the land and those who worked on it. In the wake of the collectivization campaigns carried out in the Soviet Union since the late 1920s and which had resulted in excess mortality estimated at about ten million,[5] agriculture would be organized in collective farms along industrial lines, rural factories with a much reduced work force relying on large-scale agricultural machinery and led by plan-guided managers. This programme entailed the complete re-organization of agriculture and the obliteration of the traditional German family farm.

At the end of the Second World War, somewhat over one-half of the farms in eastern Germany were less than five hectares in size, comprising less than 10 per cent of all agricultural land. At the other end of the scale, approximately 1 per cent of the farms was at least 100 hectares in size and covered about 30 per cent of the agricultural land. The majority of the large farms were in the north – Mecklenburg-Vorpommern and Brandenburg – where soils are poor, often wet, and largely forested. Further south, where high-quality soil is found, small and medium-sized farms tended to dominate. Most of these were family-run, but many required hired labourers during periods of intensive work. Technical progress was often impressive, and many of the larger farms were at the forefront in adopting modern techniques.[6] Most of the farmers we interviewed, however, had practised labour-intensive farming that relied on draught horses and oxen rather than tractors.

The Soviets and their allied governments carried out the reorganization of agriculture in eastern Germany in three distinct phases:[7]

1. 1945–1949: Forced expropriation of all farms over 100 hectares. These farmers were treated in the same manner as active Nazi members and supporters, as well as war criminals. This enforced change of land ownership has been termed 'land reform'.
2. 1948–1952: Elimination of farmers cultivating between 20 and 100 hectares, coupled with the establishment of collective farms, which – during the earliest stage – was voluntary. This period has been labelled the 'crowding-out struggle'.
3. 1952–1960: Forced collectivization of agricultural production. This process was slowed down between 1953 and 1957 and strongly enforced in 1959. This final phase would be called the 'Socialist Spring' when full collectivization was officially declared on 25 April 1960.

The ensuing narrative will recount these profound events in German agrarian history and relate them to contending cultural memories since the declaration of reunification on 3 October 1990.

Land reform, 1945–1949

In early May 1945, the first group of German communists, the Ulbricht Group, returned to Germany from exile in Moscow. Their task was to work under the Soviet Military Administration (SMA) to establish a socialist system in Germany.[8] Settling tens of thousands of *Neubauern* on expropriated land would become a central component of the wholesale reorganization of agriculture in East Germany.[9]

'Expropriation' meant that families were evicted from their *Kreis* (county). Those who were required to present themselves to local reporting centres were loaded into railroad cattle cars and transported to retention centres, often former concentration camps. Some managed to join caravans moving west and became indistinguishable from hundreds of thousands of displaced persons bound for the frontier with the American–British zone. Almost all of the 11,500 expropriated farm families eventually fled to West Germany between 1945 and 1949, either directly or via retention centres. Their abandoned homes were eventually converted into multiple one or two-room apartment buildings for *Neubauern* families.

In a special consultation with the German communist leadership in Moscow between 4 and 10 June 1945, Stalin insisted on fundamental social change in rural areas as one of the most important tasks to be performed in Germany.[10] German communists had hitherto preferred to preserve the right to private farming, but the expulsion of the owners of the large estates nevertheless became part of the founding proclamation of the German Communist Party, on 11 June 1945. Stalin and his advisors had expected the former hired workers on the large estates to rush in and take control. When this 'land reform from below' failed, Stalin ordered a 'land reform from above'.[11] By late July 1945, the Soviet Military Administration (SMA) had drafted a land reform decree and pushed for rapid implementation, and the Communist Party immediately adopted it. The Communist Party decided to launch the first wave of expropriations in Saxony -Anhalt because of the province's long and powerful communist tradition. However, support in Saxony-Anhalt was not as swift-moving as expected. Not until 3 September 1945 did the provisional government agree to the land reform decree, but then the other four East German states quickly followed, employing almost the same text.[12]

Many rank-and-file communists in rural areas were doubtful. They did not want to disrupt the ongoing harvest and preparations for the imminent spring planting season. The Social Democratic Party (SPD) preferred to keep the large farms as agricultural production cooperatives.[13] Nevertheless, Stalin disregarded any of these arguments and pushed for a rapid implementation of the reform.

Between 1945 and late 1949, the SMA took over 2.5 million hectares of land from 7,160 farmers owning more than 100 hectares, which were combined into a 'land fund' along with the 131,742 hectares from 4,537 alleged Nazi sympathizers and war criminals owning less than 100 hectares. By October 1949, when the GDR government was established, one third of the total agricultural area in East

Germany (amounting to about 3.3 million hectares, 76 per cent of which coming from large landowners) had been acquired by the SMA and put into this GDR-owned land fund.[14] This was eventually distributed as small parcels to landless agricultural workers, small-scale farmers and refugees, the *Neubauern*.

German communists administered evictions and land reform at all levels of government – local, district, provincial, and state. Local and district officers administered policies, watched over by provincial and state administrators. Some of the confiscated land was used to establish 540 state farms (*Volkseigenes Gut –* VEGs), as well as experimental agricultural stations and seed multiplication units. VEGs comprised about 500,000 hectares, while another 600,000 hectares was forest.[15] Most of the 'land reform funds' were managed by approximately 10,000 village 'land reform commissions', whose task was to re-distribute the confiscated land in an orderly process.[16] In general, a village commission consisted of five to seven individuals representing agricultural workers, small farmers, and refugees. Frequently, land was distributed by drawing lots.[17]

Approximately 70 per cent of confiscated land, about one-half of which was forested rather than agricultural land, was allocated to a variety of beneficiaries. About 1.3 million hectares was distributed among 284,673 agricultural workers, landless farmers, and assorted small farmers, many of whom were cultivating exceedingly small, non-viable parcels of land, and 763,596 hectares went to approximately 91,000 refugees from territories east of the German border. A further portion of 146,645 hectares was given to 183,261 industrial workers, to serve as small family garden plots. On average, most newly established farms were approximately eight hectares in size, much smaller than the typical German family farm.[18]

The average *Neubauern* very quickly came to realize their farms were too small to be viable. Adding to the scale issue, they lacked draught animals, agricultural inputs, and proper farm buildings. As a result, many *Neubauern* cooperated informally, in order to gain scale and maximize inputs. At first, many local and district administrators were scornful of these joint arrangements because, at that time, individual family farms were still considered the ideal.[19] Ironically, within five years these same officials would be forcing individual farmers into formal collectives. While most *Neubauern* had been happy to receive some land in order to survive in the harsh post-war years, by late 1948 about 10,000 had given up and left agriculture behind, either moving to the southern industrial zones as manufacturing began to grow or fleeing to West Germany. By 1951, an additional 67,000 individuals had left agriculture.[20] Approximately 80,000 *Neubauern* are thus reported to have quit by 1951.[21]

The SMA did not implement a land reform, as the term is commonly understood in the literature.[22] Land reform programmes do not usually just evict landowners from their homes and farms; expropriated owners are usually compensated for their loss, and recipients of the expropriated land are proven farmers or farm workers who, for the most part, have a long history of agriculture on the estate undergoing expropriation. Instead, the SMA led to evict and dispossess farmers owning more than 100 hectares of land without any pretence of compensation.

A brief reminder of the difference between 'confiscation' and 'expropriation' is essential here. The foundation of Germany's legal system dates back to Roman times. Romans *expropriated* land when it was needed for the broader public good, for example, for establishing a new town. Those whose land was expropriated were compensated. A different standard practice was *confiscation* as punishment, which would be the correct term in German juridical culture for taking the land without compensation from farmers who were guilty of owning over 100 hectares. Notwithstanding this, we will retain 'expropriation' for the sake of consistency with the current literature.

On the other hand, legal scholars are clear that international law concerning military occupation could not possibly support the confiscation of land, machinery and homes by the Soviet Military Administration between 1945 and 1949.[23] An occupying country has 'power and authority' over a conquered government and its territory, but the occupier may not alter or destroy existing legal and economic relations – though it may certainly ignore them during occupation. Once the occupying force is gone, their imposed arrangements cannot thereby acquire and sustain legal legitimacy into the future. Permanently destroying the legal arrangements concerning ownership of land, homes and machinery is not accepted by international law.

However, what was at stake during Soviet occupation was not just political and administrative control over the former enemy's territory, but a revolutionary regime overhaul as well – the property regime being at the top of the political agenda. Accordingly, the Soviets and the German communists purposefully altered the historical cadastral records of land expropriated between 1945 and 1949, and the owners' names were intentionally obliterated. As a 'constitutive act of the new order', expropriation thus involved a two-pronged act of memory: a 'trial by *fiat* of a successor regime', which symbolically severed the legitimacy roots of the past regime, thenceforth to be recalled as iniquitous, in tandem with a deliberate 'forgetting by repressive erasure' of the official memory of past legitimacy.[24]

The allocation of tiny land parcels could not possibly establish a class of small land-owning farmers with a plausible chance for success. This stands in sharp contrast to the usually acknowledged purpose of land reforms to provide ownership opportunities for landless farmers. The record is clear that the 'starvation farms' established by the SMA were soon abandoned by the recipients, thereby liberating the abandoned land for immediate consolidation into desired state or collective farms.

The crowding-out struggle, 1948–1952

During the early post-war years, owners of medium and large-sized farms had viable agricultural enterprises and they played a dominant role in rural Germany. They had adequate amounts of land, livestock, and machinery. Due to the abundance of refugees in East Germany and the great demand for food, besides meeting the SMA's obligatory delivery requirements they were able to earn a good income from their surplus production. Their economic condition gave them a strong social standing in their villages. They were often elected to positions in the various self-help organizations – both the traditional, member-owned German cooperatives and the newly established Farmers' Mutual Help Associations.[25]

However, the political situation began to change once food supplies were secured. At the first congress of the German Socialist Unity Party (SED, *Sozialistische Einheitspartei Deutschlands*) in September 1948, the remaining farmers were officially labelled as two distinct groups.[26] On one side of the divide were the *Kleinbauern*, 'working farmers' or 'small food producers', pure 'family farmers' who cultivated less than twenty hectares and did not hire outside labour. On the other side were the *Großbauern*; that is, farmers who cultivated between twenty and 100 hectares and who, during particular seasons, employed hired labourers. This latter group was deemed the new 'capitalist exploiters of labour' who would have to be destroyed.[27]

Since late 1948, a coordinated policy was gradually implemented to debase the *Großbauern*. Agricultural taxes were progressively differentiated according to farm size, whereby *Großbauern* had to pay 30 per cent higher taxes per hectare than small farmers. A progressive scale was also introduced for obligatory produce deliveries to the government, with more being required from the *Großbauern* per hectare or per animal. This progressive differentiation continued to expand during the following years: in 1950, the obligatory delivery quota had tripled for *Großbauern* compared to small farmers cultivating less than five hectares. Many *Großbauern* were simply unable to meet these increasing delivery requirements, and by failing to do so they faced penalties, from economic sanctions such as being deprived of necessary inputs to penal sanctions for economic sabotage such as fines, imprisonment, or farm confiscation. In early 1950, a new law to protect farm labourers from exploitation limited work hours and increased wages, creating an immediate labour shortage and increased labours costs for *Großbauern*.[28]

In addition to economic restrictions, the SED fought the *Großbauern's* social and political influence by excluding them from decision-making bodies in rural self-help organizations. In November 1950, traditional cooperatives were pressured to merge with the newly established Farmers' Mutual Help Associations. The machinery exchange stations voluntarily started by the *Neubauern* were taken over by new government agricultural production collectives (*Landwirtschaftliche Produktionsgenossenschaft*, LPGs), which increasingly placed the *Großbauern* at an added disadvantage.[29]

A combination of progressive taxes and delivery quotas, declining supply of inputs and unfavourable tariffs worsened the economic situation for many *Großbauern*. Farmers accused of not cultivating their land correctly were forced out, and the sanctions were reinforced with the later aggressive collectivization campaign in 1952. From 1950 to 1953, charges of economic sabotage forced 24,211 families to either sign over their farm to the emerging LPGs or face criminalization. This forced many farmers to flee to the west. With this new campaign, the government confiscated about 697,980 hectares (10.7 per cent of the arable land in East Germany), 86.2 per cent of which from *Großbauern*.[30] These lands were then turned into newly formed 'district farms', beginning in May 1951, which were intended for agricultural production, although in many cases the land remained fallow. Initially, farmers who had fled remained the legal owners until 1968, and their 'voluntarily' abandoned land remained in government custody. The abandoned land of 'republic refugees' was finally declared state property on 11 November 1968.[31]

Socialist Spring, 1952–1960

By 1952, the SED had become the official decision-making party of the German Democratic Republic. While much had changed, Stalin remained committed to some form of reunification with West Germany. But by March 1952 it became apparent that this option was no longer available.[32] The II SED Conference on 12 July 1952 adopted arrangements for the 'well-planned build-up of Socialism'. A core element of the plan was the voluntary preparation of 'Socialism in rural areas', meaning the comprehensive establishment of LPGs.[33]

By the end of 1952 there had been a slow start with regard to the formation of LPGs. 1,906 had been created, comprising 37,000 members, cultivating over 200,000 hectares, about 3.3 per cent of the agricultural area in East Germany.[34] Farmers who joined these collectives received a number of incentives and the LPGs were given priority regarding input supplies and credit. Collectivization increased rapidly from 1953. Most of this land was not acquired by small farmers joining collectives and incorporating viable family farms; rather, LPGs grew in size by incorporating the land abandoned by those fleeing to the west as well as non-viable small farms. As late as the end of 1957, this formerly abandoned land still accounted for more than half of the land cultivated by LPGs. In spite of their privileged access to agricultural inputs, the best machinery and ample credit, throughout the 1950s the LPGs were never as productive as their private competitors.[35]

The campaign to collectivize farms led to a mass uprising throughout East Germany in June 1953. The government's reaction was to use Soviet military force to gain control, but this slowed down the collectivization campaign.[36] Farmers gained the right to cancel their membership in collectives and return to individual farming, but few did so. One reason, no doubt, was that as obligatory production quotas had not been relaxed, independent small farmers with inadequate inputs would be placed at an additional disadvantage.[37] Despite the setbacks, collectivization continued to be pursued. The number and relevance of the LPGs had gradually been increasing since 1954. By the middle of 1959, there were 9,566 collectives cultivating about 40 per cent of the total agricultural land in East Germany.[38] At the end of that year, the SED leadership proclaimed the final step in achieving 'Socialism in rural areas' and threw in all sorts of incentives and threats to convince the remaining private farmers to join an LPG.[39] Party and state officials used *Freiwilliger Zwang* (voluntary coercion) to 'persuade' farmers. One farmer recalls these officials arriving several days in a row shortly before milking time. While the cows waited to be milked, the officials stayed to persuade the farmer to join the collective. Each day the officials would stay for a bit longer, until the farmer finally succumbed to the pressure and joined the LPG. The family then took whatever they could carry and joined the tens of thousands of farmers' families who fled to West Germany within four months during this period.

On 25 April 1960, the SED leadership proclaimed the end of the collectivization campaign. It was stated that the 'Socialist Spring' had arrived and farmers had at last been liberated from exploitation. Over the preceding decade, the number of family farms had declined from 750,000 to about 20,000.[40] By the end of 1960, 19,261 LPGs comprised almost one million members, cultivating over five million hectares or 84 per cent of the total agricultural land in the GDR, and yet another 8 per cent of the agricultural land was held by VEGs. What remained was partly under the control of a few remaining private farmers whose land could not easily be attached to an LPG, partly in the private plots of collective members, and 13,981 hectares belonged to the Protestant and Catholic Churches.[41]

Between 1949 and 1961, over 2.6 million refugees fled to the west,[42] one fourth to one third of whom had a farming background, comprising 180,000 to 200,000 farmers and their dependents.[43] With the construction of the 'inner border' in August 1961, leaving East Germany became much more problematic. Members of collectives showed their disagreement in more subtle ways. Slacking and sabotage rapidly increased and farmers refused to work if they did not get necessary inputs.[44] The government's initial tolerance subsided as 'the Wall' was constructed, and show trials were put on for members accused of sabotage; four of the accused were sentenced to death to 'enforce a collective spirit'.[45]

In a mere fifteen years, from 1945 to 1960, the organization of agricultural production in East Germany had been fundamentally transformed. Centuries-old

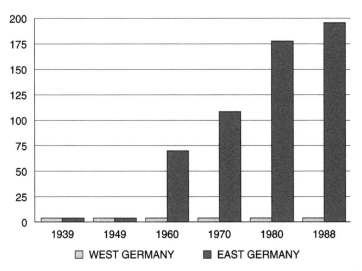

Figure 8.1 Number of employees per farm in East and West Germany, 1939–1988.

Source: A. Bauerkämper, *Ländliche Gesellschaft in der Kommunistischen Diktatur: Zwangsmodernisierung und Tradition in Brandenburg 1945–1963* (Köln: Böhlau).

successful, albeit unequal, structures had been completely dismantled and replaced with Soviet-style models. Despite the number of farmers whose farms had been expropriated or who later abandoned their property, most stayed in the GDR to become farm workers.

Managers of LPGs and VEGs ended up securing the local power and influence that had once been the large landowners', and more recently the *Großbauern*'s. In 1963–1964, both the overall economy and agricultural production improved, and collective farms were heavily subsidized in the following years, which resulted in improved living and working conditions. By 1989, when faced with the potential influence from West Germany, even the forces within East Germany who had fought for regime change were prepared to defend the collectives against de-collectivization and restitution claims.[46] Socialist policies had created a new agricultural structure, the repercussions of which have lasted to this day.[47]

Reunification: The official account

In August 1954, a West German commission declared that expropriations in the Soviet Occupation Zone were in violation of basic human rights and illegal under the West German constitution.[48] The commission's position implied that should reunification occur, the expropriated landowners would have their land restored to them. The end of the GDR in late 1989 provided the German government with the opportunity to make good on that statement and redress the effects of expropriation. East German agriculture had to be transformed to allow integration into a market economy; LPGs and VEGs were abolished and private owner-ship of agricultural assets would be reinstated. A radical change was required, which in many respects entailed a complete transfer of the West German legal and administrative system to the east.[49]

This path was not taken for several reasons. Chancellor Helmut Kohl and most German politicians were acutely aware of the widespread fear of total economic collapse in the east. Immediate action on reunification was required so that financial assistance – some of it coming from the European Union – could be mobilized as quickly as possible. Kohl had formed an alliance with Lothar de Maizière's newly emerging Christian Democratic Party in East Germany, and the ability of the CDU to dominate the political future of a unified Germany was available for the taking. There was great resistance throughout East Germany to return expropriated land to the former owners, especially to the *Alteigentümer*. Had that option been discussed more openly at the election campaigns, it would surely have undermined the electoral appeal of Kohl and his political ally de Maizière.

By January 1990, all political moves were leading towards reunification. GDR Prime Minister Hans Modrow visited Gorbachev in Moscow and received assur-ances that the Soviet Union would not oppose it. Modrow held a press conference on 30 January to announce plans for German reunification. On 21 February 1990, just three months after the Wall had crumbled, the Joint German–German Committee first sat to discuss this issue. In February 1990, all the wheels had been set in motion.

Government representatives of the United States, West and East Germany, and the Soviet Union were meeting – all eager to facilitate reunification.[50]

But it would not be easy to bring the two pieces of Germany together as far as property rights and restitution were concerned. On 1 and 2 March 1990, Modrow wrote to both Kohl and Gorbachev requesting their support for non-restitution of all expropriated private property in East Germany. And in fact, while negotiations toward reunification proceeded between the two German states, the Soviet Union's position pertaining to the restitution of confiscated land and related assets during its occupation was that it had been lawful. However, this did not amount to taking a formal stand to deny restitution to the *Alteigentümer*. The Soviets were actually avoiding taking a politically fraught position on this contentious issue. The Soviet Union did not want to be forced to pay compensation for expropriated land and buildings and, more importantly, did not want to be involved in such a fight with the German government, nor did it want any of its allies to be subjected to such questions. Clearly, the Soviets did not wish to become involved in matters that would surely come before German courts and sought to avoid further discussions and obligations that, according to them, belonged exclusively to the German government and its citizens.[51]

Nevertheless, when Klaus Kinkel, Head of the West German Department of Justice, addressed the Federal Government on 28 March 1990, he convinced the Bundestag's Committee for German Reunification of Modrow's claim that *if* the Soviet Union had insisted that land expropriated between 1945 and 1949 should not be returned to its former owners, Germany would be forced to agree so that the Soviet Union would not oppose reunification. His point was to imply that the Soviet Union actually *had* insisted on that condition. This tactic managed to create and sustain in the public's mind the assumption that restitution would pose a serious threat to reunification. Decisions by the German Constitutional Court and the European Court of Human Rights became hostage to this alleged risk.[52]

Not the least, there was great fear in the east that thousands would flood back to reclaim expropriated or abandoned farms. People who had remained in the east were concerned about their own welfare. They had been either unwilling or unable to leave and had endured an oppressive system, and there was a sense among political leaders that these people must be protected against a massive reverse migration.

Disposal of land controlled by the GDR proceeded in two ways. Historic cadastral records of farms under 100 hectares had not been altered by the Soviets or the GDR. Under GDR law, individual LPG members had retained nominal ownership, even though the effective property rights had all been transferred to the farming collectives. Names of those whose agricultural land had been given to or forced into collective farms between 1949 and 1960 remained in the cadastral records, and their land was immediately made available to them or their heirs. The restructuring of the LPGs was handled relatively quickly based on the June 1990 Agricultural Adjustment Act (*Landwirtschaftsanpassungsgesetz*). The LPGs were required to assess all of their assets, and the LPG members could decide whether the assets would be sold or distributed among them. Several options were available. Members could either start private (individual or family) farms; take their share of land and other assets (if any) into a successor organization of the LPG that could be created as a limited liability company (GmbH), a joint-stock company, or an agricultural producer cooperative; or rent their assets to someone else.[53]

In contrast, in spite of some initial optimism, it soon became apparent that a quick solution for the land which had been expropriated was not feasible. Some *Alteigentümer* began making claims even before a decision regarding restitution had been reached. They went to court to claim their rights, but were turned down by the Federal Constitutional Court in 1991 and again in 1996 and 2000. The land was never returned to its ancestral owners, even when families were able to produce official government records of their ownership. Instead, land was assigned to the 'Agency for Reprivatization of Industry in the GDR' (the *Treuhandanstalt*), whose task was to liquidate all industry, commercial buildings, agricultural property, and forests. On 17 June 1990, the East German Parliament passed the Privatization and Reorganization of State-Owned Assets Act (*Gesetz zur Privatisierung und Reorganization des volkseigenen Vermögens*; *Treuhandgesetz*), which set the legal basis for the work of the *Treuhandanstalt*.[54]

As new agricultural laws and procedures were being created by government agents, East German farmers feared for their livelihood. On 15 August 1990, as the effects of the economic, monetary and social union became evident, there was a massive rally of about 250,000 East German farmers in East Berlin, protesting the imminent collapse of farm production.[55] Politicians quickly realized that in order to restore confidence and to maintain 'social peace' in rural areas, farmers had to be assured of subsidies as quickly as possible.

The eventual denial of restitution of expropriated land was based upon what was believed to be a condition for the Reunification Treaty between East and West Germany of 31 August 1990, and the Treaty of the Final Settlement with Respect to Germany (*Vertrag über die abschließende Regelung in bezug auf Deutschland*), the 'Two Plus Four Agreement' underwritten on 12 September 1990 by the two German states and the four Allies. Without restitution, an immediate offering for sale of one million hectares would have adversely affected land prices. It was believed that sales of this magnitude should proceed gradually.[56] On 1 July 1992 the Land Settlement and Administration Company (*Bodenverwertungs- und Verwaltungsgesellschaft*, BVVG) was created as a successor organization of the *Treuhandanstalt* to administer the sale of the remaining agricultural and forest assets.[57] Initially, all agricultural land was leased on a short-term basis (one or two years). Gradually, more and more land was leased on a medium- and long-term basis (eight to fifteen years). The decision to proceed gradually would benefit returning farmers who did not have sufficient financial resources to purchase a farm outright, allowing them to lease land in order to earn enough income to purchase the farm after the lease contract expired.

Throughout the early 1990s there were intense negotiations among all political parties with respect to privatization. At the heart of the debates were competing claims to legitimacy about who should become the main beneficiaries of such privatization: the farmers who had been expropriated between 1945 and 1949 without restitution or the current cultivators. As in other transition countries, the inequality in pre-collectivization land ownership distribution may have caused a 'trade-off conflict between historical justice and social equity' and made the choice less obvious and 'more influenced by the political balance during the early phase of transition'.[58] The settlement was to a large extent contingent on the political clout of the organized interests and collective action on either side. The new *Länder* in eastern Germany exerted pressure in favour of the co-operative and corporate farms and against the positive discrimination of the *Alteigentümer*. The East German branches of the German Farmers' Union (DBV) were successful in gaining public support through campaigns undertaken by their western counterparts, tenants, and LPG-successor farms. By the time the final compromise was reached in September 1994, the *Alteigentümer* had lost the campaign for full restitution or redress and East German farmers became eligible to buy the state-owned expropriated land.[59] The coalition of farmers' unions and managers of the former LPGs enjoyed a considerable lobbying capacity and they were able to convince politicians that they could mobilize members of former collectives to join massive public demonstrations, in order to secure their interests in the privatization program. In contrast, the expropriated landowners had expected the government to protect what they perceived as their rights, as expressed in the above mentioned 1954 declaration, and they did not organize a lobbying group because they did not believe that it would be necessary.

The terms of privatization were fixed in a special programme, the Indemnification and Compensation Act of September 1994 (*Entschädigungs- und Ausgleichsleistungsgesetz*, EALG): *Alteigentümer* were only eligible either for modest compensation or to lease or purchase a small amount of their original land for a subsidized price; all farmers with a valid lease contract for state-owned land were eligible to buy such land; prices for this land would be about half of the current market prices in East Germany. Subsequently, price subsidies were considerably lowered in 2000, as a result of the European Commission imposing EU competition law because since it was open to all, the land sales programme should be considered as a market rather than a restitution process.[60]

The BVVG has since come under criticism for the slow pace of its land disposal programme since the privatization of the expropriated farmland started in 1994. By mid-2011, only about 40 per cent (approximately 389,000 hectares) of all agricultural land under BVVG control had been sold at preferential prices to former owners and to leaseholders. Another 292,000 hectares had been sold at market prices, while approximately 335,000 hectares remained under rental contracts of up to nine years.[61]

Reunification: Memories meet reality

In 2011–2012, we conducted eighty individual in-depth interviews with *Alteigentümer* and former *Großbauern* families who returned to the east after reunification. They represent more than 10 per cent of the farm families in each of the five federal states who returned to the east during and after reunification. The summarized accounts that follow from the compilation of personal interviews offer an introduction to the rich and extensive record of cultural memories covering this fraught period in German history, as seen through the eyes of this particular group, and to their narratives of how the government agencies, the local officials and the local societies met their attempts to acquire farmland and regain a foothold in what most of them regarded as their ancestral homes.

In keeping with the official view of the 1954 declaration, throughout their thirty to forty-five years in the west, those who returned had considered themselves landowners in the east. Family elders regularly used holidays and family days to kindle that memory and instruct later generations about their heritage. Those ever-replayed recollections, often laced with *schnapps*, may have become tedious in their repetition hour after hour, year after year. However, such rituals served to build up and keep alive an identity and a cultural group memory of what had been left behind and, implicitly, of a social order of ownership on which they now grounded the legitimacy of their claims.[62] Though largely landless in the west, their existence was predicated on eventually returning to their ancestral farms. While many were no longer engaged in agricultural production, they had remained involved in the upstream (input supply) and downstream (marketing and processing) sectors. Their children and grandchildren studied agricultural-related professions in agricultural economics, business and finance, law, horticulture, biochemistry, and forestry.

Alteigentümer families expelled in 1945–1946 had always been important in the village, and many of them had been patrons of their village churches. Some of those ties had never been broken. The physical absence of the families did not remove them from their former neighbours' memories, and their village obligations followed some of them wherever they went in the west. During the GDR period, they kept receiving requests from former village neighbours for help with church repairs. One family established a foundation to which they would contribute money on festive days. Those funds were then relayed through the Church network, and when supplies were unavailable in the east, materials were bought and sent instead of money.

Once 'the Wall' was torn down on 9 November 1989, even before reunification was discussed, some families began returning to what they regarded as their ancestral properties in the east. Some entered their old villages with great fanfare, while others arranged quieter returns by celebrating Christmas with other parishioners in their family's church. Others simply drove to their former homes and became spectators who merely looked around. Returning families reported meeting with mixed receptions. Some of those who attended their church's Christmas service were embraced and welcomed home by old acquaintances, but not all stories are so fondly related. Those who arrived with great fanfare were met by confused and curious residents. Villagers were aroused from their sleep by horns blowing, car lights blinking, and groups of singing and boisterous revellers hanging out of car windows. Despite the cold dark night, residents came into the streets in their nightclothes to observe the commotion. This was probably the moment when those villagers first realized how profoundly they would be affected by the open border.

Just as they recalled a version of their family's past role in the community, returnees remembered their family's farm – where the road led, the location of barns, hedgerows, and fences. But their cultural memories collided significantly with a different reality of rural eastern Germany – as well as with its peoples' own memories, an interaction which is central to our story. Families returning to the east after 1990 seeking to 're-join' communities and social settings often seemed oblivious to the fundamental transformations that had occurred during their absence. Throughout this two-generation period, physical layouts, organizations and patterns of behaviour had been dramatically altered. Private farms, both large and small, had become collective production enterprises and state farms. Most farms abandoned in the 1950s had been incorporated into LPGs and were now hardly distinguishable from one another. Farming fields, buildings and boundaries had been altered. Old property markers – hedgerows, fences, and tree lines, once landmarks of place and property relations – had been obliterated. Once fertile land was now covered with concrete pads and buildings.

For each returning family, establishing themselves in their ancestral community was a top priority. Living conditions were generally difficult and often awkward. Housing was limited and they lived wherever they could find space. A room in a boarding house, a corner of a sheep or cow barn, or a rented room from a local family often became their home. A number of the returning families rented rooms in houses that had once belonged to their family and were now owned by the local government. They began to establish relationships with those who had lived in the area throughout the GDR period. They met with members of the local community to discuss how they could work together to build a unified Germany.

It was the families who had fled later to escape the pressure of collectivization that had the easiest reception. Not only did they receive property they had abandoned, but they had also more recently been members of the local community. If their family was well remembered, the fact that local authorities removed current residents from their homes to accommodate the returning farmer did not seem to matter as much. The families expelled between 1945 and 1949, on the other hand, did not have any of their property returned. In their absence, ethnic German refugees had been settled in their village, young people had fled, and many of their peers had died.

Their local assimilation required village advocates. When they returned, they sought out people in the village who remembered their family. Those who had an easier time to assimilate had returned to villages where a large number of families favourably remembered them or their predecessors. A respected member of the village was essential to vouch for them. Sometimes the advocate was a family member who had remained, and sometimes it was someone who had worked for the expelled farmer. Frequently it was a renewed friendship from elementary school, a friend who still had fond memories of walking to school and playing together, often one whose father had worked for this returning family and who cherished their past relationship. Some of the farm labourers who had remained were loyal to their former employers; some had even been imprisoned or lived under the threat of imprisonment for having attempted to protect them. When available, such local society advocates encouraged their present neighbours to lease or sell land to the returnees to help them get started.

Besides this kind of local support, the farmer among our *Alteigentümer* who reported the most favourable experience was also fortunate in having a friend from his agricultural studies in Gottingen working at the *Treuhandanstalt* in Berlin. After the 23 April 1991 decision denying restitution, this friend faxed him indicating that he could lease an 800-hectare farm, a former VEG, on which he was able to establish himself with the help of a bank credit. However, the local residents' memories of his family were no less instrumental. His grandparents, whose rights to the land he had reclaimed, were fondly remembered in the com-munity. Although only about 30 per cent of all villagers were from families who had lived there back in 1945, their stories of his grandfather provided an important bridge to the other 70 per cent. His uncle, who was entitled to inherit the farm, had maintained a strong friendship with his elementary school classmates throughout the GDR times. His uncle's friends assured members of the community that they could trust him and that he would be a good farmer. Based on their vouching, he worked hard at establishing trust with other local farmers, reassuring them that he was only interested in obtaining former government-owned land and not their own. He worked with them to organize their farms more efficiently, swapping their scattered portions of land to make farming easier for all of them. Their 1991 arrangement still exists as we write, and this farmer serves as the president of Germany's Farmers' Union.

However, such favourable conditions did not often join together. Former village neighbours and their offspring, who had remained and were remembered from past property relations as independent farmers, tenants or farm labourers, had been turned into industrial farm workers. Many of them had first become small farmers during the Soviet-led land reform and kept memories of past land-wealth inequal-ity. Alongside them, there were the post-war *Neubauern* refugees, who shared no memories of a past neighbourhood with the returnees and kept instead the memory of the official historical narrative of land reform: that of rich and exploitive land-owners, Nazi sympathizers and war criminals on whose righteously expropriated land they or their forebears had been settled. They had all legally retained nominal landownership after joining a LPG, which the former regime had kept intact as part of its own official memory of redistribution and 'voluntary' collectivization, just as it had erased the former landownership records.

Some returnee families also carried painful memories of former neigh-bours. Those who fled to avoid collectivization returned to face former LPG managers and state security service informers, both of whom they despised. During collectivization, these families or their forebears had been under various forms of coercive pressure to join a collective, and a system of neighbourhood informers had been established by the state to report anyone who seemed inclined to flee. The authorities knew which farmers were being recalcitrant, but they could not read the mind of all of those who were seen as uncooperative resistors. This is where neighbours who could detect subtle changes in patterns of activity had become convenient accomplices of the state, and as games of deception and observation intensified, even children had been used as observers, informers, and messengers.

Conversely, those who had remained could neither anticipate how life in the west had changed their former neighbours, nor understand how profoundly they had themselves been changed by their life in the GDR. They had been taught to stigmatize the *Klassenfeind* (class enemy), a label associated with a member of an aristocratic family, someone who attended church, a family with more than two children, a farmer who privately owned agricultural machinery, etc. In other words, *Klassenfeind* was anyone 'other' to the established social order – and most significantly, almost by default, a *Wessie* (i.e., anyone from West Germany). Our returnees were locally recalled as ticking some or all of these boxes, either personally or as a class, and by definition they were all *Wessies*. As a consequence, some interviewees reported being labelled as *Klassenfeind* on arrival, which in the local social settings was a de-legitimization of their renewed claims to belong, to acquire land and to settle as family farmers.

For those who had lived through the GDR period, reunification gave an opportunity to once again become the actual private owners of land and homes. They had worked the land for two generations, and now as owners they sought to secure their holdings, their rent, or their dividends as cooperative members. A few had wielded power as managers of LPGs and VEGs, and those who controlled production also had controlled the community. As some factors at play in global agricultural markets and supply chains during the last decades favoured large-scale farming,[63] the post-privatization fragmentation of property rights provided fertile ground for land consolidation. Following privatization and the restitution of land to former owners and farm workers, property rights were reorganized under large-scale cooperatives or through leasing arrangements with corporate farms (GmbH), through the initiative of private entrepreneurs. These were often former managers of LPGs and state farms who took advantage of their management know-how, access to external advice about funding opportunities and land and produce markets, and their social capital among the locals and the regional government agencies, to launch these new capitalistic farming ventures. As a result, and contrary to the political expectations of the West German mainstream, family farming regained comparatively little ground in eastern Germany.[64] A new agro-capitalist sector rose which created powerful vested interests to be reckoned with – those of the new cooperative managers and corporate bosses, but also those of local cooperative members and farm workers whose income and jobs depended on industrial farming.

Local farmers came under intense pressure from former LPG managers to withhold their land from returning farmers. Managers of the newly created private cooperatives were often able to persuade their former comrades in the collective farms to view *Wessies* as threats, who would take their property if they let them. One interviewee told of GmbH managers going from pub to pub spreading rumours about the risk to small farmers when these *Wessies* returned, and from house to house seeking private contracts with small farmers in order to secure their land. The *Alteigentümer* and the former *Großbauern* showed themselves not so much concerned about having lost whatever influence they once had, as surprised at the level of control that the former LPG and state farm managers continued to hold over the community.

One of our interviewees came to a village in an area where his family had held land since the seventeenth century. The family saw themselves as returning home. However, to local residents they were newcomers. Many people had fled from this community to the west before the Wall had been constructed in 1961, and then after 1989 a second wave of people had emigrated. With depopulation, those who remained had formed tightly-knit communities and worked at keeping everything familiar. The former VEG manager was part of this community, and discouraged local farmers from leasing or selling any of their land to this family. Our interviewee tried to form a partnership with the former VEG manager. However, they soon became competitors, when the latter went to work for the *Treuhandanstalt* and later the BVVG. As a local government agent he could use his position to his advantage. The returnee farmer faced conditional obligations to acquire land: he had to purchase outdated GDR farm equipment that he did not want, could not use, and had to pay to have it taken away. And while he had to wait for years to get the approval to buy more land, which exposed him to rising prices, the former VEG manager was able to obtain land immediately.

Notwithstanding this, families returned because they wanted to re-establish their farms, to be close to their ancestral land, and to restore their sense of place in the local community. They turned to the *Treuhandanstalt* and later to the BVVG, as well as to local government agencies to gain access to land, buildings, and agricultural machinery. There they encountered government agents who were often vague about the status of land. One threatened a returning farmer with arrest for accepting an offer from the office clerk to look at the computer inventory of available land; perhaps the farmer's real offence had been finding out that the actual inventory for distribution was considerably larger than what the agency had reported.

Concluding remarks

In late spring 1945, the Soviet Military Administration launched an elaborate programme to eliminate the legacy – the cultural memory – of those who had laboured for centuries to create a vibrant agriculture in eastern Germany. The underlying aim was to replace family farms with large industrial agriculture relying on wage labour. Private ownership of land was the first impediment, followed later by the resistance of small independent farmers. Land confiscation, mass eviction and repression would be the instruments utilized. German communists would prove eager enablers, implementers, and enforcers. The past order of land ownership was tried by a *fiat* of the new regime, and its official memory was coercively erased to be replaced with a new set of official memories and the cultural memories of those who had taken the place of the expropriated landowners.

Upon reunification, those contradictory memories collided as the divergent social interests in land property organized themselves into action, both at the level of state politics and local everyday life. Had the two German governments acted in accordance with international law, the choice would have been a simple one. They could quite easily have acknowledged that the SMA had been a powerful squatter with the obvious ability to control all of eastern Germany. Mikhail Gorbachev was certainly of this view. However, while some of the furniture, libraries, and art work taken by Soviet soldiers and officers and subsequently removed to the Soviet Union has slowly been returned over the years, the confiscation of land, homes, and agricultural machinery went into a separate 'account' in the eyes of the German government and the European Court of Human Rights.

The post-war regime in East Germany succeeded in creating a new order of land ownership and a change in agrarian structure. That the latter persisted to a large extent after the regime change in 1990 reflects the existing balance of power between the different claimants. The 'incumbent' farmers and farm managers in place in the latter days of the GDR were able to mobilize effectively against the claims of the main group of 'invaders', threatening to disturb the transition process. If these *threats* from the decollectivized farmers had failed, it is likely that the current agricultural system in eastern Germany might resemble more the family-farm model of West Germany rather than the agro-industrial structures that still recall the imported Soviet tradition.[65]

And so today, almost seventy years after that comprehensive assault on German culture and society, the former GDR would appear – superficially at least – to be following along the path envisioned by Stalin. The vast majority of farms are indeed industrial in both scale and in capital intensity. Most farm workers are wage-labourers. The rural countryside has been emptied of peasants. Of course, these large industrial farms are now private, rather than government owned, and they have replaced all other agricultural entities. However, as the underlying factors that have led to the increasing scale of European farms during the last decades combined with the social and technical structures left behind by de-collectivization, the agricultural landscape of eastern Germany has retained a distinctly Soviet flavour.

Rural communities are fragile. Families who lived through the GDR period witnessed large-scale emigration before 1961, and then again after 1989. Many villages are bereft of young people. Those who remain are protective of what little is left of their community. Interestingly, their commitment to the recent past has so far precluded receptivity to the very collaborative opportunities that could revitalize their community. In the face of this, families who were expropriated or left under threat of collectivization, and might have the most compelling reasons to return and invest, have met with indifference, resistance, and hostility. The Soviet legacy of *Klassenfeind* continues to legitimize local vested interests and stifles social and economic integration.

At an official level, as members of these rural communities, many local government officials were able to enforce these demonizing attitudes in the normal line of their employment. Often, local agents of the *Treuhandanstalt*/BVVG, instead of being willing to work with returning farmers to liquidate the former GDR agricultural assets so much in demand, have created adversarial relationships that have prevented the implementation of their official mandate. The alarming inconsistency in the behaviour of these government officials raises questions about whether they were (are) ignorant of official policies, whether procedures for processing claims actually exist, or whether these local officials have been subject to proper oversight.

Nevertheless, we have found a few cases of the successful integration of returnees, in which pre-existent local memories of their families and of past social relationships served them as a strategic social resource on which they were able to lean, in order to generate trust, garner support and overcome resistances from both the community and official agencies.

A truly historic opportunity still awaits eastern Germany. Future generations would be justified in asking to what extent this legacy is German – or Soviet?

Notes

1 I. Iriarte and J. M. Lana, in chapter seven, provide another example of memories of dispossession being used in social disputes over property rights. (Editors' note.)
2 Cited by R. Conquest, *Harvest of Sorrow: Soviet Collectivization and the Terror Famine* (New York: Oxford University Press, 1986), p. 20.
3 A. Bauerkämper, 'Von der Bodenreform zur Kollektivierung: Zum Wandel der ländlichen Gesellschaft in der Sowjetischen Besatzungszone Deutschlands und DDR 1945–1952', in H. Kaelble, J. Kocha and H. Zwahr (eds), *Sozialgeschichte der DDR* (Stuttgart: Klett-Cotta, 1994), pp. 119–43, quoted from p. 119.
4 Conquest, *Harvest of Sorrow*, pp. 20–1, 49.
5 M. Livi-Bacci, 'On the human costs of collectivization in the Soviet Union', *Population and Development Review*, 19:4 (1993), pp. 743–66. The mid-range estimates are of 9.5 and 9.7 million, respectively, according to Western and Eastern European model life tables (p. 751). Cf. L. E. Hubbard, *The Economics of Soviet Agriculture* (London: Macmillan, 1939), pp. 117–18.
6 J. von Kruse (ed.), *Weißbuch über die 'Demokratische Bodenreform' in der Sowjetischen Besatzungszone Deutschlands: Dokumente und Berichte* (Munich: Vögel, 1988 [1955]), p. 12.
7 J. Schoene, *Das Sozialistische Dorf: Bodenreform und Kollektivierung in der Sowjetzone und DDR* (Leipzig: Evangelische Verlagsanstalt, 2011); E. Tümmler, 'Die Agrarpolitik in Mitteldeutschland: Historische Entwicklung der Landwirtschaft in Mitteldeutschland und ihre Agrarpolitische Konzeption', in E. Tümmler, K. Merkel, and G. Blohm (eds), *Die Agrarpolitik in Mitteldeutschland und ihre Auswirkung auf Produktion und Verbrauch Landwirtschaftlicher Erzeugnisse* (Berlin: Duncker & Humblot, 1969), pp. 1–167; K.-E. Wädekin, *Sozialistische Agrarpolitik in Osteuropa*, vol. 1: *Von Marx bis zur Vollkollektivierung* (Berlin: Duncker & Humblot, 1974).
8 von Kruse, *Weißbuch*, p. 15.
9 G. Last, *After the 'Socialist Spring': Collectivization and Economic Transformation in the GDR* (New York: Berghan Books, 2009), p. xxi.
10 J. Laufer, 'Die UdSSR und die Einleitung der Bodenreform in der Sowjetischen Besatzungszone', in A. Bauernkämper (ed.), *'Junkerland in Bauernhand'? Durchführung, Auswirkung und Stellenwert der Bodenreform in der Sowjetischen Besatzungszone* (Stuttgart: Steiner, 1996), pp. 21–35, on p. 22.
11 Schoene, *Sozialistische Dorf*, pp. 50–1.

12 Mecklenburg-Pomerania on 5 September, Brandenburg on 6 September and Saxony and Thuringia on 11 September. Bauerkämper, 'Von der Bodenreform zur Kollektivierung', pp. 80–2.
13 Bauerkämper, 'Von der Bodenreform zur Kollektivierung', p. 122.
14 W. Bell, *Enteignungen in der Landwirtschaft der DDR nach 1949 und deren Politische Hintergründe: Analyse und Dokumentation* (Münster-Hiltrup: Landwirtschaftsverlag, 1992), p. 85; K.-F. Thöne, *Die agrarstrukturelle Entwicklung in den Neuen Bundesländern: Zur Regelung der Eigentumsverhältnisse und Neugestaltung Ländlicher Räume* (Köln: Verlag Kommunikationsforum Recht, Wirtschaft, Steuern, 1993), p. 15.
15 H. C. Löhr, *Der Kampf um das Volkseigentum: Eine Studie zur Privatisierung der Landwirtschaft in den Neuen Bundesländern durch die Treuhandanstalt (1990–1994)* (Berlin: Duncker & Humblot, 2002), p. 19.
16 Tümmler, 'Agrarpolitik in Mitteldeutschland', p. 24.
17 Bauerkämper, 'Von der Bodenreform zur Kollektivierung', p. 122.
18 Bell, *Enteignungen in der Landwirtschaft*, p. 86; T. Bergmann, *Agrarpolitik und Agrarwirtschaft Sozialistischer Länder* (Stuttgart: Plakat-Bauernverlag, 1973), p. 111.
19 J. Schoene, *Landwirtschaftliches Genossenschaftswesen und Agrarpolitik in der SBZ/DDR 1945–1950/51* (Stuttgart: Ibidem, 2000), pp. 20–1.
20 Schoene, *Sozialistische Dorf*, p. 81.
21 Löhr, *Kampf um das Volkseigentum*, p. 20.
22 W. C. Thiesenhusen (ed.), *Searching for Agrarian Reform in Latin America* (Boston: Unwin Hyman, 1989).
23 D. A. Jeffress, 'Resolving rival claims on East German property upon German unification', *Yale Law Journal*, 101:2 (2012), pp. 527–49.
24 P. Connerton, *How Societies Remember* (Cambridge: Cambridge University Press, 2006), p. 7; P. Connerton, 'Seven types of forgetting', *Memory Studies*, 1:1 (2008), pp. 59–71, on p. 60.
25 Bauerkämper, 'Von der Bodenreform zur Kollektivierung', p. 122.
26 The SED resulted from the forced merger, in April 1946, of the German Communist Party and the Social Democratic Party.
27 H. Prange, *Bauernschicksale: Die Landwirtschaft im Osten Deutschlands seit dem Zweiten Weltkrieg* (Dößel: Janos Stekovics, 2007).
28 Bauerkämper, 'Von der Bodenreform zur Kollektivierung', p. 134; Bell, *Enteignungen in der Landwirtschaft*, p. 55; Prange, *Bauernschicksale*, p. 32; Schoene, *Sozialistische Dorf*, p. 93.
29 Bauerkämper, 'Von der Bodenreform zur Kollektivierung', p. 134.
30 Bell, *Enteignungen in der Landwirtschaft*, pp. 55, 78.
31 'Republic refugees' refers to those who fled to West Germany. K. V. Hagedorn, B. Beckmann, B. Klages and M. Rudolph, 'Politische und ökonomische Rahmenbedingungen für die Entwicklung ländlicher Räume in den neuen Bundesländern', in A. Becker (ed.), *Regionale Strukturen im Wandel* (Opladen: Leske und Buderich, 1997), pp. 355–500, on p. 445; Thöne, *Die Agrarstrukturelle Entwicklung*, p. 49; Tümmler, 'Agrarpolitik in Mitteldeutschland', p. 54.
32 J. Schoene, *Frühling auf dem Lande? Die Kollektivierung der DDR-Landwirtschaft*, 3rd edn (Berlin: Christoph Links, 2010), pp. 88–91.
33 Tümmler, 'Agrarpolitik in Mitteldeutschland', p. 54.
34 Tümmler, 'Agrarpolitik in Mitteldeutschland', p. 87.
35 U. Kluge, 'Die Affäre Vieweg: Der Konflikt um eine sozialistische Agrarbetriebslehre', in U. Kluge, W. Halder and K. Schlenker (eds), *Zwischen Bodenreform und Kollektivierung: Vor- und Frühgeschichte der 'Sozialistischen Landwirtschaft' in der SBZ/DDR vom Kriegsende bis in die Fünfziger Jahre* (Wiesbaden: Steiner, 2001), pp. 195–212, on p. 212; von Kruse, *Weißbuch*, p. 144.

36 Stalin's death on 5 March 1953 had also decreased the government's pressure on collectivization, but only temporarily.
37 Prange, *Bauernschicksale*, p. 39.
38 Tümmler, 'Agrarpolitik in Mitteldeutschland', p. 88.
39 Tümmler, 'Agrarpolitik in Mitteldeutschland', p. 93.
40 Schoene, *Sozialistische Dorf*, pp. 130–5.
41 Tümmler, 'Agrarpolitik in Mitteldeutschland', pp. 87–8, 94; Wädekin, *Sozialistische Agrarpolitik*, p. 147.
42 Thöne, *Agrarstrukturelle Entwicklung*, p. 20.
43 A. Wolz, 'The organisation of agricultural production in East Germany since World War II: Historical roots and present situation', *Discussion Papers*, 139 (Halle (Saale): IAMO, 2013), at www.econstor.eu/handle/10419/83981 [last accessed 10 March 2016].
44 Schoene, *Frühling auf dem Lande?*, p. 227.
45 Schoene, *Frühling auf dem Lande?*, p. 291.
46 Löhr, *Kampf um das Volkseigentum*, p. 22.
47 Schoene, *Frühling auf dem Lande?*, p. 304.
48 C. Paffrath, *Macht und Eigentum: Die Enteignungen 1945–1949 im Prozess der Deutschen Wiedervereinigung* (Köln: Böhlau, 2004).
49 G. Lehmbruch, 'Verbände im Ostdeutschen Transformationsprozeß', in W. Bührer and E. Grande (eds), *Unternehmerverbände und Staat in Deutschland* (Baden–Baden: Nomos, 2000), pp. 88–109, on p. 88.
50 Paffrath, *Macht und Eigentum*, p. 24.
51 Paffrath, *Macht und Eigentum*.
52 Paffrath, *Macht und Eigentum*.
53 O. Wilson and B. Klages, 'Farm restructuring in the ex-GDR: Towards a new farm model?', *Journal of Rural Studies*, 17:3 (2001), pp. 277–91, on pp. 278–9; A. Wolz, M. Kopsidis and K. Reinsberg, 'The transformation of agricultural production cooperatives in East Germany and their future', *Journal of Rural Cooperation*, 37:1 (2009), pp. 5–19.
54 Beckmann, V. And Hagedorn, K. 'Decollectivization and privatization policies and resulting structural changes of agriculture in eastern Germany', in J. F. M. Swinnen, A. Buckwell and E. Mathijs (eds), *Agricultural Privatization, Land Reform and Farm Restructuring in Central and Eastern Europe* (Aldershot: Ashgate, 1997), pp. 105–60, on p. 118.
55 E. Stuhler, *Die Letzten Monate der DDR: Die Regierung de Maizière und ihr Weg zur Deutschen Einheit* (Berlin: Christoph Links, 2010), pp. 155–9.
56 G. A. Wilson and O. J. Wilson, *German Agriculture in Transition: Society, Politics and Environment in a Changing Europe* (Houndsmill: Palgrave, 2001), p. 131.
57 G. Wegge, 'Eine nicht geprobte Welt-Uraufführung', in Agrarsoziale Gesellschaft (ed.): *Zeitzeugen Berichten: Wir Waren Dabei – Aufbau von Agrarverwaltungen und -Institutionen in den Neuen Bundesländern 1990/1991* (Göttingen: Pachnicke, 1999), pp. 348–67.
58 A. H. Sarris, T. Doucha and E. Mathijs, 'Agricultural restructuring in central and eastern Europe: Implications for competitiveness and rural development', *European Review of Agricultural Economics*, 26:3 (1999), pp. 305–29, on p. 308.
59 Beckmann and Hagedorn, 'Decollectivization and privatization policies', pp. 125–6; Wilson and Klages, 'Farm restructuring', pp. 284–5.
60 B. Forstner and F. Isermeyer, 'Transformation of agriculture in East Germany', in S. Tangermann (ed.), *Agriculture in Germany* (Frankfurt AM: DLG, 2000), pp. 61–90; Wilson and Klages, 'Farm restructuring', p. 287.
61 BVVG (Bodenverwertungs- und Verwaltungs GmbH), Press release, 'BVVG hat fast 1,3 Millionen Hektar privatisiert', 8 July 2011, pp. 2–3, at www.bvvg.de/Internet/waktuell.nsf/vbroinfo/dPDFPM54_webaktuell/$File/pm54a.pdf [last accessed 10 March 2016].

62 Connerton, *How Societies Remember*, pp. 39–40.
63 K. Deininger and D. Byerlee, 'The rise of large farms in land abundant countries: Do they have a future?', *World Development*, 40:4 (2012), pp. 701–14.
64 J. N. Choi, A. Wolz and M. Kopsidis, 'Family farm ideology and the transformation of collective farms in East Germany, 1989–2005', in R. Congost and R. Santos (eds), *Contexts of Property in Europe: The Social Embeddednes of Property Rights in Land in Historical Perspective* (Turnhout: Brepols, 2010), pp. 247–66.
65 J. Djenderedjian and D. Santilli, in chapter four, provide another example of the implementation of a new set of formal property rights being moulded by the pre-existing social and agrarian structure. (Editors' note.)

9 Property rights in land

Institutions, social appropriations, and socio-economic outcomes

Rosa Congost, Jorge Gelman and Rui Santos

Introduction

Our argument in this final discussion chapter starts out from two assumptions. The first one is that the weight of the processes, mediating between a given institutional innovation affecting property rights, on the one hand, and its economic and social outcomes in different societies, on the other, is the result of the concrete social appropriations of institutional rules and norms. That is, of how, by whom and to what purposes they are actually used to legitimize the power inherent to property relations, or resistance to that power.[1] The second, is that social appropriations result from historical processes engaging multiple agents, and are too deeply embedded in social contexts to be reduced to an account of the interests and actions of the state and elite organizations, important though these doubtlessly are.

This chapter has four sections, throughout which we will draw on the approaches and findings of the preceding substantive chapters to illustrate our discussion, followed by a few concluding remarks. The first section states the need to replace tautological reasoning, which has often marred research about 'property', with a historical analysis that takes into account the historicity of all concepts of property. We illustrate this by briefly discussing and contextualizing two rival concepts of property in historical and social scientific discourse, namely those of an absolute right over things and of a bundle of rights regulating people's relationships regarding things. The second section questions the relationships between institutions, organizations, and social action, and draws on the 'bundle of rights' approach to discuss the reduction of the concept of property rights to that of institution. We propose instead that it should be derived from that of social relations in order to analyse agency, power, and legitimation and to understand the functions of institutions therein. The third section discusses the concept of path dependence in the light of the preceding arguments, mainly through the work of Douglass North and his associates, arguably the most sophisticated attempt from within new institutional economics to address its own shortcomings. The fourth section argues for a relational realist approach to property, which deals with historical processes of appropriation and expropriation. We argue that such an approach may help overcome the a-critical use of stereotyped dichotomies, which over-simplify the social relations underlying such processes and how they affect wider socio-economic outcomes. Finally, our concluding remarks summarize the main ideas presented in the chapter.

Historical analysis *versus* tautological reasoning: On the historicity of all concepts of property

The dominant views among neo-institutionalists consist of considering *a posteriori* that 'good' and 'efficient' institutions are those found in countries that have experienced enrichment processes, and conversely, that those institutions found in countries which have failed to develop their economies are 'bad' and 'inefficient'. Because the causal direction is mostly assumed *post hoc*, and it is inferred from, and tested on cases selected by sampling on the dependent variable, the reasoning is tautological[2] – a kind of argument which, as Pierre Vilar denounced, tends to justify the existing social order,[3] be it in developed countries or among countries on the world stage. Moreover, the theory is hardly falsifiable. Even when institutions that worked in developed economies fail to perform efficiently in other economies, that can be blamed on the inefficiency of the latter's wider 'institutional matrix', and, as a last resort, on 'cultural heritage'.

There is hardly any need to expand on the well-known centrality of property rights in neo-institutionalist economic theories. Property is often assumed in its contemporary common sense meaning, as an a-historical, 'natural' category towards which human history evolved by purging its concrete manifestations of their imperfections. But to take any generalized discourse on past or present property outside of its social and economic context will prove a serious hindrance to historical analysis. The current vocabulary constantly lays traps for historians and social scientists, which we must detect and untangle. On the one hand, the very term 'property *rights*', if used a-critically, compels us to acknowledge as rights, in a normative sense, practices of land use and exclusion that, however naturalized and legitimized they may be by present-day intuitions, resulted from privilege and abuse, which we would hardly consider to based on the rule of law.[4] Conversely, it may lead us to treat as malfeasance, as illegitimate customs, and certainly not as rights, past land uses that in their day and place were quite legitimate, and which were often expropriated by states acting under legal definitions of what property *should* be as a *natural right*: 'The law can simply refuse to recognize a person's property right ... as in the extinguishment of "uncertain" and "unreasonable" common rights during enclosure'.[5]

Furthermore, adjectives such as 'perfect' and 'absolute', often used as attributes of an abstract and universal concept of property, have reinforced the ideology of the superiority and the ultimate achievement of that abstract category, be it on economic, political or moral grounds. Such historical and social science discourse has tended to naturalize the idea that property rights have evolved (or they *should* if and where they have not) towards that ideal of perfection. In spite of their apparent neutrality and universality, however, such concepts, with which we must deal in our studies, are in fact the product of specific historical contexts in which they were articulated and designed, which explains both their success and their change. We will now briefly address two contrasting ideas of property in this light, namely those of absolute perfect property and of property as a bundle of rights.

> There is nothing which so generally strikes the imagination, and engages the affections of mankind, as the right of property; or that sole and despotic dominion which one man claims and exercises over the external things of the world, in total exclusion of the right of any other individual in the universe.[6]

This famous quote from Blackstone's *Commentaries* epitomizes the idea of absolute property, just as it was starting on its way to ideological dominance in Europe in the mid-eighteenth century. As idealized in it, property is the attribute of one individual (more specifically, a man) and consists of his exclusive and entire dominion over a thing. Significantly, the appropriation of land for agricultural use played a pivotal role in the justification of absolute property, as indeed property itself did in the genesis of civil society with its 'long train of inseparable concomitants':[7] states and government, law and enforcement, public religion, the useful arts, and science. Absolute property in land became the seed of all human liberty and progress:

> And thus the legislature of England has universally promoted the grand ends of civil society, the peace and security of individuals, by steadily pursuing that wise and orderly maxim, of assigning to every thing capable of ownership a legal and determinate owner.[8]

Abstraction played a major part in the historical construction of this ideal of property, which proved highly performative in changing social structures, along with the appropriation of resources. It became pervasive in England and France at the end of the eighteenth and the beginning of the nineteenth century, and swiftly extended to other countries. It actually overrode differences between the two main European legal traditions: rulers in England and the newly born American Republic promoted absolute property in land through acts and jurisprudence based on common law, while those in France used the Roman Law tradition and, from the nineteenth century on, the Civil Code, as most states in continental Europe would do in the course of time. In both legal traditions, jurists used and reshaped a discourse on progress which identified absolute property, however distributed, with the interests of society at large. Most of the above chapters bear witness to its spread in the late eighteenth and the nineteenth centuries.

The success of this paradigm was partly due to its abstract nature, which allowed it to justify land property policies adopted in the late eighteenth and the early nineteenth centuries, which were quite contradictory regarding their social implications – from enclosures and the abolition of communal rights in England, to the abolition of feudal rights and the expropriation and sale of national assets in post-Revolutionary France. This is probably why in the former case it was a popular protest that denounced absolute property in defence of customary rights, whereas in the latter it was the aristocrats who played that part in defence of their privileges of rank. In fact, some French counter-revolutionary discourses were more radical – in the sense that, like the English anti-enclosure protest, they brought up political issues of class struggle over the appropriation of land – than much French Enlightenment and revolutionary discourses that held on to the abstract virtues of absolute property.

One of the dogmas that most favoured the superiority of absolute property was the idea, which we can find in both Quesnay and Adam Smith, that large-scale farming based on it provided the most benefits across the whole of society, by increasing overall wealth and relying on markets to distribute it. This provided the ideological justification to support large land ownership where it existed and oppose land reform, as well as to expropriate and privatize common rights in land and abolish various types of customary ownerships and contracts. The concepts of perfect, absolute property and of economic growth were constructed by abstracting from coterminous historical processes of expropriation and increased social inequality regarding access to land, as evidenced in the case studies on Buenos Aires in chapter four by Djenderedjian and Santilli, on Spain in chapter seven by Iriarte and Lana, and on Sweden by Morell in chapter two. However, the cases of Denmark also in chapter two, of Santa Fe in chapter four, and of Madeira by Câmara and Santos in chapter five, suggest that the balance of power in such transitions could end up affording smaller peasants and farmers some degree of hold over land rights, even within frameworks of persistent structural inequality.

The latter case explicitly involves bringing in the alternative approach to the Blackstonian concept of absolute private property, that of property as a 'bundle of rights', which largely informed the development of new institutional economics and 'law and economics' scholarships, as epitomized in an equally famous quote from Coase: 'We may speak of a person owning land and using it as a factor of production, but what the land-owner in fact possesses is the right to carry out a circumscribed list of actions'.[9]

According to its critics, Coase's redefinition of property stemmed from the success of the legal realist school in law studies, which since the 1920s had succeeded in imposing this doctrine of property: 'property consists of nothing more than the authoritative list of permitted uses of a resource – posted, as it were, by the state for each object of scarcity'.[10] In this sense, '[i]t is not *the* resource itself that is owned; it is a bundle, or a portion of rights to *use* the resource that is owned'.[11] Besides being delimited, the bundle of property rights in an asset may be distributed among several parties, without the physical asset itself being partitioned. This 'bundle' metaphor eventually developed in two quite different ways, both related to the idea of a social function of property but with opposite implications, from social reformism to a renewed faith in market efficiency in promoting social welfare.

The notion of a social function of property is linked to the name of the French scholar and publicist Léon Duguit, who was influenced by Durkheim's theory of organic social solidarity and who wrote in 1912 that 'ownership is no longer the subjective right of the owner; it is the social function of one who detains the wealth'.[12] In a reviewer's words, '[a]s Blackstone represents "despotic ownership", so Duguit has come to represent property's "social function"',[13] in line with the roughly contemporaneous reformist views of early American economic institutionalists like Commons and Veblen, among others. As the American economist Frank Knight wrote in 1921, the feeling regarding the large property-owner was that '*[h]e is really a social functionary now*'.[14]

According to Merrill and Smith, the first legal realists in the US were reformists arguing against absolute property as a natural right, in order to allow the state to intervene in the reallocation of property rights to optimize social welfare. This was a time of structural change in the shaping of modern corporate capitalism in the US and in Europe, which, in Schumpeter's words, 'by substituting a mere parcel of shares for the wall of and the machines in a factory, takes the life out of the idea of property'.[15] It was also a time of intense social struggle, when the response to economic and social crises led state policies away from the golden age of invisible hand liberalism and further towards interventionism.[16] In this context,

> the motivation behind the realists' fascination with the bundle-of-rights conception was mainly political. They sought to undermine the notion that property is a natural right, and thereby smooth the way for activist state intervention in regulating and redistributing property.[17]

Both legal realism and early economic institutionalism then converged on relativizing property rights to harness wealth creation and distribution in the interest of higher social purposes – a political view of the social function of property underlying much of what has since been called 'welfare capitalism', but which, as Morell shows in chapter two, had deeper roots in pre-modern forms of regulating property rights: a practical pattern of political conflict resolution by handling land property as a divisible bundle of rights developed in Sweden since the early modern period, which kept being used to regulate successive processes of disputed rights, up to present day disputes over the functions of land within a post-industrial welfare society.

The bundle of rights approach was later refashioned in a very different context and to quite different purposes. Put briefly, the goals became those, on the one hand, of making a theory of organizations and firms amenable to general economic theory, including the search for the most efficient allocation of property rights in firms' assets to different corporate actors; and on the other hand, of designing laws to facilitate the delineation and enforcement of property rights and transactions, as well as the prevention or redressing of negative externalities at the minimum cost. This entails a quite different political idea about the social function of property, namely that of making markets more efficient by reducing transaction costs and devising incentives to maximize wealth creation in and between complex organizations. The approach taken by Locatelli and Tedeschi concerning Lombardy in chapter three is close to this view. According to them, the introduction of the land cadastre and associated fiscal policies from the second half of the eighteenth century brought about better delineation and securitization of the landowners' and tenants' bundles of rights, decreased transaction costs in land and credit markets and boosted economic growth in what was already one of the most productive agrosystems in Europe.

The latter approach to the 'bundle of rights' concept, set out to accomplish much the same task for property and the governance of corporate capitalism, as the doctrine of absolute property had accomplished for land and capital ownership just before industrialization and during its earlier stages; that is, to achieve the most perfect legal delineation of discrete property rights allocated in each bundle and to enforce them efficiently, in the interest of securing property, aligning the incentives of 'agents' (whether corporation managers or capitalist tenants) with the interests of the 'principals' (shareholders or landowners), and easing market transactions to allocate assets more efficiently. Ironically, this came at the cost of sacrificing the ideal absoluteness of property. But also, and more strategically from our point of view, new institutionalists after Coase arrived at this point by abstracting property rights as stylized institutions, enshrined in law and court rulings, away from the social relations and action that their very initial definition entailed, and of which legal legitimation is but one dimension, important though it may be.

Institutions, social relations, and agency

It is of key interest to our point to elaborate on the relationship between institutions, social relations, and agency. Institutions do not act. They are 'the grin without the cat, the rules of the game without the players', to quote from a textbook in new institutional economics; in sociological terms, 'a virtual world of rules/norms which . . . are instantiated only when actors draw upon them in order to act or interact in specific situations'.[18] North's, by now standard, definition of institutions as 'the humanly devised constraints that shape human interaction' emphasizes constraint.[19] However, institutions both constrain *and enable* action.[20] Their effects on society and the economy are mediated by how social agents, pursuing different interests and endowed with unequal resources, are not just constrained by rules and norms, but also able to process or evade institutional constraints and to use them as empowering tools in their (inter)actions. It is in this sense that we speak of the 'social appropriation' of property rights, meaning the ways in which individual or collective agents make institutions 'their own' through their effective agency, using socially sanctioned rules and norms to legitimately appropriate resources, to constrain the actions of others concerning those resources, and conversely to resist being constrained by others.

Standard new institutional economic theory postulates that the relevant social agents are organizations, defined as 'a group of individuals pursuing a mix of common and individual goals through partially coordinated action' – with a special emphasis, put by North and his associates, on elite organizations.[21] However, it is not only organizations who act and choose. Focusing solely on organizations assumes away individual and non-organized collective action embedded in everyday social relations. Unless, that is, a rather loose definition of 'organization' is stretched to mean virtually all forms of collective action and social interaction, even such collectives as 'a market community',[22] the concept being thereby rendered virtually useless as an analytical tool. Social networks and *ad hoc* groups such as the 'English crowd' are not organizations which either act or make choices as discrete actors, yet their participants partially coordinate their individual goals, choices and actions and act collectively.[23]

New institutionalists have rightly highlighted the importance of informal institutions (for example, binding customs enforced through social control) alongside formal ones, such as the law and the judicial system, and they have theorized about the relationships between them.[24] This is important, but it still begs the issue. Informal institutions and their interaction with formal ones remain a grin without the cat, unless their interplay with social structures and relations is empirically examined, rather than presumed. The rather fuzzy definitions of 'informal institutions' to comprise not just normative systems but also underlying values, shared beliefs and world views, tends to make this a wildcard notion that lends itself to all sorts of *ad hoc* explanations, as we shall see in the following section on path dependence. As Portes argues, neo-institutional theorists conflate different aspects and levels of abstraction under the same definitions, as well as the cultural and structural dimensions of social phenomena, thereby obscuring both their differences and their relationships.[25]

Focusing solely at the nation-state level, moreover, usually ignores the variance between national and local level institutions, power structures and contexts of action.[26] This sidesteps the part of non-elite social agents, groups and communities in adopting, adapting and resisting institutions and institutional innovation in the concrete social contexts where their actions take place. Serrão and Rodrigues in chapter one, Câmara and Santos in chapter five, Garrido in chapter six and Bromley and Wolz in chapter eight, all remind us that in local social orders, agents hold context-specific power and their (inter)actions are also constrained and enabled by local level institutions. The everyday practice the latter legitimize may subvert and even overtly oppose macro-level power structures and institutions, in ways that organizations such as the state can barely control, let alone coerce.[27] Thus the divergent results of formally identical institutions are contingent on how these are embedded in concrete social relations and in their change over time.[28] It is very much at this level, and not just at the macro-political level of the state and national elite organizations, that institutionalized rules, norms, and roles are acted upon, and that social and economic outcomes emerge out of social relations.

Following on from the previous argument, we would challenge the definition of property as merely an institution, which abstracts a normative and, quite frequently, legal and state-centred view of property, largely bypassing concrete property relations and their social contexts.[29] We propose instead a relational realist view, focused on the dialectics of social appropriation and expropriation.[30] This entails an understanding of property rights as social relations – in the Weberian sense of courses of action that are made probable because they are carried out by a plurality of social agents, who reciprocally refer the meanings of their actions[31] – rather than as simply the abstracted institutions that frame those meanings. This is actually in line with the basic definitions of new institutional economics: 'property rights do not refer to relations between men and things but rather, *to the sanctioned behavioral relations among men that arise from the existence of things and pertain to their use*.[32] Thus defined, property is legitimized power (as different from non-legitimized power of access);[33] that is, the socially sanctioned ability that asset owners possess to constrain the behaviour of others in respect of those assets. Domination, consisting of the probability that this power is obeyed, varies with the extent to which it is perceived as legitimate and therefore consented to within a given historical context (i.e., to the extent that it constitutes authority).[34]

Therefore, property is not just an institution, but rather a set of social power relations that manifest themselves in everyday social action, and which are legitimized by formal and informal institutions, enforced by organizations and social control. This definition carries with it both the distinction and the relationship between values at a deep cultural level; a social order (again in the Weberian sense, which implies *a probability* of compliance)[35] consisting of rules, norms, and roles, at an intermediate institutional level; the structural power relations pertinent to each context of action, and the concrete social relations in which institutional rules, norms, and roles are (re)interpreted and (re)acted upon according to the agents' variable goal orientations and power resources.[36]

When dealing with culture, the most sophisticated neo-institutional economists tend to assume a direct relationship between stereotyped cultural traits, often presented as 'national cultures', and action – paradoxically, the sort of over-socialized conception for which economists and rational action theorists used to blame sociology, and which sociological theory itself has long denounced.[37] Even when they pay attention to smaller-scale phenomena, and attempt to explain resistance to change by the counter-action of group-specific institutions, neo-institutional theories still rely on norms and values as the explanatory variable, to the detriment of the analysis of power, social relations, and agency.[38] We believe instead that the productive way to include cultural values and shared beliefs, alongside rules and norms, in an analytical framework of property rights, is to problematize and research empirically how such cultural elements translate and are actively reinterpreted, through the bias of legitimation, into power relations and purposive individual or collective action.

How institutions come to operate in practice – including their economic outcomes – depends on which agents appropriate their legitimacy and how they act upon this, as shown throughout several historical cases brought together in this book; and also on the extent to which this is socially consented to or disputed and resisted against – possibly by using competing cultural sources of legitimacy such as local or group-specific institutions, the 'moral economy', and collective memories of dispossession, but the point is precisely that in order to justify cultural explanations we still have to ascertain if, how, by whom and to what effects such cultural constructs are actually used, as illustrated by Iriarte and Lana in chapter seven and by Bromley and Wolz in chapter eight.[39]

Formally identical interventions in property rights regimes may produce different effects depending not just on the pre-existing values and institutions, but also on the social relations and power structures upon which they were overlaid.[40] It is

in the contingent histories of how property rights were adapted to social and historical contexts, appropriated by specific individuals and groups and expropriated
from others, that we should seek to understand their effective outcomes. In this
sense, within the field of new institutional economics, a distributional conflict
theory of institutions is more appealing than the standard theory based on efficiency.[41] We find a good example of conflict-based analyses in Alston, Libecap
and Mueller's studies of institutional failure in Brazil. According to them, the
inconsistency between Brazilian civil law and constitutional rules on land reform
generated insecurity in property rights both for the landowners, whose land could
be seized and expropriated if not usefully occupied, and for the squatters, whose
right to the land they had seized was enforceable by the land reform agency under
constitutional rules, but disputable in courts under the civil law. As a result,
violence and deforestation are shown to be viable strategies for both parties to
secure their existing or claimed rights, and the allocation of land through tenancy
contracts to be discouraged. Historically, the long-lasting pressure for land reform
in Brazil is presented as the inheritance of Portuguese colonization, with the
granting of large tracts of frontier land to influential parties and the resulting
social asymmetry between large landowners and landless peasants – which leads
us to the next section.[42]

Institutions, path dependence, and global history

The idea of path dependence looms large in new institutional economic history,
particularly in the overarching theoretical framework developed by Douglass
North and his collaborators since the late 1980s. It purports to account for the
observed long-lasting differences in economic growth across economies. The
essence of this meta-theoretical narrative is that most societies have not harnessed
the potential for modern sustained economic growth, as did a minority of indus-
trialized Western nations, because somehow the former resisted adopting institutions that economize on transaction costs, facilitate trade and cooperation, and
allow competitive markets to evolve so as to allocate production factors in the
most efficient ways; and above all, institutions that are able to adapt continuously
to ever changing circumstances.

According to this theory, in most historical and contemporary countries, centralized and redistributive societies with insecure property rights tend to perpetuate
their 'perverse' incentive systems. However, a few de-centralized societies with
competitive markets and polities somehow evolved out of that state and became
able to sustain growth. 'Understanding the transition is the holy grail, for it is the
process of modern social development.'[43]

As an analytical tool for that purpose, North borrowed the theory of path
dependence from technology studies. The original concept is that once a technology has been adopted by a large number of users, the costs involved in changing
it may eventually block later alternatives, regardless of their higher efficiency, and
therefore the historical sequence of events may lead to a 'lock-in' around less
efficient technologies.[44] If one substitutes 'institutions' for 'technology', the role

of path dependence in the neo-institutionalist meta-narrative becomes clear. Each country's individual history has set an institutional matrix that generates economic and political advantages for the ruling elites and their organizations, by limiting access to economic and political resources. The incumbent elites therefore have no incentives to change those institutions and indeed strive to keep them, regardless of their overall efficiency.[45] Because the elite coalitions hold the power, the resources, and the redistributive capacity to garner social support, the social system gets locked into those institutions. Rather than their persistence, the real historical puzzle the theory faces concerns the extraordinary historical circumstances which allowed the unlikely transition to take place from 'limited access orders' to competitive and efficiently adaptable 'open access orders'. Variations on this kind of argument are to be found in some of the most influential writing in economic history concerning global differences in economic development.[46]

At this point, the theoretical meta-narrative draws on analytical narratives of successful breakthroughs, looking for the critical junctures and processes that led a handful of north-western European nations to shift their course towards 'open access social orders'.[47] The transition from limited to open access orders was a difficult one, which required contingent power disequilibria to create the incentives for some of the elites to promote institutional innovations. For example, the historical sequence in seventeenth-century England, leading from the Crown's fiscal rapacity under the Stuarts to the Glorious Revolution and the resulting constitutional accountability of the Crown, bringing about more secure property rights and creating the 'doorstep conditions' for England to later make the incremental transition into an open access order.[48]

The theory then expands to the global scale by adopting what we might call the 'institutional export model': as European countries created worldwide empires, new colonial societies, later to become independent nations, were built upon their home-grown institutional matrices. Some, like England's colonies in North America, inherited institutions conducive to open access orders and carried on accordingly along the path of economic development. Others, like the Iberian colonies in Latin America, were burdened with institutions upholding limited access orders. The latter either never tried to adopt 'good' institutions, or when they did their positive effects were blocked by the inherited institutional matrix of informal norms, world views and shared beliefs, by which those societies persisted on the underdevelopment path set out by their former colonizers.[49] At the global level, therefore, path dependence means the export of historically divergent institutional matrices and of the correlative chances for economic development, which set up the initial conditions for the new nations' paths into the modern world and the successive waves of globalization. To put it bluntly, as the initial hypotheses about the economic outcomes of more precisely defined institutions failed, the theory evolved to blame that on 'their culture' without really going through the trouble of investigating how specific institutional rules and norms are actually used in concrete social relations, let alone how the latter relate to the assumed cultural values and beliefs.

The way North, Wallis and Weingast deal with ownership in colonial societies plainly reveals the kind of West-centrism and Eurocentrism often denounced by proponents of a global history.[50] Since most colonial societies have not entered the stage they call 'open access order', only the United States deserve a section in their chapter on successful transitions.[51] A note in the chapter on England shows, in a very concise and significant way, the authors' line of reasoning. They begin by stating that '[a]s De Soto ... and the larger development literature emphasize, establishing well-defined and easily transferrable ownership rights to land remains a significant problem in many parts of the world today'. The note to this states that:

> The export of English land law to the American colonies is a centrepiece of most economic histories of the New World. English land law provided an institutional and legal basis for a relatively equal distribution of freehold land in the American colonies, while Spanish and Portuguese land law led to the creation of large estates and unequal distribution of land throughout what would become Latin America.[52]

Thus, according to the authors, the economic success of the United States is due to its British colonial past, as compared with the failure of the Ibero-American colonies.[53] However, if we go beyond sweeping generalizations to examine the historical detail, we find many examples of the United States profoundly changing and actually rebelling against the legal ground rules for ownership rights exported by the British. There were anti-feudal revolts that were unknown to Britain, and jurisprudence sanctioned expropriation measures that do not in the least conform to the principle of secure property rights. On the other hand, the 'principle of discovery' which justified the occupation of Native American land was actually borrowed from the Spanish. Social struggles and overt violence between Native Americans and European settlers, slave owners and slaves, farmers, ranchers, and gold and oil miners, and so forth, played a key role in this whole process; almost all were struggles over land rights, the results of which were then institutionalized in law and formal land titles. If the exported British model involved protecting property rights, then many ownership rights were eventually violated in the United States, as in most British colonies and indeed in Britain itself. In Daunton's words,

> North's account of secure property rights is curiously partial. The creation of secure property rights in Britain entailed not only protection of state creditors but also the transfer of clan lands in Scotland into the private property of powerful landowners, the displacement of Irish lords by English settlers, and the erosion of the rights of English peasants. The transfer of secure property rights from Britain to its colonies had its counterpart in the disruption of the property rights of native Americans which was extended to many parts of Asia and Australasia. What was security to one person was theft to another.[54]

Moreover, many expropriations were justified in the name of the common good, which suggests that some institutions which allegedly had been 'good' in Britain would have been 'bad', had they been functioning in full force in the United States. The same may be said of important differences within Britain itself, as between and within former British colonies.[55]

Just as the explanation for the successes of the United States and other former British colonies cannot be put forward that superficially, so the failure of the former Iberian colonies cannot be assumed to simply result from the export of the ownership model of their former mainlands. As Djenderedjian and Santilli show in chapter four, it was the implementation of fully delineated, exclusive and enforceable property rights in the Buenos Aires province, certainly inspired by the British model, which eventually enhanced and congealed land-wealth inequality at a much higher level than the 'traditional' modes of imperfect property. The contrast they make with the neighbouring province of Santa Fe, where the same Argentinian political system established quite different rules for land allocation resulting in lesser inequality, shows that to speak of a wholesale 'Spanish legacy' obscures significant differences in the interests and strategies at stake. In Brazil, the colonial institutions also admitted a plurality of property rights, both those underlying *latifundia* and those legitimizing customary peasant tenancies and emphyteutical landholdings. Such plurality certainly made for insecurity in property rights; however, when the time came to secure them according to the principle of absolute and exclusive property, complex political struggle during the nineteenth century dictated which were acknowledged and which were expropriated. Rather than settling land conflicts, this fuelled new ones that remain ablaze.[56]

In both Buenos Aires and Brazil, the political implementation of the liberal model of property selected some amongst the different possibilities to legitimize rights afforded by the traditional colonial inheritance, and in both it ended up legitimizing extensive inequality in land rights. In Brazil, however, the specification and securitization of land property was much feebler than in Buenos Aires, where a full-fledged land registry system was put in place. To put down all these similitudes and differences to the presumed effects of inherited informal institutions, shared beliefs, and world-views, sidesteps the need to bring in concrete social structures, power relations, agents and contexts of action, and how these played out in actual historical processes.[57]

North's view on path dependence at the global level also relies almost exclusively on one-way transfers from metropolises to colonies. However, as Serrão and Rodrigues show in chapter one, the migration of Portuguese emphyteusis to India, Ceylon and Mozambique was far from a static one-way transfer. Instead, the Portuguese rulers used the plasticity of emphyteutical property rules to accommodate them to the aboriginal institutions and power relations, to gain political control over the territory and rent and/or direct control over productive processes, trade routes and resources. As local institutions were translated into the Portuguese legal vocabulary, new normative forms and practices evolved out of this miscegenation, and what the authors term Indo-Portuguese emphyteusis was successively adapted to different and evolving local appropriations and sets of economic opportunities, for instance adapting in Mozambique from control over traditional chieftaincies for exploiting rents and slaves, to a contract with an international capitalist company to explore international market opportunities. Across all these cases, Portuguese institutions undeniably formed an imprint, but in return they were profoundly reshaped by the translation of local institutions and power relations into them, and by the successive practical appropriations made of them.

Summing up, the neo-institutionalist dominant take on the concept of path dependence ultimately treats the processes of social reproduction and change as black boxes. We believe that it is only by opening up those black boxes and delving deeper into concrete social processes that we can give history back its due. Several chapters in this book besides the above mentioned by Serrão and Rodrigues may be read in this light, whether or not they have made explicit use of the concept of path dependence.

Morell in chapter two, points to path dependence in the aforementioned practical model of conflict resolution that the Swedish state consistently applied, when facing evolving demands on the social functions of land and related social interests. The result seems to be a regime of property rights, highly adaptable to social demands over the centuries, but because of that, they also remain very open to public and political contestation, and it is tempting to speculate on whether and how this may have affected land markets. The results emphasize the cognitive dimension of learning and of decision routines in policy making, which seem to have led to a stable pattern of change over time; and also, at points, how different agents went about not just struggling or lobbying for realignments of property rights, but also actively appropriating what rights were available in novel ways.

Locatelli and Tedeschi's narrative (chapter three) of the effects of the land cadastre in Lombardy from the eighteenth century onwards, how it secured property rights and provided tax incentives for productive land use, gives an account of path dependence mostly in line with that of North's. As we see it, the main point is not that such institutional innovations were a path-changing event, but rather that they were one further step on a trajectory that had previously been entered into. The cadastre introduced positive changes because it built upon a set of pre-existing cultural factors and socio-economic structures that had evolved since at least the late Middle Ages. This was also contingent on coevolving and mutually reinforcing socio-economic processes, which makes the region's history overall rather unique and, rewording the authors' conclusions after North, a clear-cut illustration of 'adaptive efficiency'. Nevertheless, the essay significantly highlights the role that non-elite groups and organizations such as rural trade unions played in this outcome. Further research will certainly provide more detail as to how the newly defined property rights were actually reworked and appropriated by the different parties, namely concerning the reciprocal strategies of landowners, lessees and farm labourers in the capitalistic farming sector, and of landowners, sharecroppers and labourers in the peasant farming sector.

As we have argued previously, chapter four by Djenderedjian and Santilli contributes to problematizing the 'cultural heritage' explanation in North's theory of path dependence at the global scale. While its main explanatory argument remains within a neo-institutional framework, it nevertheless emphasizes often neglected distributive outcomes: the system of property rights implemented in Buenos Aires in the final third of the nineteenth century crystalized a part of the property rights, previously allocated through different forms of concessions of public land, as a full property structure, in the context of a very extensive production regime. When soon after production became much more intensive and capitalized in response to world market opportunities in the 'first global age', land value increased and the associated inequality in wealth widened. The comparison with Santa Fe suggests that differences in productive allocations and the relative influence of regional coalitions of interests led to differences in land appropriations, which the implementation of the new property rights regime eventually amplified. Nevertheless, it cannot be ruled out that the inequality structure may have been nuanced by the allocation of property rights through a lease market, for the assessment of which further research would be needed on land rent flows and the terms and details of tenancy relationships. However, this was admittedly outside the scope of the study, which rests on the absolute rather than the 'bundle of rights' concept of property.

Chapter five by Câmara and Santos on the *colonia* in Madeira goes into some detail about the rules and the incentives contained in the contract, in order to understand the possible appropriation strategies of landowners and tenants to gain or keep control over property rights, and then explores practical adaptations in the course of the nineteenth century, when both parties faced changing economic and legal circumstances. The results suggest two kinds of path dependent results: the once efficient contract survived longer than might be expected in the wake of economic and political changes, and even as it waned it still left its imprint in a pulverized land property structure. Both kinds of effects are tentatively related to the agents' strategies and the courts' rulings concerning the adaptation of the customary norms within the new economic and legal context; further research is needed on everyday property and contract management, household strategies, and litigation to consubstantiate those hypotheses.

Finally, in chapter eight Bromley and Wolz describe how political negotiations at the state level, leading to land re-privatization in eastern Germany within the wider context of political reunification, ended up acknowledging the claims of the social interests in place over the 'historical' claims of former landowners expropriated under the communist regime. This outcome is attributed to the difference in mobilization, organization and consequent political lobbying capacity between the competing claimants. Even though the juridical nature of property rights was profoundly changed, its effects were scarce on the farming organization and landscape, because the newly allocated private property rights were rearranged under large-scale agricultural cooperatives and corporate enterprises. Thus far the argument remains within the neo-institutional framework. Departing from it, the study goes on to explore the actual social agency of returnees in striving to gain a foothold in local communities, and of local villagers, farm managers and authorities towards blocking their access to land legally open for purchase – albeit somewhat one-sidedly, since the only 'voice' in the study is that of the returnees. While explicitly focused on cultural memories, the analysis is very much about how all parties use them, along with formal rules, organizational power and everyday social relations, to legitimize their claims.

Regardless of the different approaches of these several chapters to this topic, they have all contributed to suggesting historical processes by which social arrangements built at one stage restricted the set of possible choices and conditioned change at later stages. In all cases, history clearly mattered – but then, where does it not matter? The counterfactual assumptions implicit in assessing which alternative trajectories would have been open otherwise and whether they would have been more efficient (and come to that, for what purpose), as required by the strict theoretical definition of path dependence, are hard to posit and harder still to test. However, if historians and social scientists are to make any sense of this, we believe it is in the detail of such processes that we may expect to understand the 'social dynamics (involving social interactions among economic or political agents) that are characterized by positive feedbacks and self-reinforcing dynamics', to recover the precise formulation of one of the leading proponents of the concept,[58] and more importantly, to make the social analysis of property rights a part of the comparative endeavour of a social and economic world history.[59]

Reality or metaphor? A relational realist approach to property rights

As we have pointed out, one feature common to all the neo-institutionalist discourse on property is that the concept is articulated at the level of institutions alone. In line with what we have stated earlier about institutions, 'perfect property' – as indeed all things perfect – has been construed as an abstraction away from social practice.

Abstraction requires an exercise of imagination. Imagining absolute property over vast expanses of land in a nation-state, and even at an imperial scale entails a system of 'legibility', control and enforcement that would not often be available as that discourse was emerging.[60] Imagining a bundle of perfectly delineated property rights allocated to different persons in the most efficient way entails abstracting from the power relations presiding over that allocation and in turn reinforced by it. Indeed one might ask, as E. P. Thompson did about 'the market', whether we are in fact conceptualizing reality or forcing a metaphor – in Thompson's own word, a 'superstition' – on it.[61] In the historical process leading to modern capitalist societies, out of the social appropriation relations standing at one historical time and place, some objects, subjects and modes of appropriation were abstracted as the 'real', 'natural' and 'legitimate' meanings of 'property'; while others – no matter how grounded in previous social practice and legitimized by pre-existing institutions – were declared to be 'trespass' and 'abuse'.[62] A *numerus clausus* of legitimate property forms was explicitly built into civil law systems and by court practice into common law systems.[63] These legal templates of property became the dominant metaphor for property relations. To the extent that they came to embody a 'natural grammar' of property, they are of essence

192 Congost, Gelman and Santos

a-historical in their terms, if by no means in their origins. Not surprisingly, the *numerus clausus* principle is at the core of the arguments of essentialist criticism against the relativism of the bundle of rights approach in law and economics.[64]

Moreover, a significant part of globalization as a process was the progressive import of liberal property templates into new and very different contexts to those in which they had originated, such as the Argentinian pampa in chapter four and Madeira in chapter five, or brought back into contexts which had since experienced radically different property relations, as in eastern Germany in chapter eight. Their implementation met (and still meets) with varying degrees of resistance, as they were imposed, adapted and hybridized by practical compromise, according not only to the inherited cultural norms and blueprints, but also, critically, to the concrete power relations at play, as shown in the above-mentioned chapters and also in chapters two on Scandinavia and seven on Spain.

There is nothing about the idea of *numeri clausi* of property forms that feels inherently alien to a sociologist or a historian. It is a plausible enough hypothesis that all historical societies had some such standardizing and legitimizing menu, in law or in custom, for the prevalent power relations concerning the appropriation of resources.[65] Or rather, several such menus may have coexisted in more or less conflictive ways, according to the varying social scales and forms in which binding rules could be set, as suggested by the overlaying of European emphyteusis on diverse aboriginal land rights across all the colonies of the Portuguese Indian empire, in chapter one. Our point is that the abstraction, articulation and enforcement of such templates for property – their contents, how, to what extent and by whose actions they became dominant, how and by whom they are or were resisted – must be empirically studied and analysed as social processes within their own terms and contexts, and only then classified for comparative purposes.[66]

That is why, in spite of insightful criticism, we still feel the bundle of rights approach to be more operational when it comes to understanding 'the heterogeneity and plasticity of property [. . . and how] it can be deployed toward an endless variety of purposes'.[67] Taking currently dominant templates of property (or rather, the way they are idealized) for granted remains a major epistemological obstacle, either directly as a fit-for-all descriptive metaphor or indirectly as a yardstick against which to assess all societies' social appropriation arrangements concerning efficiency, perfection, and ultimately the very existence of property. Echoing calls in earlier social historiography to contextualize the 'principle of property' and its outcomes,[68] historians and social scientists should bring forth evidence on how such 'templates' of property rights historically varied, were construed, upheld, resisted against, changed and appropriated, and to what social and economic effects.[69] Only such analyses may bring us understandings of how and why some objects could be appropriated and expropriated in specific ways in some contexts and not in others,[70] some subjects could hold property and not others, some appropriations gained or lost acknowledgement and enforcement as property rights, or new categories of legitimate objects, subjects and appropriations were socially constructed and old ones destroyed to meet newly prevalent ideals, needs, interests, and power balances.[71]

How can a relational realist approach to property rights, such as we propose, contribute to repositioning relevant historical problems, and redress the effects of using un-problematized abstract notions of property?

The processes involved in the social appropriation of natural resources have largely (though not always, it should be stressed) been correlated with processes of expropriation by the state, stemming from a belief in the superiority of one ideal of property over other existing forms, or that some kinds of land occupation and use were outside the conceptual realm of property. This led to a number of conceptual dichotomies, which have mainly been used to justify this sort of operation, as for instance those of possession *versus* property, feudal *versus* modern property, individual or private *versus* collective or common property, and ultimately of whole historical societies having *versus* not having property as a recognizable idea or institution. Many such dichotomies have become an accepted part of historical discourse. However, to the extent that they oversimplify historical reality and frame research problems within a biased and a-historic outlook, historians should object to any analysis of the social dynamics of property that is anchored in those simple dichotomies. Analysing the history of property requires a global perspective able to overcome a Eurocentric, linear and tautological vision of history as the convergence of imperfect forms of property towards a perfect one. At the same time, this should allow historians to engage in a dialogue with social scientists on subjects of great current importance.

Some examples from early modern European history may help to illustrate this. For instance, one very common historiographical topic is the idea of a generalized expropriation of the peasantries throughout Western Europe during the modern era. This idea, which ran through the 1960s–1970s debates on the transition from feudalism to capitalism and the justly famous 'Brenner debate',[72] was consistent with this having been a first step towards proletarianization in the old regime, which seemed to suggest that the impoverishment of the majority had been the normal path to economic 'progress'. But up until now, we historians have scarcely asked ourselves whether and how sectors of the European peasantry managed a way out of poverty, whether and how 'new middle classes' emerged out of peasant groups. Rather than just explaining peasant expropriation, the analysis of diverse dynamics of social appropriation/expropriation should help us detect – if, when and where they occurred – processes whereby some within the poorest sectors were empowered in property relations, which would be difficult to capture otherwise.

Such historical concerns can also be linked to the present issues of fighting poverty in developing countries. Neo-institutionalist theories have also influenced development policies and anti-poverty aid programmes around the world. In 2008, a High Commission was created within the United Nations for the 'legal empowerment' of the poor, partly inspired by De Soto, the economist cited above by North, Wallis and Weingast and who in turn cites North. De Soto's was a very simple proposal: the poor, who often live on the margins of legality, should be able to formalize their deeds of ownership, in order to have the land allocated to the most efficient uses through market mechanisms and to allow landowners to access credit and build up capital.[73]

Significant criticism to the UN Commission's and similar approaches to land property and governance, such as those upheld by the World Bank under the so-called 'Washington consensus', has since pointed out that those policies take generalized propositions for granted, regardless of the realist analysis of the historical and social contexts for their application, failing to take into account the actual social relations and practices of land ownership and tenure. Many development scholars and practitioners refer to the need to ensure and improve the means the poor have of effectively and enduringly accessing land, rather than formalizing full individual land ownership, commodifying land and liberalizing markets. By decoupling formal property rights from informal institutions and social structure, such policies can in fact disempower poor landowners and make access to land less secure for them.[74] Case studies in Africa have concluded that, as a backlash:

> Far from dispelling tension and confusion, neoliberal efforts to clarify and enforce rights of ownership have often added to them ... [I]ntersecting tensions over eligibility for land access and political participation have contributed to a resurgence of appeals to tradition and historical precedent to validate claims to land and citizenship. Far from substituting 'modern' political economies ... for 'traditional' particularisms, neoliberal interventions appear to have reinvigorated particularity and custom as bases for legitimizing claims to property, citizenship and authority both within and without the purview of the state.[75]

A relational realist perspective will also help overcome simplistic historical interpretations arising from the abuse of the feudalism *versus* capitalism dichotomy. Almost all of the many misconceptions this brought about can be traced back to the assumption of an ideal, progressive form of property, which required a liberal revolution in order to impose itself on society and eradicate backward, 'imperfect' forms deemed to be 'feudal'. This explains, for instance, why historians have long conceived of the emphyteusis, in all its various forms, as a feudal legal figure, thereby lending it a strong connotation of archaism in the transition to agrarian capitalism.[76]

However, we know that in the early modern period, emphyteutic practices have provided a sizable part of the population in certain areas with significant property rights in land. As recalled in chapter three, businessmen in medieval and early modern Lombardy who invested in large lease-farming used a form of emphyteutical contract as a step up the property ladder, on their way to becoming a landowning elite.[77] A similar process happened in late eighteenth- and early nineteenth-century southern Portugal, which played an important part in the region's agricultural modernization and growth.[78] In many regions in Mediterranean Europe, emphyteusis formed the basis for a model of agrarian growth driven by market-oriented specialization. While urban and rural elites certainly have played a part in these processes, the leading role was often the peasants', who took advantage of the wide property rights which this kind of contracts afforded them to clear uncultivated and often wooded land in order to undertake commercial farming. Madeira's contract of *colonia* studied in chapter five, though not emphyteutic in nature, is another example of an 'archaic' contractual form proving highly effective in agrarian growth, much like the *rabassa morta* contract in Catalonia and the *livello* in some areas in Alpine Lombardy.[79]

The private *versus* common property dichotomy also lends itself to much oversimplification of historical processes. It goes without saying that the privatization of common property rights through legal or *de facto* enclosure, contracts letting them out to private persons, or through suppression of collective rights in private land, on the one hand, as well as the communalization or restriction of private rights through compulsory rotations, rights of access, eminent domain, nature and landscape conservation, zoning laws, etc., on the other, have been part and parcel of the historical dynamics of land property to this day. However, we should beware of shutting these processes within simple dichotomous categories and of lending them preset meanings and consequences, irrespective of the social contexts and processes in which they take place. Hardin's 'tragedy of the commons' is the most notorious example of such oversimplifications, displaying the commons as either a free-for-all buffet open to unrestrained use by myopic egoists, or as a pool of resources managed under socialist rule. The only other way he conceived of managing a commons meant its sheer destruction as such – 'the privatism of free enterprise'.[80] His response to criticism in 1998 was not in the least nuanced by the accumulated evidence that the 'mutual coercion mutually agreed upon' needed to sustain common resources has in fact been widely achieved by endogenous and often informal community institutions, through arrangements that only the wildest stretch of imagination might define as either 'socialism' or 'the privatism of free enterprise'.[81]

As shown by Morell in chapter two, Locatelli and Tedeschi in chapter three, and Garrido in chapter six, natural resources, such as woodlands and water, as well as agricultural land during specific times of agricultural cycles, have varied amply in their status as ownable 'things'. Specific actions concerning them (some sticks in the bundle, for example, grazing and gleaning, collecting and timbering, hunting and fishing, passing through and roaming) were variably acknowledged and their allocation has been disputed among communities, lords, private and collective users, organizations, and the state.[82] The very identity and status of subjects holding legitimate entitlements in commons has been disputed and redefined according to power relations at play, as can be seen in the account of the boundaries of entitlements to common water in chapter six and the description of memories of privatization in chapter seven – sometimes to such a degree of exclusion that common rights eventually became private and indeed were forgotten.[83]

Privatization too is neither a simple category nor one that rests on state institutions alone. Like communalization, it can take different paths and forms, leading to different consequences according to the power balances in different historical settings. In the pampa region in Argentina, a combination of strong local consuetudinary legitimacy, weakness of central state and local power relations blocked the large landowner's claims to eradicate customary (collective or individual) rights during the first half of the nineteenth century,[84] which however did not preclude significant agricultural growth, as is also shown in chapter four. In several cases in the eighteenth and nineteenth centuries, identical state rules for the privatization of commons and the 'perfecting of property' were refracted by the local political and social structure, social alliances and strategies, and cultural legitimacy into a variety of forms and degrees of privatization – including non-privatization and even contractual arrangements to re-establish communal control over formally privatized land, as pointed out in chapter two.[85] Where property rights were privatized, this met with mixed results. A new set of opportunities might open up for the lower rural classes to engage in commercial farming, improving their standards of living and agricultural productivity on the whole, as in the Baden Palatinate.[86] On the other hand, the management of resources might actually deteriorate because of unfettered private overexploitation, which under common appropriation had been checked by some degree of social control by the community and the insecurity of returns to investment in land clearance, as pointed out in chapter three, concerning the Lombard Alpine areas.[87]

Thus, the paths leading from a variety of common property rights arrangements to a variety of private ones and from institutional arrangements to economic, social and environmental outcomes are not made intelligible either by a simple 'common *versus* private' dichotomy, by the institutions themselves, let alone formal state institutions, or by the actions of elite organizations. While all these undoubtedly mattered, one again has to get down to the detail of social structure, social relations and agency in order to understand such processes.

Conversely, to idealize common property rights as egalitarian and denounce all claim to privatization as a move to seigniorial or capitalist exploitation may prove to be an equally harmful trap.[88] Among collective rights in land, there have been some, such as gleaning, which had a highly redistributive capacity and could be approximated to an actual 'poor law'; whereas others, as was frequent with grazing, could disproportionately benefit a few individuals or entities. In a different sort of idealization, an important institutionalist school of thought in economic history, inspired by Ostrom's theory, has devoted its efforts to vindicating common property as being efficient, depending on its institutionalized modes of governance in specific historical contexts. Chapter six makes a clear point against such idealizations of the irrigation communities in eastern Spain, be it on moral and political grounds concerning egalitarianism, or on theoretical grounds concerning Ostrom's formalization of governance principles, which, in spite of its heuristic value, Garrido's critical contrast with historically ascertained practices shows to be partially flawed.

From a social, rather than economic history perspective, it has been argued that the commons emerged in Europe, during the later Middle Ages and the turn of the early modern era, as a 'silent revolution' resulting from collective action.[89] It should be evident at this point that we do not take issue with collective action as a relevant *explanans*. Nevertheless, one should beware of the assumptions underlying the *explanandum*. Within the frame of the private *versus* common dichotomy, the very need to explain the historical emergence of commons as a 'revolution' inadvertently carries with it the assumption that private property 'was there' to begin with, and as such it begs no explanation by social agency. This way of stating the historical problem tends rather to strengthen the view of private property as the 'natural order of things' and the commons as some sort of 'collective deviance'. Such an assumption may prove just as harmful to the theoretical understanding of historical processes as that of the privatization of commons resulting from 'natural progress'.

Similarly, early modern laws upholding peasant communities' right to glean in privately-owned land have been depicted as an expropriation of private rights by the state.[90] However, the state's legislative action may just as well be understood as a response to the pressure of private landowners, seeking to exert an ever tighter check on locally institutionalized collective uses and, ultimately, to expropriate such collective property rights. This amounts to saying that collective action driven by individualist values may in some contexts, and sometimes just as 'silently', have challenged collective property practices and relations which had, up to then, been legitimized by the established moral economy and the institutions based on this.

Therefore, a realist conception of property as a social relationship implies assuming that diverse social processes of appropriation and expropriation of land and related resources are possible in different historical contexts, and that changes in those processes may take a plurality of paths that are irreducible to those mapped out by the aforementioned dichotomies. It also means that we should be able to look at property relations as changing realities that both result from wider social changes and may in return cause them. Our view is not simply that property relations are the product of history, which is a truism, but rather that we need to ask new sorts of questions about their history. Otherwise, we risk disregarding or not even looking for important evidence in our research, as well as forcing our assumptions on such evidence as we do collect.

We can illustrate with two of the most widely-researched national processes, the historiography over which has had the most impact on property studies around the world. The abolition of feudal rights in revolutionary France can be looked at as either the expropriation of the former ruling classes' property rights, or as a a recovery and enhancement of the peasants' own rights. Similarly, land occupation in the United States can be seen as either a process in which the concept of property was created and exclusive property rights were appropriated by a variety of contending agents and groups, often striving to expropriate each other; or as a process of expropriation of the native inhabitants' own rights to the territory and the use of land, for want of the 'true' concept of property and of productive use, under newly imposed property rules. Our point is that historical analyses should focus on *both* appropriation and expropriation as coevolving political and social practices. Their dialectic relationship, we argue, was at the heart of what really happened to land property across both the old and the new nation.

Put more generally, when looking at changes in property rights, what some may see as the recovery of usurped rights, the more efficient allocation of such rights, or indeed the creation and allocation *ab initio* of effective property, others will regard as the expropriation of individuals or collectives. Therefore, a historical inquiry that, as a matter of methodology, takes appropriation and expropriation together as two terms of a dialectical relationship is best suited to check ideological bias in the way we frame the research problems and select and interpret the data. Setting aside whatever beliefs one has about the property forms at stake in each case, or the sympathy one may feel towards this or that among the contending groups, appropriation and expropriation should be systematically related in the historical analysis of such processes – with emphasis on the plural.

First and foremost, we must not assume from the outset that in each case there was but one uniform process, guided one-sidedly by the elite, the state and the law. It follows from our premises that researchers should ask how far the outcomes have differed, according to the extent to which the local institutions and power balances enabled each of the various agents and groups with interests at stake to appropriate the new rules, to prevent rivals from appropriating them, and to resist being expropriated. Historical social science has to acknowledge the complexity of the problems experienced, the social resources used, and the diversity of roles played by all social groups, without neglecting the agency of those (be they feudal lords, large landowners, poor peasants, non-European peoples, or any other kind of intervening social groups) who had previously appropriated land resources by different social relations and under different rules, and were eventually excluded from the newly institutionalized concepts of property.

Concluding remarks

We have argued for an approach to property rights that goes beyond the perspective on property as an institution, whether formal or informal, which is prevalent in the new institutional economics literature, and builds on the analytical potential of the initial definition of property rights as social relations. Concurrently, we have argued for the view of property as a bundle of rights and against the revival of the absolute concept of property under a *numerus clausus* of property forms defined *a priori*. We did not claim that these do not exist, but rather that any such property templates that have become institutionalized in a given space and time are themselves social constructions, which both express and legitimize power relations among individual and collective social actors. We have labelled this approach a relational realist perspective on property rights, stressing as a methodological consequence the need to consider their historical dynamics as a dialectical relationship between appropriation and expropriation.

Changes in property relations take place at local and global, as well as national and intermediate levels, in the course of which some have to cede some rights in favour of others as result of dispute, conflict and negotiation. Institutions do not have a stand-alone explanatory power, regardless of how they are concretely acted upon in social relations. They are but one component, albeit necessary, in the analysis of social structures, relations, and agency. Placing explanatory models at the abstract level of institutions seriously risks a fallacy of misplaced concreteness.

Neither should we take for granted institutional hegemony by the state and elite organizations, since competing sources of legitimacy can coexist in the same society, which may complement, dispute or ignore those upheld by the state, even forcing them to adapt and change. To acknowledge this should lead to dynamic and empirically grounded analyses of practice in relation to rights in land and their dispute, and to take stock of the diverse institutional forms – new and old, legal and customary – that coexisted and how they were appropriated, that is, purposively used to support and dispute claims to legitimacy in specific historical contexts. This should allow us to assess not just how land and related resources, but also the institutionalized norms themselves, were socially appropriated by some and expropriated from others, as devices to confer authority on property relations or contest such authority, thus differentially enabling some social agents and groups and constraining others. While differences and trends in social structure and culture doubtlessly matter, we therefore stressed the need to research concrete agency for understanding the actual economic and social outcomes of institutionalized property rules and norms.

Taken together, the chapters in this book display a rich and vibrant, if by no means exhaustive, array of outlooks on these issues. They leave us wishing for more focused analyses of the effective appropriation/expropriation of property rights. If ours are relevant questions to be asked, more effort is needed to clarify and operationalize them and, hopefully, to build up cumulative knowledge about them. If the reading has served to stir scientific curiosity in this direction, the book will have accomplished its purpose.

Notes

1 R. Congost and R. Santos, 'From formal institutions to the social contexts of property', in R. Congost and R. Santos (eds), *Contexts of Property in Europe: The Social Embeddedness of Property Rights in Land in Historical Perspective* (Turnhout: Brepols, 2010), pp. 13–36; R. Santos and J. V. Serrão, 'Property rights, social appropriations and economic outcomes: Agrarian contracts in southern Portugal in the late 18th century', in G. Béaur, P. R. Schofield, J.-M. Chevet and M. T. Pérez Picazo (eds), *Property Rights, Land Markets and Economic Growth in the European Countryside (Thirteenth–Twentieth Centuries)* (Turnhout: Brepols, 2013), pp. 475–94.

2 M. Daunton, 'Rationality and institutions: Reflections on Douglass North', *Structural Change and Economic Dynamics*, 21:2 (2010), pp. 147–56, on p. 151.

3 P. Vilar, 'Histoire du droit, histoire totale', in *Une Histoire en Construction: Approche Marxiste et Problématiques Conjoncturelles* (Paris: Gallimard and Les Éditions du Seuil, 1982), pp. 265–91.

4 R. Congost, *Tierras, Leyes, Historia: Estudios sobre la 'Gran Obra de la Propiedad'* (Barcelona: Crítica, 2007), pp. 253–78.

5 J. Getzler, 'Theories of property and economic development', *Journal of Interdisciplinary History*, 26:4 (1996), pp. 639–69, on p. 657.

6 W. Blackstone, *Commentaries on the Laws of England in Four Books* (1753), vol. 1 (Indianapolis: The Liberty Fund), 2011, p. 304, at http://files.libertyfund.org/files/2140/Blackstone_1387-01_EBk_v6.0.pdf 2011 [last accessed 10 March 2016].

7 Blackstone, *Commentaries*, pp. 307–8.

8 Blackstone, *Commentaries*, pp. 311–12.

9   R. H. Coase, 'The problem of social cost', in R. H. Coase, *The Firm, the Market and the Law* (Chicago and London: University of Chicago Press, 1990), pp. 95–156, on p. 155.

10   T. W. Merrill and H. H. Smith, 'What happened to property in law and economics?', *Yale Law Journal*, 111:2 (2001), pp. 357–98, on p. 366.

11   A. A. Alchian and H. Demsetz, 'The property rights paradigm', *Journal of Economic History*, 33:1 (1973), pp. 16–27, on p. 17, emphases in the original.

12   L. Duguit, *Les Transformations Générales du Droit Civil depuis le Code Napoléon* (Paris: Félix Alcan, 1920).

13   M. C. Mirow, 'The social-obligation norm of property: Duguit, Ahyem, and others', *Florida Journal of International Law*, 22 (2010), pp. 191–226, on p. 195.

14   F. H. Knight, *Risk, Uncertainty, and Profit* (Boston: Hart Schaffner & Marx and Horghton Mifflin Co., 1921), p. 359, emphasis in the original.

15   J. A. Schumpeter, *Socialism, Capitalism and Democracy* (Oxford and New York: Routledge, 1994, p. 142).

16   M. J. Horwitz, *The Transformation of American Law, 1870–1960* (Oxford: Oxford University Press, 1992).

17   D. C. North, J. J. Wallis and B. R. Weingast, 'A conceptual framework for interpreting recorded human history', *NBER Working Paper Series*, 12795 (Cambridge MA: National Bureau of Economic Research, 2006), p. 365, at www.nber.org/papers/w12795.pdf [last accessed 10 March 2016].

18   E. G. Furubotn and R. Richter, *Institutions and Economic Theory: The Contribution of the New Institutional Economics* (Ann Arbor: University of Michigan Press, 2000), p. 7; N. Mouzelis, 'Social and system integration: Lockwood, Habermas, Giddens', *Sociology*, 31:1 (1997), pp. 111–19, on p. 114.

19   D. C. North, *Institutions, Institutional Change and Economic Performance* (Cambridge: Cambridge University Press, 1990), p. 3.

20   W. R. Scott, *Institutions and Organizations: Ideas and Interests* (Thousand Oaks: Sage, 2008), p. 50.

21   North, Wallis and Weingast, 'Conceptual framework', pp. 12, 14. See criticism of North's and the new institutionalist theories (and lack thereof) about institutions, organizations and their relationships in J. Faundez, 'Douglass North's theory of institutions: Lessons for law and development', *Legal Studies Working Paper*, 2014/13 (Warwick: Warwick University School of Law, 2014), at http://dx.doi.org/10.2139/ssrn.2493052 [last accessed 10 March 2016], and A. Portes, *Economic Sociology: A Systematic Inquiry* (Princeton: Princeton University Press, 2010), pp. 48–70.

22   Furubotn and Richter, *Institutions and Economic Theory*, p. 7.

23   M. Granovetter, 'Economic action and social structure: The problem of embeddedness', *American Journal of Sociology*, 91:3 (1985), pp. 481–510; E. P. Thompson, 'The moral economy of the English crowd in the eighteenth century', *Past and Present*, 50 (1971), pp. 76–136.

24   J. Ensminger, 'Changing property rights: reconciling formal and informal rights to land in Africa', in J. N. Droback and J. V. C. Nye (eds), *The Frontiers of New Institutional Economics* (San Diego: Academic Press, 1997); North, *Institutions, Institutional Change*, pp. 40–5; S. Pejovitch, 'Formal and informal rules: Conflict or cooperation?', *Journal of Markets and Morality*, 2:2 (1999), pp. 164–81.

25   Portes, *Economic Sociology*, pp. 48–51.

26   R. L. Hopcroft, 'The importance of the local: Rural institutions and economic change in preindustrial England', in M. C. Brinton and V. Nee (eds), *The New Institutionalism in Sociology* (Stanford: Stanford University Press, 1998), pp. 277–304.

27   V. Nee and P. Ingram, 'Embeddedness and beyond: Institutions, exchange, and social structure', in Brinton and Nee, *New Institutionalism*, pp. 19–45, on pp. 36–7; J. C. Scott, *Weapons of the Weak: Everyday Forms of Peasant Resistance* (Yale: Yale

University Press, 1985); J. C. Scott, *Seeing like a State: How Certain Schemes to Improve the Human Condition Have Failed* (Yale: Yale University Press, 1998).

28 Faundez, 'Douglass North's theory', p. 53.

29 S. M. Borras Jr and J. C. Franco, 'Global land grabbing and trajectories of agrarian change: A preliminary analysis', *Journal of Agrarian Change*, 12:1 (2012), pp. 34–59; C. M. Hann, 'Introduction: The embeddedness of property', in C. M. Hann, *Property Relations: Renewing the Anthropological Tradition* (Cambridge: Cambridge University Press, 1998), pp. 1–47.

30 We use 'relational realism' as opposed to 'theoretical realism', after M. Somers, 'Symposium on historical sociology and rational choice theory: "We're no angels": Realism, rational choice, and relationality in social science', *American Journal of Sociology*, 104:3 (1998), pp. 722–84, esp. on pp. 766–72.

31 M. Weber, *Economy and Society: An Outline of Interpretive Sociology* (Berkeley: University of California Press, 1978), pp. 26–8.

32 Furubotn and Pejovitch, *Institutions and Economic Theory*, p. 1139, emphasis in the original.

33 J. C. Ribot and N. L. Peluso, 'A theory of access', *Rural Sociology*, 68:2 (2003), pp. 153–81.

34 B. C. Carruthers and L. Ariovich, 'The sociology of property rights', *Annual Review of Sociology*, 30 (2004), pp. 23–46, on pp. 23–4, 29; Getzler, *Theories of Property*, p. 655; T. Sikor and C. Lund, 'Access and property: A question of power and authority', in T. Sikor and C. Lund (eds), *The Politics of Possession: Property, Authority and Access to Natural Resources* (Chichester: Wiley-Blackwell, 2009), pp. 1–22; Weber, *Economy and Society*, pp. 36–8, 212–15.

35 Weber, *Economy and Society*, pp. 31–2.

36 Portes, *Economic Sociology*, pp. 51–5.

37 Granovetter, 'Economic action'; D. H. Wrong, 'The oversocialized conception of man in modern sociology', *American Sociological Review*, 26:2 (1961), pp. 183–93.

38 Ensminger, 'Changing property rights'; Pejovitch, 'Formal and informal rules'.

39 For instance, E. P. Thompson, *Whigs and Hunters: The Origins of the Black Act* (London: Allen Lane, 1975); T. M. Buoye, *Manslaughter, Markets and Moral Economy: Violent Disputes over Property Rights in Eighteenth-Century China* (Cambridge: Cambridge University Press, 2000).

40 S. M. Borras Jr and J. C. Franco, 'Contemporary discourses and contestations around pro-poor land policies and land governance', *Journal of Agrarian Change*, 10:1 (2010), pp. 1–32, on p. 9.

41 S. Ogilvie, 'Whatever is, is right? Economic institutions in preindustrial Europe', *Economic History Review*, 60:4 (2007), 649–84.

42 L. J. Alston, Gary D. Libecap and B. Mueller, 'Land reform policies, the sources of violent conflict, and implications for deforestation in the Brazilian Amazon', *Journal of Environmental Economics and Management*, 39 (2000), pp. 162–8; L. J. Alston and B. Mueller, 'Property rights, land conflict and tenancy in Brazil', *NBER Working Paper Series*, 15771 (Cambridge MA: National Bureau of Economic Research, 2010), available at www.nber.org/papers/w15771 [last accessed 10 March 2016]. Their view on the colonial origins of land conflict in contemporary Brazil is largely corroborated by M. Motta, *Right to Land in Brazil: The Gestation of the Conflict* (Rio de Janeiro: Editora da UFF, 2014).

43 North, Wallis and Weingast, 'Conceptual framework', p. 6.

44 W. B. Arthur, 'Competing technologies, increasing returns, and lock-in by historical events', *Historical Journal*, 99:394 (1989), pp. 116–31; P. A. David, 'Clio and the economics of QWERTY', *American Economic Review*, 75:2 (1985), pp. 332–7.

45 North, *Institutions, Institutional Change*, pp. 92–104.

46 For example, D. Acemoglu, and J. A. Robinson, *Why Nations Fail: The Origins of Power, Prosperity and Poverty* (New York: Crown Business, 2012).

47 D. C. North and B. R. Weingast, 'Constitution and commitment: The evolution of institutions governing public choice in seventeenth-century England', *Journal of Economic History*, 49:4 (1989), pp. 803–32.

48 B. R. Weingast, 'Why developing countries prove so resistant to the rule of law', in J. J. Heckman, R. L. Nelson and L. Cabatingan (eds), *Global Perspectives on the Rule of Law* (Oxford and New York: Routledge, 2009), pp. 28–51; Acemoglu and Robinson, *Why Nations Fail*, pp. 182–212.

49 Acemoglu, Johnson and Robinson, *Why Nations Fail*; D. C. North, 'Institutions', *Journal of Economic Perspectives*, 5:1 (1991), pp. 97–112; North, *Institutions, Institutional Change*, pp. 103, 116.

50 For example., M. Geier and C. Bright, 'World history in a global age', *American Historical Review*, 100:4 (1995), pp. 1034–60; K. Pomeranz, 'Political economy and ecology on the eve of industrialization: Europe, China, and the global conjuncture', *American History Review*, 107:2 (2002), pp. 425–46.

51 They did, however, co-edit another book with case studies of countries with limited access orders, mostly former colonies, in which Chile and South Korea stand out as the successful transitions. D. C. North, J. J. Wallis, S. B. Webb and B. R. Weingast (eds), *In the Shadow of Violence: Politics, Economics, and the Problems of Development* (Cambridge: Cambridge University Press, 2012).

52 Both quotes are from D. C. North, J. J. Wallis and B. R. Weingast, *Violence and Social Orders: A Conceptual Framework for Interpreting Recorded Human History* (Cambridge: Cambridge University Press, 2009), p. 77. Besides North and collaborators, the cited authors are J. R. T. Hughes with D. Acemoglu and S. Johnson with J. Robinson.

53 This argument was fully developed by North in *Institutions, Institutional Change*, pp. 101–3 and in D. North, *Understanding the Process of Economic Change* (Princeton: Princeton University Press, 2005), pp. 108–15.

54 Daunton, 'Rationality and institutions', p. 155.

55 Daunton, 'Rationality and institutions'; Horwitz, *Transformation of American Law*.

56 W. Dean, 'Latifundia and land policy in nineteenth-century Brazil', *Hispanic American Historical Review*, 51:4 (1971), pp. 606–25; R. M. Fonseca, 'A *Lei de Terras* e o advento da propriedade moderna no Brasil', *Anuario Mexicano de Historia del Derecho*, 17 (2005), pp. 97–112; Motta, *Right to Land*; M. Pedroza, *Conflicts of Property Rights of Land in Brazil: The Moral Economy of Carioca Tenancies* (New York: Edwin Mellen Press, 2015).

57 As critically pointed out in the otherwise praising review by R. Bates, 'A review of Douglass C. North, John Joseph Wallis, and Barry R. Weingast's *Violence and Social Orders: A Conceptual Framework for Interpreting Recorded Human History*', *Journal of Economic Literature*, 48:3 (2010), pp. 752–6.

58 P. A. David, 'Path dependence: A foundational concept for historical social science', *Cliometrica*, 1 (2007), pp. 91–114, on p. 92.

59 K. Pomeranz, 'Social history and world history: From daily life to patterns of change', *Journal of World History*, 18:1 (2007), pp. 69–98.

60 Scott, *Seeing like a State*.

61 Thompson, 'Moral economy', p. 91.

62 F. Sánchez Salazar, 'La redefinición de los derechos de propiedad: A propósito de los decretos sobre cercados de las Cortes de Cádiz', *Historia Agraria*, 39 (2006), pp. 207–40.

63 T. M. Merrill and H. Smith, 'Optimal standardization in the law of property: The *numerus clausus* principle', *Yale Law Journal*, 110 (2000), pp. 1–70.

64 T. M. Merrill, 'Property as modularity', *Harvard Law Review*, 125 (2012), pp. 151–63, on p. 154; H. E. Smith, 'Property as the law of things', *Harvard Law Review*, 125 (2012), pp. 1691–726, on p. 1698.

65 R. Santos, 'Direitos de propriedade fundiária e estratificação social rural: Um contributo sociológico', in A. Garrido, L. F. Costa and L. M. Duarte (eds), *Estudos em Homenagem a Joaquim Romero de Magalhães: Economia, Instituições e Império* (Coimbra: Almedina), pp. 277–93.
66 As advised by E. Ostrom, 'Design principles of robust property rights institutions: What have we learned?', in G. K. Ingram and Y. Y. Hong (eds), *Property Rights and Land Policies* (Cambridge MA: Lincoln Institute of Land Policy, 2009), pp. 25–51, on pp. 27–8.
67 Merrill, 'Property as modularity', p. 153.
68 E. P. Thompson, *Customs in Common* (London: Merlin Press, 1991); Thompson, *Whigs and Hunters*; Vilar, 'Histoire du droit'.
69 As in, for example, P. Schofield and B. van Bavel (eds), *The Development of Leasehold in Northwestern Europe, c. 1200–1600* (Turnhout: Brepols, 2009).
70 On modes and practices of expropriation, L. Lorenzetti, M. Barbot and L. Mocarelli (eds), *Property Rights and their Violations: Expropriations and Confiscations, 16th–20th Centuries* (Bern: Peter Lang, 2012).
71 Carruthers and Ariovich, 'Sociology of property rights', pp. 33–4; Congost and Santos, 'From formal institutions'.
72 T. H. Aston and C. H. E. Philpin (eds), *The Brenner Debate: Agrarian Class Structure and Economic Development in Pre-Industrial Europe* (Cambridge: Cambridge University Press, 1985).
73 For example, H. De Soto, *The Mystery of Capital: Why Capitalism Triumphs in the West and Fails Everywhere Else* (New York: Basic Books, 2000). To be fair, North did distance himself from simplistic neoliberal policy recommendations that have often selectively used his ideas. Faundez, 'Douglass North's theory', pp. 48–50; cf. North, *Understanding*, pp. 21 and 122.
74 Borras and Franco, 'Contemporary discourses'; Borras and Franco, 'Global land grabbing'; D. W. Bromley, 'Formalising property relations in the developing world: The wrong prescription for the wrong malady', *Land Use Policy*, 27:1 (2009), pp. 20–7; Ensminger, 'Changing property rights'; C. N. Musembi, 'De Soto and land relations in rural Africa: Breathing life into dead theories about property rights', *Third World Quarterly*, 28:8 (2007), pp. 1457–78; J.-P. Platteau, 'The evolutionary theory of land rights as applied to Sub-Saharan Africa: A critical assessment', *Development and Change*, 27:1 (1996), pp. 29–86; E. Sjastaad and D. W. Bromley, 'Indigenous land rights in Sub-Saharan Africa: Appropriation, security and investment demand', *World Development*, 25:4 (1997), pp. 549–62.
75 S. Berry, 'Property, authority and citizenship: Land claims, politics and the dynamics of social division in West Africa', in Sikor and Lund, *Politics of Possession*, pp. 23–45, on p. 40.
76 Long-term contracts like emphyteusis proved very versatile and they were widely used, under different names, throughout Europe. R. Congost, G. Béaur and P. Luna (eds), *Almost Landowners: Emphyteusis and Other Long-Term Practices in Europe (16th–20th centuries)* (Turnhout: Brepols, forthcoming).
77 D. F. Dowd, 'The economic expansion of Lombardy, 1300–1500: A study in political stimuli to economic change', *Journal of Economic History*, 21:2 (1961), pp. 143–60.
78 Santos and Serrão, 'Property rights'.
79 R. Congost, 'The social dynamics of agricultural growth: The example of Catalan emphyteusis in the eighteenth century', and L. Lorenzetti, 'Property relations, socio-economic change and the state: the Valtellina in the nineteenth century', both in Béaur et al. (eds), *Property Rights*, respectively on pp. 439–54 and 179–94.
80 G. Hardin, 'The tragedy of the commons', *Science*, 162:3869 (1968), pp. 1243–8; G. Hardin, 'Extensions of "The Tragedy of the Commons"', *Science*, 280:5346 (1998), pp. 682–3.

81   F. Esteve Mora and J. H. Ortego, 'Régimen comunal y economía moral en el Antiguo Régimen: La lenta transformación de los derechos de propiedad en Madrid, siglos XV–XVIII', and J. Izquierdo Martín, 'En nombre de la comunidad: Antropología de la propiedad en el Antiguo Régimen', both in R. Congost and J. M. Lana (eds), *Campos Cerrados, Debates Abiertos: Análisis Histórico y Propiedad de la Tierra en Europa (Siglos XVI–XVX)* (Pamplona: Universidad Pública de Navarra, 2007), pp. 173–200 and 53–73 respectively; E. Ostrom, *Governing the Commons: The Evolution of Institutions for Collective Action* (Cambridge: Cambridge University Press, 1990); E. Ostrom, 'Community and the endogenous resolution of common pool problems', *Journal of Theoretical Politics*, 4:3 (1992), pp. 343–51.

82   R. W. Hoyle, 'Securing access to England's uplands: Or how the 1945 revolution petered out', in Congost and Santos, *Contexts of Property*, pp. 187–209; Thompson, *Whigs and Hunters*.

83   J. M. Lana-Berasain, 'Forgotten commons: The struggle for recognition and property rights in a Spanish village, 1509–1957', *Rural History*, 23:2 (2012), pp. 137–59; Congost, *Tierras, Leyes, Historia*, pp. 253–78.

84   J. Gelman, 'Derechos de propiedad, crecimiento económico y desigualdad en la región pampeana, siglos XVIII y XIX', *Historia Agraria*, 37 (2005), pp. 467–88.

85   M.-D. Demélas and N. Vivier (eds), *Les Propriétés Collectives Face aux Attaques Libérales (1750–1914): Europe Occidentale et Amérique Latine* (Rennes: Presses Universitaires de Rennes, 2003); N. Grüne, 'Transformation of the commons in rural south-west Germany (8th–18th centuries)', *Historia Agraria*, 55 (2011), pp. 47–74; I. Iriarte Goñi and J. M. Lana Berasain, 'Concurrencia y jerarquización de los derechos de apropiación sobre los recursos: Bienes comunales en Navarra: Siglos XVIII–XX', in Congost and Lana, *Campos Cerrados*, pp. 201–31; J. M. Lana Berasain and I. Iriarte Goñi, 'The social embeddedness of common property rights in Navarra (Spain), sixteenth to twentieth centuries', in Congost and Santos, *Contexts of Property*, pp. 83–103; Sánchez Salazar, 'Redefinición de los derechos de propiedad'.

86   Grüne, 'Transformation of the commons'.

87   T. De Moor, 'La función del común: La trayectoria de un comunal en Flandes durante los siglos XVIII y XIX', in Congost and Lana (eds), *Campos Cerrados*, pp. 111–39; R. Santos and M. J. Roxo, 'A tale of two tragedies: The commons of Serra de Mértola in Alentejo (southern Portugal) and their privatization, eighteenth to twentieth centuries', in B. van Bavel and E. Thoen (eds), *Rural Societies and Environments at Risk: Ecology, Property Rights and Social Organisation in Fragile Areas (Middle Ages–Twentieth Century)* (Turnhout: Brepols, 2013), pp. 115–44; P. Tedeschi, 'Common land in eastern Lombardy during the nineteenth century', *Historia Agraria*, 55 (2011), pp. 75–100.

88   D. R. Curtis, 'Did the commons make medieval and early modern rural societies more equitable? A survey of evidence from across Western Europe, 1300–1800', *Journal of Agrarian Change*, Early View (published online 27 February 2015), at http://onlinelibrary.wiley.com/enhanced/doi/10.1111/joac.12101 [last access 10 March 2016].

89   T. De Moor, 'The silent revolution: A new perspective on the emergence of commons, guilds, and other forms of corporate collective action in Western Europe', *International Review of Social History*, 53:S16 (2008), pp. 179–212.

90   L. Viardi, 'Construing the harvest: Gleaners, farmers and officials in early modern France', *American Historical Review*, 98 (1993) pp. 1424–47.

Index

absolute ownership 33–6, 38, 42, 48, 74, 81, 83, 177–80, 182, 188, 190–1, 198
Acemoglu, D. 10
Africa 4, 9, 12, 19–26, 92, 194
agency 2, 26, 69, 177, 182–5, 196; theory 182
Agrarian Technical Committee, Ministry of Labour, Spain 135
agriculture 4–5, 7, 13, 17, 22–4, 179–80, 189–90, 194–6; Buenos Aires 74–9, 83–7; East Germany 154–65, 167, 169–72; Lombardy 54–61, 63, 65–9; Madeira 92–8, 100, 103, 105; Scandinavia 32–41, 45–9; Spain 116, 118–20, 126, 132–6, 138, 146–50
agronomics 67, 69, 182
Ahmadnagar Sultanate 13
Alicante 111, 114–15, 119
allemansrätt 42–3, 49
Alps 40, 54–6, 59, 62, 64, 67, 195–6
Alston, L.J. 185
Alteigentümer 154, 163–7, 169–70
alternative land uses 32–53
amortization 58
Andalusia 133, 137–8, 141–7
Anderson, R.L. 113–14, 118–19
appropriation 1–3, 6, 10–12, 15, 22–3, 115–17; Buenos Aires 81; institutions 177–204; Lombardy 54, 68–9; Madeira 91; Portuguese Empire 26; Scandinavia 32, 35–6, 46, 48–9; social 177–99; Spain 111–15, 120, 122, 124–8, 132, 134–6, 142–3, 145, 148–9
Aragon 127, 140–1
Argentina 5, 74, 83, 85, 188, 192, 195
aristocracy 15–16, 18, 60, 65, 133, 170, 179
Asia 9, 12, 24–6, 187
Åström, A. 42–3

Atlantic 9, 12, 16, 22, 25, 78, 92
Australasia 187
Austrian empire 54–5, 57–9, 61–4, 68

Baltic 37
banks 58, 67
Basque region 133
Bayly, C. 11
beaches 41, 43–4, 48
Berge, E. 47
Bergslagen 38
Bijapur Sultanate 12
biodiversity 33, 46, 48
Blackstone, W. 179–80
Bonde, C. 32
Borriana 117, 122–4
boundaries 55, 76, 81, 84, 113–15, 127, 135, 142, 144, 168
bourgeoisie 133
Brazil 12, 22, 185, 188
Brenner debate 193
Britain 10, 40, 43–5, 93, 187–8
brokers 114, 116
Bromley, J.E. 7–8, 183–4, 190
Buddhists 16–17
Buenos Aires 5, 74–90, 180, 188, 190
Bundestag 164
bundle of rights 177, 179–82, 190, 192, 198
bureaucracy 17, 61

cadastral system 5, 54, 57–9, 61, 63, 68, 80–1, 159, 164, 181, 189
Câmara, B. 6, 180, 183, 190
capitalism 1, 7, 10, 23, 25, 181–2, 189, 191, 193–4, 196; Buenos Aires 86; East Germany 160, 170; Lombardy 55, 58–9, 68; Spain 132
Carlesjö, G. 41, 43

For Product Safety Concerns and Information please contact our EU
representative GPSR@taylorandfrancis.com
Taylor & Francis Verlag GmbH, Kaufingerstraße 24, 80331 München, Germany